DAILY LIFE IN RUSSIA
under the Last Tsar

St Basil's Cathedral, Moscow, at the end of the century

Daily Life in Russia
under the Last Tsar

HENRI TROYAT

TRANSLATED BY MALCOLM BARNES

Stanford University Press
Stanford, California

Stanford University Press
Stanford, California
Original French edition, *La Vie Quotidienne en Russie
au Temps du Dernier Tsar*, © 1959 by Librairie Hachette
English translation © 1961 by George Allen & Unwin Ltd.
Originating American publisher: The Macmillan Company, New York, 1962
Reissued in cloth and paper by Stanford University Press in 1979
Printed in the United States of America
Cloth ISBN 0-8047-1037-6   Paper ISBN 0-8047-1030-9
(previously ISBN 0-02-62025)
Last figure below indicates year of this printing:
88   87   86   85   84   83   82   81   80   79

PREFACE

Undoubtedly I should have followed the usual pattern of this series of books by handling my subject like a historian, but the period and the land that I was asked to describe seemed so close to me – because of my parents' tales and my own childhood memories – that from the moment I started work I felt unable to present the living world that I bore within me in a systematic manner. I have therefore done my best with the necessity of dividing this confused totality of impressions into clearly defined chapters: administration, the nobility, the clergy, the bourgeoisie, the people ... I have even been shameless enough to invent a traveller in the process of discovering Russia for himself and my readers. I derived amusement and sorrow from his disappointments. In short, instead of treating the past as if it were dead matter, I have tried to animate it by giving it the colour and vitality of a contemporary report.

For the date of this journey beyond the frontier, it seemed to me logical to choose the year 1903, which is characteristic of the last days of absolutism. In the following year, in fact, the Russo-Japanese War shook the country's faith in its army and its sovereign, and immediately afterwards a revolution, followed by strikes, stirred Nikolas II to make his first liberal concessions. The Russia of the Duma was already no longer the Russia of the old régime. Under an apparent administrative stability there was a sickness and an anguish which could only end in the tragic events of 1917.

Having decided that the year 1903 was the best period for a description of pre-revolutionary Russian society, I also saw myself obliged to restrict my investigations in terms of space. In a land as vast and as diversely peopled as Russia, the variety of customs was much more noticeable than in any other European land, and 300 pages would not have sufficed had I wished only to compare the life of a peasant from the Tula region with that of his brothers in the Ukraine, the Kuban, the lower Volga, the shores of the Caspian Sea, or the confines of Siberia. Since the most Russian city in Russia was incontestably Moscow, it was by penetrating into the different circles of that city that I strove to catch the innumerable aspects of daily life in the Tsarist empire.

I do not deny the imperfections of such a method. My documentation is certainly incomplete and arbitrary. It was drawn equally from didactic writings and from the tales of contemporaries who were worthy to be trusted.

A day will come when better-qualified writers than myself will draw up the complete catalogue of human activity in Russia on the eve of the First World War. While we wait for this enormous compilation, I beg the reader not to see anything more in my book than a sentimental promenade through the past of a land that is little known.

CONTENTS

PREFACE   *page* 5

TABLE OF WEIGHTS, MEASURES, MONEY   8

I *Arrival*   13

II *Family Party*   23

III *Russian Promenade*   30

IV *Entertainment and Dining Out*   40

V *Baths, 'Traktirs' and Night Shelters*   51

VI *The Orthodox Church*   63

VII *The Workers*   87

VIII *The Army*   108

IX *The Different Social Classes and the Administrative Machine*   127

X *The Law*   147

XI *Moscow's Many Faces*   159

XII *The Tsar and his Entourage*   174

XIII *The Peasants*   195

XIV *Nizhny-Novgorod*   215

XV *The Volga*   226

BIBLIOGRAPHY   233

INDEX   236

Pood = approximately 36 lb. avoirdupois.

Verst = approximately ⅔ mile, or more exactly 3,500 feet. 100 versts = 66 miles 520 feet.
1 *verst* = 500 sagenes; 1 *sagene* = 3 arsheens; 1 *arsheen* = 16 verchoks. Thus 1 sagene = 7 feet; 1 arsheen = 28 inches; 1 verchok = 1¾ inches.

Rouble = (100 kopecks = 1 rouble) 51½₵ in 1903. Thus 10 roubles = $5.15, 100 roubles = $51.50, and 1,000 roubles = $515.00.

ILLUSTRATIONS

	St Basil's Cathedral, Moscow	*frontispiece*
1.	Workers' quarters in Moscow	*facing page* 48
	Railway police on the Trans-Siberian line	
	Second-class carriage at the end of the train	
2.	The Kremlin and the Moskvaretsky Bridge	49
	The Spass Gate of the Kremlin	
3.	The market-place of Kitaï-Gorod, Moscow	96
	Moscow street scene	
4.	Moscow shops	97
	Moscow street scene	
5.	Muscovite Workers	112
	Workers' dwellings in Moscow	
	Artillerymen of the Guard	
6.	Workers' dormitory in St Petersburg	113
	Interior of a St Petersburg *traktir*	
	Interior of a shelter in the Khitrovka, Moscow	
7.	A colporteur	144
	Around the Samovar	
	A rich Russian merchant	
	The wife of a rich Russian merchant	
8.	Monks of the St Serge Monastery, Moscow	145
	Children's nurse in traditional clothing	
	A market in Moscow	
9.	Tsarkoe Selo, St Petersburg	160
	Bridge and church of St Isaac, St Petersburg	
10.	Entrance to the Palace of Tsarkoe Selo	161
	The Chinese Theatre at Tsarkoe Selo	
	On the banks of the Neva, St Petersburg	
11.	Nikolas II and the Empress Alexandra	192
	The Winter Palace, St Petersburg	
12.	Nizhny-Novgorod with the barges gathering	193
	A street scene in Nizhny-Novgorod	
13.	A peasant family at the table	208
	A young peasant conscript leaves to join the army	
14.	Emigrants at Chelyabinsk Station	209
	Russian emigrants at the station at Samara	
	Volga steamship	

DAILY LIFE IN RUSSIA
under the Last Tsar

CHAPTER I

ARRIVAL

In the train – Formalities – Russian railways and roads – Moscow – Conveyances, roads, churches, the hotel – The calendar

A FLAT white landscape had been slipping past the misted windows of the train for many hours. The engine whistled mournfully in the snow-covered plain, while beneath the traveller's feet the rails rumbled and jarred. He was alone in his compartment, and to while away the time had opened on his knees a small book in a red binding, a Baedeker of Russia published in 1902. He had bought it on the eve of his departure; filled with maps, itineraries, prices and practical advice, it was indispensable to all who were going to take a look at the Slav world.

In these early years of the century, when the railways were bringing people and cultures closer together, Russia alone seemed to stand apart distrustfully. Although our traveller would not have needed a passport to go to Paris or Berlin, he had to ask for one to go to Moscow. Reason for travelling: business. Age: 26 years. Status: bachelor. Permanent address: 14 Littlefields Avenue, London. Surname and first names: Russell, Edward Paul John. Seals, stamps, signatures. . . . Nor did the formalities end there. In Moscow he would have to exchange his passport for a residential permit, which must be renewed at the end of six months, and when he wanted to return home his papers would only be handed back in exchange for a certificate from the district police superintendent, stating that there was no objection to his departure. Luckily, according to Baedeker, hotel-keepers took responsibility for these procedures at a charge that varied between 30 and 90 kopecks.[1]

Although exasperated by all these irritating formalities, Russell had to admit that when he crossed the frontier the customs officers who had examined his bags and the men who

[1] See p. 10 for table of dollar equivalents.

had looked at his passport had been reassuringly correct in their behaviour. The officer in charge of the passport officials bore himself with a certain pride and spoke a little French: he wore a long greatcoat, had an upward-curling moustache, and carried a sword. The railway staff wore dark clothes, baggy trousers, black boots and fur caps. It was at Wirballen (Verjbolovo) that they had first been seen. The passengers had had to change trains because the Russian railway gauge (1·524 m.) was wider than that of other European railways, except the Spanish. Fear of invasion was ever-present.

In Russia the first-class carriages were blue, the second-class were yellow and the third green. In the first-class compartments two wide seats with removable backs could be turned into four couchettes for the night. There were special carriages for non-smokers and ladies, and on the main lines, like the one from Warsaw to Moscow, there were even sleeping-cars. Before reaching any main station the guard passed through the train to warn passengers. Those who wished to get down on to the platform locked their compartments or asked an attendant to look after their baggage. They could find refreshment in the station buffets, almost all of which had some gastronomic speciality new to a European palate. The samovar was steaming and there were piles of *hors-d'œuvres*. The white-aproned waiters hurried from table to table where tired travellers' heads bent over their food. The train would start again after the bell had been rung three times: first as a warning, again ten minutes later, and when it had rung a third time the train moved off.

It was 1,067 versts (710 miles) from Wirballen to Moscow, a journey of thirty hours. Russell was rather sorry that he had reserved the whole compartment to himself, for the price of luxury was solitude: a supplement of six roubles so as to have no one to talk to. At the prevailing rate of exchange this amounted to less than thirteen shillings. His gaze faltered over Baedeker's grey text. He knew already that European Russia and Siberia formed an empire of 129,000,000 inhabitants; that supreme authority was held by the Tsar, Nikolas II; that the established church was the Orthodox Church; that in church architecture the Byzantine style was supreme; that 'popes' were married and wore their hair long; that the national drinks were tea, kvass and vodka; that serf-

dom had been abolished in 1861; but that the greatest of the
noble families and the leaders of industry and commerce
made a great display of their wealth. A few words gathered
from travellers' tales formed the basis of his vocabulary:
moujik, knout, troika, izba, barin, etc.

Russell, the son of a prosperous textile merchant, had suc-
cessfully concluded his studies in law and accountancy. He
spoke French, and was interested in art, politics and social
questions. There were no problems about his future; but
before taking him into the business, his father had decided
to send him to Russia to complete his education. This land
held promise of gigantic development. Moreover, Russell
would not be at a loose end in Moscow, for his parents had
commended him to Alexander Vassilievitch Zubov, a big
Moscow textile merchant who had recently visited the
Russell firm on a buying trip. When Zubov had heard that
young Russell was planning to pay a visit to Russia, he had
offered him advice and hospitality. Russell wondered how
sincere this friendly man's proposals were. But he had not
taken the train just in order to meet this Russian again; his
father's instructions had been vague but serious: 'stay there
as long as necessary. Make yourself familiar with the ways of
the country. See what there is to be done there. At the
moment, rather than in the future, I have less need of you
here than in Moscow.'

These words echoed in the young man's ears while the
train rolled along towards the ancient capital of the Tsars. It
was his first big journey. He had been on the move for more
than two days. At times he thought he might be dreaming,
and that he might wake up at home in his own room, with the
old servant, Gertrude, vigorously drawing the curtains on a
vista of roofs, rain and smoke. But the minutes passed and the
wheels went on turning and the frosted window still framed
the same patch of white and foggy earth over which the birds
flew silently. How vast this country was! How far apart the
towns and how few the roads! Russell recalled some statistics
recently consulted. With its population of 129,000,000 people,
Russia had only 19 cities of more than 100,000 inhabitants.[1]

---

[1] Only St Petersburg and Moscow had more than one million inhabitants.
Warsaw had 638,000, Odessa 405,000, Lodz 315,000, Riga 282,000, Kiev
247,000, Kharkov 175,000.

In European Russia and Russian Poland there were only 15,000 miles of roads that were surfaced from end to end; 3,300 miles of roads paved throughout; and 340,000 miles of roads neither surfaced nor paved, and impracticable in fact in times of rain or thaw. As to the Russian railway system, with its 25,000 miles of track, it was no greater than that of Britain. Russell was not unaware that, since the Crimean War, an enormous amount of foreign capital had been invested in the Russian Railway Co.[1] This fact to some extent reassured him. Even a foreigner moved along on machinery paid for with money from home. In general, the Russian Government entrusted the construction of new lines to private companies and gave them help in their activities, either by assuring a normal interest to the shareholders, funds in the form of assistance, or by guaranteeing its debentures. But the State also became its own contractor, or in advance bought back lines that belonged to joint-stock companies. Anyway, according to the concessions, the Government settled the technical conditions of their construction very precisely and fixed the tariffs for the transport of passengers and goods.[2] Nevertheless, for obscure reasons, Russian stations were situated a long way from the towns. According to legend, when in 1842 Nikolas I decided to build the line from St Petersburg to Moscow, there were so many arguments among the engineers entrusted with laying out the route that the potentate then seized a ruler, traced a straight line on the map between the two capitals and, looking angrily at his engineers, declared: 'You will lay the track along this line and no other.' The result, it is said, was to leave Novgorod about forty miles south of the main line and to bring about the rapid decline of Moscow's former rival.

Telegraph poles slid past Russell's eyes. He struggled against sleep. The compartment was overheated, but outside the cold was fierce enough to freeze the saliva in one's mouth. Russell was glad that he had brought flannel under-

[1] This company was authorized to exploit the Nikolas railway (St Petersburg–Moscow), then to construct the lines from St Petersburg to Warsaw and Wirballen, and Moscow to Nizhny-Novgorod.

[2] Until the promulgation of the law of May 8, 1889, private companies fixed their own tariffs freely, which involved the public and railway agencies in a real chaos of contradictory figures.

clothes with him, a cat-skin waistcoat and thick woollen socks.

As to overcoats, Baedeker recommended buying one in Russia, lined with fur. This advice was followed by the laconic note: 'Do not hesitate, in second-rate shops, to offer 10 to 20 per cent less than the price asked (35 per cent in the Caucasus).' Were Russian shopkeepers robbers? The following advice gave Russell some anxiety: 'In small hotels it is as well to have a pillow, bed-linen and insect powder.' But he would not be going to a 'small' hotel, for he had already chosen the Slavyansky-Bazar, which Baedeker rated a first-class establishment.

Perhaps he should have warned Alexander Vassilievitch Zubov of his arrival? He had not wished to do so for fear of disturbing him, but also in order to be rather more free about his accommodation and in his first look at the city. He would wait a day or two before telephoning his Russian contact. It was an extraordinary fact that, according to Zubov, there had been a telephone service in Moscow since 1882.[1] For a land that some people regarded as backward, this was rather an achievement.

From time to time a village of snow-covered wooden houses loomed up in the distance. Birches, firs, frozen ponds, a sledge gliding across the country behind a small dark horse. At minor stations the gates were watched by women with round weather-beaten faces, their heads covered with a kerchief, a horn slung round their shoulders bandolier-fashion, and felt boots on their feet. On the platforms of the main stations uniforms were everywhere: policemen, soldiers, railwaymen, students, all were dressed, it seemed, in military fashion. Was it true that in Russia half the men wore the distinctive dress of their profession?

On the whole the men were tall, with an air at once gentle and martial, which was very attractive. The memory of Napoleon, which had already come to Russell's mind as the train crossed the Berezina, returned at the approaches to Borodino, where the terrible battle of the Moskva had been

[1] The first apparatus put into service were by Bell-Blek, but from 1888 apparatus by Erikson of Stockholm were employed throughout the territory.

fought. This Moskva, or Moscow River, was slowly crossed on a bridge which roared and trembled. The end of the journey was drawing near. People were stirring in neighbouring compartments. Russell ventured into the corridor and wiped away the mist from a small patch of window; then suddenly, very far away, in a region made unreal by fog, sun and snow, he saw the gilded domes of Moscow.

✳   ✳   ✳   ✳

As he emerged from the station, Russell came face to face with the city and its low buildings, its dirty snow, its muffled figures, and the distant clamour of a thousand bells. A white-aproned porter hurried along in front of him with one case on his shoulder and one in his hand. In the forecourt stood a line of small sleighs with their drivers shouting to attract customers. The porter wanted to stop at the first in the line, but Russell resolutely chose another, for Baedeker had made it clear that an *izvozchik* standing at the station entrance always asked more than his fellows farther off. They all wore long greatcoats. Their massive figures were of one piece with their sleighs. At the end of the line an enormous pot-bellied individual, well-wrapped up, crushed the seat with his great weight. A curious black hat like an inverted chamber-pot came down to his eyes. Locks of filthy hair hung down over his ears. His steel-blue eyes sparkled above his reddish beard. His nose was blue with cold.

'Slavyansky-Bazar,' Russell said to him resolutely.

The face of the driver melted into a toothy smile. He stretched his arm out in a welcoming gesture and jabbered a few incomprehensible words. But Russell, warned by Baedeker, refused to climb into the sleigh until he knew what it would cost. An argument began between the driver, who spoke violently in Russian, and Russell, who persisted in repeating in his own language: 'Fix a price, or I will go to someone else!'

A sympathetic traveller came forward as interpreter. He was young, well dressed and dictatorial. Several times Russell heard on his lips the terrible word *gorodovoi*; since crossing the frontier it was impossible not to know that this meant 'policeman'. Eventually the quarrel died down and the interpreter said to Russell: 'He wants forty kopecks. It's a reasonable price. Good-day, sir.'

Thus reassured, Russell was profuse with his thanks and climbed into the sleigh, in which the porter had already placed the cases. Two ten-kopeck pieces passed into a hand that was black with dirt. The porter bent double in a deep bow and Russell wondered if he had given too much. The driver clicked his tongue and the small, shaggy horse dragged at the shafts. The runners grated on the packed snow and they were off. The Russian cold, dry and sharp, seized Russell's tender face. Curled up on his seat, he screwed up his eyes in the icy air where the shining crystals danced.

The streets were full of life. On the pavements, which had been scraped clear and were flanked with thick banks of snow, men dressed in European fashion, striking military figures and elegant women with their hands buried in muffs, jostled with kerchief-wearing matrons and moujiks with unkempt beards; and tattered *tulups*,[1] who were still living as in the time of Peter the Great. The buildings were painted in soft colours. Here and there above the roofs rose blue domes studded with gold. Over the shopfronts were the strange characters of the Russian alphabet, but was it for the benefit of foreigners or illiterate Russians that each shop bore also an unmistakable sign representing the articles to be found inside? Signs which depicted strings of sausages, placid cattle in a pasture, yellow biscuits, a scarlet hat, a gun, a giant boot. Innumerable sleighs glided rapidly along the roadway between these two rows of pictures; sumptuous or modest, they jostled one another to the creaking of the runners and the jingle of the harness, the horses blowing jets of vapour through their nostrils. Fragments of ice, torn from the road by their hoofs, bombarded the snow-screens of the sleighs.

The driver turned to Russell and said: 'Tverskaya!'

Evidently he wished to point out that they were in Tverskaya Street. According to Baedeker's map, this important thoroughfare led to the Red Square and the Kremlin, and Baedeker was right. Here was a two-way arch, each passage surmounted by a pointed tower. Between the two stood the

[1] *Tulup*: overcoat of uncured skin, with the fur turned inside.

Iberian Chapel, its entrance obstructed by a group of tramp-
ling, mumbling worshippers. The driver removed his hat and
crossed himself in a slow and ample fashion which passed,
singularly, from forehead to chest, and from right shoulder
to left.

Suddenly the walls drew apart, the view widened, and all
the pictures of the Kremlin that Russell had ever seen in
books of travel, in illustrated papers and on postcards, came
together in a single vista, motionless and grandiose. The
Kremlin wall, its battlements notched in the shape of swal-
lows' tails, enclosed a prodigious variety of scaly bulbs,
gilded domes, pinnacles and turrets with collars of bright
stonework. Yet, it was not behind these ramparts, but at the
far end of the vast snowfield, that the city's strangest structure rose. Was it a church . . . or an avalanche of toys that
had fallen upon the earth from the sky and lay there in
disorder, brilliant with all the colours of childhood?

On a number of white drums St Basil's Cathedral thrust
upwards a group of dissimilar and asymmetrical domes,
shaped like pineapples, turbans, onions and pumpkins. Gold,
blue, red, yellow and green streamed from top to bottom of
the edifice, which was surmounted by orthodox crosses. 'So
there it is, the heart of Russia,' Russell said to himself, and
he deplored the fact that since the days of Peter the Great
the Tsars should have had themselves crowned in Moscow
but should have lived obstinately in St Petersburg. Overwhelmed by the picturesqueness of the spot, he would like
to have seen all the passers-by in boyar costume, or peasant
costume at least. Was it because of the blood that was spilt
there throughout the centuries, on that very spot, that it had
been named the Red Square? This romantic idea appealed to
him, for he did not know that in Russian the words 'beautiful'
and 'red' are synonymous, that *Krasnaya devitsa*, for example,
means 'a beautiful girl', and that *Krasnaya ploshchad* can
be translated as either 'the red square' or 'the beautiful
square', with a definite preference for the latter?[1] After a

[1] It was only in the second half of the seventeenth century that the Kremlin Square, surrounded by beautiful new buildings, was given the name of
Krasnaya ploshchad, in other words 'the beautiful square'. Until then it had
been known as *Pozharnaya ploshchad*, or 'the square of fires', with allusion to
the numerous fires which destroyed the wooden shanties at this spot.

slight detour to allow the traveller to admire the monument to Minin and Pozharsky, who conquered the Poles and liberated Moscow in 1612, the driver turned back, drove his sleigh into Nikolskaya Street, passed yet another cathedral, two monasteries, and the ancient printing works of the Holy Synod, and halted before the Slavyansky-Bazar.[1]

He had scarcely paid his driver and crossed the threshold than he was no longer in Russia, but in a luxurious and cosmopolitan place with mirrors, chandeliers, red carpets, white shirt-fronts, bows and smiles. The finest apartment cost twenty-five roubles. But one could live more modestly under the same roof. Wisely, Russell chose a very suitable room at five roubles a day. There was not the slightest local colour in this room, which was papered yellow with a floral design and furnished in heavy mahogany. The lighting was electric. There was hot and cold running water in the wash-basin, and double windows because of the cold. Russell sat down on a leather settee, took a notebook from his pocket and wrote the date: January 17, 1903. 'Have arrived in Moscow. Everything all right.' Then, raising his eyes, he noticed a calendar on the wall, showing the figure 4.

Being an orderly man he prepared to correct the mistake by tearing off the leaves and then suddenly stopped as an idea struck him: the Russians had kept the Julian calendar, which was thirteen days behind the Gregorian calendar adopted by the West.[2] So Russell was in Moscow even before he had left home and he was beginning again the month that was already nearly half-finished in Western Europe. The impression of having lived backwards during his journey seemed so strange to him that for a long while he stood as if astounded, unable to distinguish the past from the present, suspended in a chronological void. He had put his watch right at Wirballen, and the time there was fifty-nine minutes

[1] At the entrance to Nikolskaya Street stood the Kazan Cathedral; by its side was the Za-Ikono-Spassky (The Saviour behind the Ikons) monastery, and farther off the Greek convent of St Nikolas, and opposite, the Blagoyavlensky (Epiphany) monastery.

[2] The Julian calendar, established by Julius Ceasar forty-six years before the Christian era, was adopted by the first Nicaean Council in 325 as the basis of the Christian year. This calendar was thirteen days behind the Gregorian calendar adopted successively by all the western peoples. A century earlier the gap had been only twelve days.

behind that at Moscow. So it was high time to have lunch! This prospect whetted Russell's appetite. After a hurried toilet he stood before his mirror and saw himself younger by thirteen days, slender, elegant and clear-complexioned, with curly brown hair and a neat moustache above a gourmand's lip.

CHAPTER II

FAMILY PARTY

A Muscovite family – The traditional patronymic – The two forenames – The Russian cuisine – The importance of tea – The samovar

AFTER he had bought a fur-lined coat and visited the Kremlin, Russell telephoned Zubov, who reproached him for not announcing his arrival earlier and asked him to lunch the same day.

The Zubov family was numerous and prosperous, and lived in a two-storied house near the Nikitskaya Gate. Beside Alexander Vassilievitch, who was a stout, pink-skinned man of fifty, with a fair beard and a playful sense of humour, his wife, Tatiana Sergeyevna, seemed strangely pale, gentle and dreamy. They had a son Nikolas of fourteen years, restless and talkative, who wore the black-belted grey uniform of a gymnasium pupil, a nineteen-year-old daughter, Helen, and one a little older – Olga – who was married to her father's partner, Paul Egorovitch Sychkin. She had just had a baby. The young couple lived in the house next door. Paul Egorovitch Sychkin had a bald and oblong head, pince-nez spectacles, an infallible memory and a passion for statistics. His conversation was sprinkled with dates and figures, and it did not take Russell long to realize that control of the Zubov firm was effectively in this meticulous man's hands, while the easy-going Alexander Vassilievitch was content to agree with his son-in-law's decisions and enjoy the benefits of freedom from worry.

Everyone in the family spoke a refined French under the fond eye of a governess who came from Dijon, plump Mlle Joze. When Olga's baby reached the age when he would be stammering his first words, Mlle Joze would take him in hand in order to teach him 'the language of Voltaire'. For the time being he was still in the care of an old nanny, the *niania*, a person indispensable to any Russian household.

This *nyanya*, like all of her kind, was a peasant who had

come to the city when young and had worn herself out looking after children without hoping for anything but their love.
Illiterate, superstitious, talkative and tirelessly devoted, it
was she who spent the whole night at the bedside of some
young scamp; who grovelled before the ikon, repaired the
broken toys, wiped away tears and blew noses after a fit of
misery, and pleaded for her charges when their parents were
too severe; and when sleep was slow in coming, she would
lean over the little bed by the wavering flame of a nightlight
and in low voice tell the story of some episode in the lives of
the saints, or some legend in which invincible knights fought
for princesses against their would-be ravishers.

Despite her numerous virtues, the *nyanya* was rarely
allowed at her master's table, and Russell, though he heard
speak of the woman who had brought up Helen, Olga, and
Nikolas before being passed on to little Andreï, had no opportunity to see her that day. But the conversation soon took a
less intimate turn, for the Zubovs had invited some friends to
lunch. Their arrival produced a lively atmosphere in the
room; they were four — two single men and a married couple.
Russell had heard that in Russia men kissed each other on the
lips to wish each other good-day. But this was another mis-
taken idea. They simply embraced. And the way in which
they greeted the ladies was most elegant: they clicked heels
in a military fashion before bowing to kiss hands.

Alexander Vassilievitch made the introductions. The new-
comers seemed delighted to meet Russell. They gathered
round him and asked him about life at home, about the
theatres and the exhibitions.... Flattered by their interest,
Russell began to swagger. Alexander Vassilievitch then decided that he could not continue to treat his guest so for-
mally. In Russia everyone was known by two forenames, his
own and his father's. Thus Alexander Vassilievitch meant
Alexander, son of Vassili. Tatiana Sergeyevna meant Tatiana,
daughter of Serge. Even if you had met someone only once
and long ago, you had, at the risk of being considered ill-
bred, to remember his double forename. This everyday
mnemotechnical exercise seemed quite exhausting to Russell,
for at home he need only remember the addresses and
telephone numbers of his acquaintances.

Alexander Vassilievitch Zubov was delighted. What was Mr Russell's usual forename? John? And his father's? Paul. In future, therefore, he would be Ivan Pavlovitch.

'Ivan Pavlovitch, we are delighted to welcome you!'

'The pleasure is all mine, Alexander Vassilievitch,' Russell replied.

The company broke into smiles. Ivan Pavlovitch felt that he had been russified to the core and asked for further information. Was it true that in Russia the family name changed in gender according to whether it applied to a man or a woman? The reply was in the affirmative. Thus, one of Alexander Vassilievitch Zubov's daughters was Helena Alexandrovna Zubova, and the other, the wife of Paul Egorovitch Sychkin, was Olga Alexandrovna Sychkina. The widow of Mikhailovsky, one of their friends, was Anna Grigorievna Mikhailovskaya.

They lingered for a while in the drawing-room, which was crowded with Napoleon III furniture, green plants and modern paintings in heavy gilded frames. But at last the double doors opened and a delicious odour titillated Russell's nostrils.

In the dining-room, which was very big and bright, a special table had been laden with *hors-d'œuvres* or *zakuski*. Bottles of iced vodka shone above an extraordinary display of eatables, which Alexander Vassilievitch enumerated for his guest: fresh caviar, pressed caviar, herring fillets, cucumbers in brine, smoked sturgeon, balyk, sucking-pig in horseradish, cold salmon, and little warm patés of meat, cabbage, fish, etc. Astonished by this abundant prologue to the real meal, Russell watched the other guests, who were helping themselves to whatever they fancied and washing each mouthful down with a bumper of vodka.

'Never drink vodka without eating something on top of it,' said the master of the house.

Ivan Pavlovitch followed this advice. At each draught of spirit his throat burned and a line of fire passed through his stomach. He quickly reached out for the *zakuski* to smother the fire with a blanket of caviar. The vodka called for food, and the food called for vodka. From one small glass to another, Russell had the impression that the noise in the room was increasing, that it was gayer, lighter and warmer. Alexander Vassilievitch started to tell him about the Russian cuisine. Many of the dishes in this cuisine were controlled by the seasons and by religion. Thus, a delicious cake of sweetened white cheese, *paskha*, and a sort of brioche, *kulich*, were only served at Easter; *bliny* – pancakes with cream and caviar – only appeared on the table on meat days; for *okroshka* – cold soup, sourish and aromatic, with scraps of fish and flakes of ice – one had to wait till the summer, and the return of the larks was celebrated on March 9 by making little bread rolls shaped like birds (*zhavoronki*) with raisins for eyes. But there were innumerable other dishes which could be eaten all through the year: *borsch* (a soup of cabbage and meat, served with cream); the various *kulibyaki* of meat, rice and fish; the *côtelettes de Kiev, côtelettes Pozharsky, pelmeni* . . . without counting all the products of the French cuisine, which were much enjoyed in Russia. Many houses boasted of having a French chef in their employ. Most of the time the meals were mixed: half-Russian, half-French. Evidence of this could be found in an anonymous gourmet's book called *The Gastronomic Notebooks of St Petersburg*. This book, of which only 100 copies were printed, was a collection of all the important menus which the author had enjoyed during his long life. Alexander Vassilievitch Zubov showed Russell this work: dinners at the English Club, at the home of Prince Lobanov, at the home of Count Vorontzov, and so on. Sixteen covers served by two, 200 covers served by twenty. . . . Hazel-grouse cutlets *à la Russe* together with quail pies with truffle *à la Périgueux*, little Volga sterlets, or *rastegai* of salmon, with chicken *à la Montmorency*.

The great wines were all French, but there were very good Crimean vintages. To attract the connoisseurs, champagne had to be, not iced, as in France, but positively frozen, so that needles of ice could be seen suspended in the bottle. Of vodka, a spirit made from grain, there were several kinds; from ordinary white vodka to peppered vodka, *pertsovka*, and in between a more savoury vodka, *zubrovka*, so named because the herb which gave it its bouquet was much sought after by an animal in process of extinction, the zubr, a species of aurochs or bison.

At his host's invitation, Russell tasted three vodkas in turn in order to compare them, and his eyes filled with tears. With a brave effort to stay lucid, he asked his neighbour if the common people fed and quenched their thirst in this fashion. The answer was that the fare of the common people was of course simple, *shchi* (sour cabbage soup), *kasha* (buckwheat gruel), *borsch* and black bread formed the basis of their ordinary meals. Both in summer and winter their preference was for vodka, but they liked *kvass* too, a less expensive drink made by fermenting barley. Finally, tea was so important to the national life that instead of a 'tip' or *pourboire*, one said in Russia *nachai*, which means 'for tea'. Throughout the provinces the samovar was the centre of the household, the symbol of relaxation and well-being. Its name was derived from two Russian words: *samo*, itself, and *varit*, to boil. Thus it was not a vessel for making tea but for obtaining and keeping boiling water. Russell, who during his journey had already seen numerous samovars in buffets, learned that these pot-bellied and gleaming copper urns were traversed by a vertical chimney with a small grate for holding live charcoal at the base. The water, poured in at the top, surrounded the chimney and got hot from contact with it. A teapot, filled with concentrated tea, was kept warm on the top of the samovar. To get boiling water at any hour of the day, all you had to do was to turn on the tap. A curious detail was that men drank their tea from glasses and women drank theirs from cups. The glasses were mounted in stands with handles so that they could be picked up without burning the fingers. All classes of society followed this custom: in the big houses these stands were real pieces of skilfully carved silver. Peasants, workers and shopkeepers did not sugar their tea, but slipped a piece of sugar into their mouths and kept it there by clever manipulation of the tongue while the warm drink passed into their throats. This way of drinking tea was called *v prikusku*.

While Russell listened to these explanations, he felt he was choking with an abundance of alcohol and food. Someone offered him a Russian cigarette (*papirosa*) with a long cardboard mouthpiece. The tobacco had a sweet oriental flavour. Even the ladies smoked. The sound of the voices was deafening. Russell, stupefied and nauseated, thought long-ingly of a long siesta in his room. But Alexander Vassilievitch took him amicably by the arm. It was time to go to table.

Convinced that he could swallow nothing of this meal, Russell was surprised to feel his appetite return at the sight of a jellied sturgeon. Two *maîtres-d'hôtel*, dressed in black, with white cravats and gloves, glided behind the chairs. Their manner of serving was perfectly European, but their faces had the prominent cheekbones and the slanting eyes of the conquering Mongols. Rhine wine was poured into the glasses. Conversation was general. They spoke of a certain Chekhov, whose last play had been a great success, of Chaliapin, a deep bass singer, Sobinov, an extraordinary tenor who was Chaliapin's rival with the female public, and of some celebrated dancers, Pavlova and Kchessinskaya, over whom the Moscow and St Petersburg theatres were quarrel-ling. It was apparent that there was jealousy between the two great cities. According to Alexander Vassilievitch Zubov, the people of St Petersburg criticized the Muscovites for their coarse joviality and their puerile insouciance, while the Muscovites criticized them for their false western elegance, their haughtiness and their pretentiousness in regarding themselves as the centre of the universe.

'Moscow', said Alexander Vassilievitch, 'is the old Russia of merchants, artisans and artists. St. Petersburg is the new Russia, artificial and formal, governmental. Some day the Tsar will have to come back to live in Moscow.'

Russell signified assent while he cut up a chicken cutlet *à la Kiev*, full of melted butter, which spread warm and steaming over his plate. After dessert – a pineapple jelly beaten up in champagne and topped with a fruit macedoine – the men returned to smoking their long cigarettes with cardboard tubes. Coffee was not served in the drawing-room, but on the table in the dining-room. Though the cups were nothing special to look at, Russell admired the little inlaid silver spoons which were, according to Helen, his neighbour, of a special Russian style. The liqueurs were international: cognac, chartreuse, framboise and kümmel.

It was four in the afternoon when they left the table. Russell's tongue was on fire and he felt he had all the Kremlin's domes in his stomach. The other guests seemed happy and comfortable. One after the other they approached their hostess and kissed her hand to thank her for having fed them so well. This custom seemed so strange to Russell that he hesitated a little before conforming to it. But Tatiana Sergeyevna responded to his gesture with a gracious smile and, without knowing exactly where his feet were taking him, he found himself back in the room with the great green plants. Outside the snow was falling, and here, in hothouse warmth, were palms and exotic ferns. It was Sunday in Russia and Saturday in England. Nobody was in a hurry to leave. In response to the entreaties of those around her, Helen sat down at the piano and sang a very languorous tzigane ballad.

CHAPTER III

RUSSIAN PROMENADE

Domestic life – Servants' pay – A schoolboy's morning – The cares of a domesticated lady – A sleigh-ride – Troikas – Philippov's patisserie and Elisseyev's food store – Muscovite bazaars – The fire service

RUSSIAN hospitality was no mere phrase: after inviting Russell to lunch or dinner several times, Alexander Vassilievitch Zubov begged him to come and live with them. A guest room was at his disposal. It would be so much nicer than at the hotel. Russell accepted the offer eagerly, for he was anxious to know about life in a big Muscovite house.

His host told him how, in his parents' happy days, before the abolition of serfdom, the house swarmed with servants whose functions were ill-defined. Now that times had changed they had to restrict themselves. The family had only one chef in its service, an assistant cook, two valets, two chambermaids, a laundress, a sewing-maid, a coachman, a groom and an odd-job man. It was the coachman who received the highest wages: 40 roubles a month (about £4 14s). The chef and the valets made shift with 25 roubles and the head chambermaid with 15 roubles. As this staff was insufficient to maintain the establishment, Alexander Vassilievitch had made a contract with a tiler who inspected the roof at the beginning and end of the winter, with a German clockmaker who undertook to wind up all the clocks in the house, with a stove-setter who occupied himself with the central heating, and with a polisher who regularly came with his men to polish the parquet floors and clean the tiles. The cellar and the storeroom were crammed with drink and foodstuffs. Provisions were bought for several months in advance: mountains of potatoes, and barrels of sauerkraut and herrings. In the stable were four horses, including a pair of Orloff trotters which had cost 2,500 roubles (approx. £265) and were the envy of all Moscow. In the carriage shed were two sleighs, a landau, a calash and a small hunting-brake. But unknown to his wife, Alexander Vassilievitch dreamed of acquiring a motor-car: a Mercedes-Simplex with 'side-doors'. This would appear next year. Between now and then the Germans would have improved their machines further.

'I don't like the Germans,' he said, 'but one has to admit that they are ingenious. Do you know, my dear Ivan Pavlovitch, that in Old Russian the words "German" and "foreigner" are synonymous? In the old days a *Nemets* was a German.'[1]

Every day Alexander Vassilievitch rose at eight, before his wife. The family took breakfast all together in the dining-room. But young Nikolas had already swallowed his last slice of bread when the grown-ups sat down to table: prayers at the gymnasium began at eight-thirty and lessons at nine. The numbering of the classes in Russia began with the first and ended with the eighth. So Nikolas, who was in the fifth, had to endure three more years of tiresome discipline before achieving the free life of a student. While waiting for the pleasures of such promotion, his daily hope was to see the thermometer go down to minus 20° Reaumur.[2] Then the firemen would hoist white flags on their watch-towers, the official signal for leave of absence because of the cold. The schools would close their doors and throughout the city the schoolboys would pray secretly that the temperature would stay where it was. Unfortunately, this kind of holiday was rare and Nikolas left to face the snow and the blackboard, leaving his parents, his sister, Mlle Joze and John Russell seated in the warmth with the aroma of tea and jam.

On rising, Tatiana Sergeyevna wore a champagne-coloured wrap, buttoned to the neck, with lace at the wrists. Alexander Vassilievitch sported a cashmere dressing-gown. A piece of transparent material covered his upper lip. He removed this muzzle before sitting down, to reveal a soft and shining moustache, as if drawn by the brush of a Chinese artist. He was visibly glad to be in good health, closely shaved, with flawless nails and a sound set of teeth. Close to his plate were

---

[1] Etymologically, *nemets* was connected with *nemoi* (mute). In popular speech the term was applied to those who could not speak Russian, in other words foreigners, and especially Germans.

[2] Twenty degrees of frost Réaumur would equal 45° of frost Fahrenheit.

some letters and the morning papers: *Moskovsky Listok* and *Russkaya Vedomost*.... After some refreshment he peered at the envelopes, grumbling 'Nothing interesting,' and stuffed them into his pocket. Then he lit a cigarette, opened a news-sheet and commented on the headings for the benefit of those present. His partner would have been at the office a long time already and he could not make up his mind whether to go there himself. He would gladly have stayed for another hour in the family circle if his valet had not come to announce that the sleigh was ready.

'Ah! Very well,' he said, stretching himself.

His glance faded, a sigh escaped his thick red lips, and just for a moment he resembled his son about to leave for school.

Having accompanied her husband to the entrance-hall, received his kiss and listened to the ritual 'Au revoir, angel!' Tatiana Sergeyevna was soon caught up in the many cares of a lady of quality. The valet came to show her the suppliers' bills and to tell her about a recent dispute between the two chambermaids. The cook followed him, bringing suggestions for the menus of masters and servants. Servants had a separate diet, healthy and abundant; they required soup and meat at every meal. Next came Olga in a great hurry to seek her mother's advice: Prascovie, little Andreï's nurse, required large helpings of caviar for lunch, for she was obliged, she said, to eat a salty diet and drink copiously so that her milk should be beyond reproach.

'That's girl's impossible!' cried Tatiana Sergeyevna. 'Give her herrings, they'll have the same effect. Threaten to send her away if she insists! What a pity you cannot feed your child yourself!'

Prascovie was a robust peasant girl with a comely face and firm full bosom. The Zubov's doctor had sounded her, had analysed her blood and milk, and had declared her fit for the job. In accordance with custom, Olga had provided the nurse's outfit, which comprised a red satin skirt, another blue one, underclothes, nightclothes, white aprons, a Russian diadem with multicoloured ribbons, and a necklace of unbreakable beads which the baby could bite without danger.

'When I think of all we have done for her!' Olga sighed.

Finally she hurried off to a fitting, and Tatiana Sergeyevna returned to her own affairs. The florist, with whom the Zubovs had a contract for the regular decoration of their rooms, delivered armfuls of fresh flowers which had to be tastefully arranged in the vases. Then came the masseuse, an athletic matron with short hair and the spectacles of a professor. While she kneaded her client's body with her hands she reported the latest gossip. Scarcely had the masseuse finished her work than a manicurist replaced her at Tatiana Sergeyevna's bedside. The hairdresser awaited his turn in the neighbouring room. From time to time the telephone rang, friends suggested dinner, a sleigh-ride, a visit to a fashion house. . . . With her ear to the receiver and her eyes in the mirror, she gossiped happily with a friend as idle as herself, while the man flourished his curling-irons above her head.

❋ ❋ ❋ ❋

For form's sake, Russell sometimes went to the Zubov store to study the way its business was run. But despite the size of the counters, the number of its clerks and the variety of materials on the shelves, he did not feel strange in this big Muscovite establishment. From one country to another, the working methods were the same. The only notable differences from things at home were that the salesmen measured materials by the arsheen[1] and that Russian book-keepers did their calculations on an abacus. This was definitely no place for Russell to spend his time if he wished to profit by his stay in Moscow. Rather than grow bored in the afternoon in the stale smell of cloth, Russell preferred to go with Tatiana Sergeyevna and Helen on their trips round the town or for sleigh-drives across the Petrovsky Park.

Snow and sunshine. The finest turnouts met in the avenues. Between the passing lines of vehicles people greeted one another or exchanged shouts, or waved their hands as they went by. Some carriages were drawn by high-strung trotters, driven by enormous coachmen in blue or green greatcoats. But there were also lowly hired sleighs, calashes mounted on

[1] See page 10 for list of American equivalents.

runners, and little boxes carried swiftly along by horses with black flowing manes. The wind whistled around Russell's ears. Curled up opposite Tatiana Sergeyevna under her bearskin cover, his head down between his shoulders, his eyes running and his nose frozen, he was divided between wonder and fear. Troikas were seeking to pass one another to the rapid tinkling of little bells. The drivers sat upright on their seats, with arms outstretched and beards like snowy sponges. They shouted at their horses to encourage them.

Thanks to the information given him by Russian friends, Russell was not unaware of the way in which such an equipage was harnessed. Although harnessed in line abreast, a troika's three horses ran in different styles. Only the centre horse ran in shafts. A wooden arch surmounted its neck. Held on two reins, this horse was the active, well-balanced, serious element in the group. Its role was to trot straight ahead with its head up, while the other two horses had to gallop at its sides in a free and spirited fashion, their heads turned outwards and their muzzles down towards the snow. The driver handled these two with only one outer rein each, and a single strap connected each of them with the shaft-horse. Thus the three horses, in their silver harnesses, their steaming blankets and their bells, spread like a fan in front of the light sleighs. The Zubovs' carriage was drawn by a pair of trotters, but Tatiana Sergeyevna decided that one evening they would hire several troikas and go together to a famous restaurant near Moscow.

The drive to the Petrovsky Park often ended with a skating session on the Priesnienskie Ponds. Near the Zoological Garden one could hear the rumble of sleighs in the twilight mists as they glided up the frozen slopes, the grating of the chains that dragged them, laughter and the sound of an orchestra playing waltzes for the skaters. This orchestra was accommodated at the edge of the pond, in the shelter of an enormous plaster shell. The rink was surrounded by lighted globes. Elegant ladies circled upon the ice with their hands buried in their muffs. Others, clinging to chairs, uttered cries of fear, while military gentlemen swirled around them, their hands on their hips, their teeth shining and their moustaches stiff with frost. One big gentleman with side whiskers pushed a chair on skates, in which a pale and chilly beauty lolled. Russell, who knew how to skate, was glad to prove to his northern friends that, although he lived in a temperate climate, he was as skilful as they were in the art of propelling himself on the frozen surface of the pond. Around him the light of the lamp-standards transformed the mist into a sort of scintillating aurora, powdery and unreal. He dashed forward; he flew; he was no longer cold; he was a Samorzed, a Laplander.

After this exercise they all went together to the Café Philippov, which stood at the corner of Tverskaya Street and Glinichevsky Street. Oh! the comfortable warmth, the delicious perfume, that welcomed them over its threshold! It was said that old Philippov's fortune was made on the day when, having delivered some rolls to the Governor of Moscow, the latter had called him along to show him a spider that had been cooked in the dough. Without a sign of concern, Philippov had munched the spider, saying:

'It's a raisin, Your Excellency.'

'Since when have you been putting raisins in the rolls?'

'Since today, Your Excellency. It's an innovation. . . .'

When he returned home the patissier had grabbed a box of raisins and had cast them in handfuls into the dough that was ready for the oven. Some hours later, as proof of his good faith, he sent the Governor further rolls picked out with black spots. Next day all Moscow wanted to taste them. The fashion had been started. Philippov doubled his business; his son enlarged it and increased its specialities. There Russell could taste all sorts of pies with meat, cabbage, eggs, mushrooms, cream cheese or jam, complicated cakes, succulent tartlets, *kalachi*, *saiki*, black bread, brown bread and even white bread.

Another spot sacred to gastronomy was the immense Elisseyev store, named the Temple of Bacchus, stuffed with exotic fruits and fine wines. A crowd of buyers jostled before a display of pineapples, bananas, coconuts, grapes and flasks with multicoloured labels. The proprietor claimed to have gained the Legion of Honour at the Paris Exhibition of 1900 for the excellence of the vintages he had shown there. Whether that was true or not, his buttonhole was decorated with the red ribbon. In Moscow, meanwhile, the success of his business had been almost endangered by fussy officialdom. He had been trading for several years when some officials had been warned that he was contravening certain police regulations: no one might sell wines and spirits within a radius of forty-two sagenes (about 100 yards) of a church. Now, the door of the nearest church was within the prohibited distance from the store. Ordered to stop his trade, Élisseyev had avoided the problem by taking all his bottles to the far end of the store and making a new entry into Kozitsky Street. By thus separating the paths of those going to the temple of God and those going to the temple of Bacchus, he put himself right with the authorities and kept his customers.

Under the guidance of the Zubovs, Russell visited other stores: food stores, fashion, fur and jewellery shops. They seemed to him to be as well kept on the whole as those in Paris or London. But his preference, for picturesqueness, was for the Ryady bazaars on the Red Square. These huge three-floored buildings were intersected by passages, galleries and staircases, and entirely lit by electricity. This labyrinth sheltered more than a thousand shops with incredible displays of laceware, lacquer-ware, undressed skins, knives, enamel-ware, table-covers, antique clocks.... Bearded and booted merchants, standing in the doorways, called upon passers-by to enter. The crowd was indolent and poorly dressed. There were no fixed prices for the articles in the windows. The least scrap of cloth and the crudest wooden bowl were the excuse for interminable arguments. Beside a ragged peasant, searching amongst remnants, a young woman, wrapped in a sumptuous sable coat, was examining delicate Bruges lace through her lorgnette. As Russell was speaking French with Tatiana Sergeyevna, a jeweller offered them his silver articles, insisting on the fact that the quality of the silver used in Russian jewellery was better than that of French silver, but he was careful to say that with articles made of gold the reverse was the case.

Not far away, bordering upon the Theatre Square, was an even stranger market: Okhotny Ryad. Along the open-air stalls, overburdened with foodstuffs, dawdled a motley mob of housewives. With shawls over their heads, felt boots on their feet and baskets on their arms, they felt the chickens, the fish and the meat with both hands. Hens cackled, and piglets squealed in their cages. Sturdy hunters, festooned with hares, ducks and pheasants, wandered about among the crowd offering their game. An itinerant veterinary surgeon, with his apparatus hanging from his belt, took off his boots and pushed a cat into one of them head-first, so as to be able to castrate him more conveniently. Some old gossips surrounded him, serious and contemplative. The cat howled. Its owner crossed himself. Vendors of hot drinks poured their tea and *sbiten* into glasses for one kopeck a time. This boiling brew, with a honey basis, was the special choice of coachmen, who froze all day long upon their seats. But Tatiana Sergeyevna dissuaded Russell from tasting it. Moreover, she did not like these vulgar gatherings and always turned back to the shops she preferred, at the Marshals' Bridge on the Lubyanka Street and Tverskaya Street. When she felt she had made too many purchases, she called upon a messenger to carry the packages. There were messengers almost everywhere, in front of the big hotels, the luxury shops, the museums, the theatres and the restaurants. They were recognizable by the red bands round their caps. Friendly, quick and resourceful, they would deliver a letter, or obtain information about train times, or book seats for a concert. . . .

One day, as Russell and Alexander Vassilievitch Zubov were leaving the Reinhard tobacconist's shop where they had bought some cigars, a hurricane swept past them: the fire brigade! At the head of the formation galloped a big fellow in a copper helmet, armed with a long whip. His cheeks were puffed out and his eyes were fierce as he sounded the horn. Carriages scattered and pedestrians fled in disorder at his approach. Behind him red sleighs glided madly by, packed with helmets, ladders, hoses and axes. . . . In a twinkling, the brigade had vanished.

'The fire is in the Myasnitskaya district,' said Alexander Vassilievitch.

'How do you know?' Russell asked.

'Because three white balls have been hoisted on the fire brigade's watch-tower. That's the sign for Myasnitskaya. For

Gorodskaya it is one ball, for Pyatnitskaya four balls. . . . See for yourself. . . .'

Indeed, above the roofs the tower of the Tverskaya barrack could be seen, with three balls at its mast.

'At dusk,' Alexander Vassilievitch went on, 'the balls are replaced with lanterns. A watchman walks about the top of the building day and night. As soon as he perceives smoke in the distance he gives the alarm by sounding a bell and putting out balls or lanterns corresponding to the district. If the fire is very large a red flag or a red lantern is added to the usual signal. Then all the fire-brigade barracks are mobilized. . . . The firemen who have just passed came from the Tverskaya fire-station.'

'How do you know that?'

'By the horses' coats. Each barrack has its own colour for the teams. The horses of the Tverskaya barrack are all piebald, those of the Arbatskaya barrack are all bay, those of the Lakimskaya are all dapple-grey, those of the Sretinskaya are all roan with white tails and manes. . . . The Muscovites are very proud of their fire-brigades. . . .'

While talking, he turned into a cross-road and Russell saw that at this point the road and pavement were covered with fresh straw.

'That's because there's a sick person in one of these houses,' said Alexander Vassilievitch. 'The porter has put down straw to deaden the noise. Between ourselves, they could have done without it, for the snow deadens it all anyhow. But what can you do? It's a custom with us. When my daughter was in childbirth, I too made them spread straw. Ah! you were right to come to Moscow in the winter, dear Ivan Pavlovitch! It's the best time to see the town!'

Alexander Vassilievitch interrupted himself to point to a cloud of birds that were covering the sky. They were arriving in black, cawing masses from all points of the compass.

'What's going on?' Russell asked.

'Those are the crows coming home.'

'Coming home?'

'Yes, they roost in the towers, on the roofs, on the domes of the Kremlin. In five minutes they will all have settled. When the sun goes down the birds go to sleep and civilized man begins to live. You don't know the Moscow nights yet, Ivan Pavlovitch. I shall undertake your education. Tonight we'll go to the Salomonsky Circus, tomorrow to the Grand Theatre and the day after to the Moscow Arts Theatre, then next to the Korch Theatre and after that to the Little Theatre. . . .'

With his otter-skin cap jauntily set over one ear and his chin in the fur collar of his greatcoat, Alexander Vassilievitch was filled with satisfaction.

CHAPTER IV

ENTERTAINMENT AND DINING OUT

Moscow theatres – Different kinds of coachmen – The Merchants' Club – Supper at the Strelnya – Tzigane singers

COMPARED with Moscow's Grand Theatre, Covent Garden was a charming little chocolate-box. Russian ostentation overflowed in the building's gigantic dimensions. As he got down from the sleigh and prepared to make for the imposing pillars at the entrance, that were covered with hoar-frost and lit by the milk-white globes of the candelabra, Russell felt that the Tsar in person was about to welcome him at the door. The sleighs lined up to take their turn in front of the peristyle. Policemen shouted orders in hoarse voices. Coachmen swore as they dragged at their reins. Clouds of steam rose from the horses' flanks. In the flickering light of the carriage lamps, footmen were busy helping some general with white side-whiskers to get down, or some young woman, dusted with snow, who laughed as she shook her fur coat.

The bright vestibule hummed like a beehive in the sun. Bald heads, diadems, bare shoulders, sombre dress-coats, uniforms starred with decorations – a whole mass of people sparkled, glittered, swirled around, gossiped and drifted slowly away towards the great glass door which led to the auditorium. Tatiana Sergeyevna and her daughter, who were both in evening gowns, exchanged greetings with their friends. This was a ballet night, and all the season-ticket holders were there. The performance would begin at eight. Alexander Vassilievitch, as a Muscovite of rank, had rented his box for the season.

An attendant in red and gold uniform, decorated with the black imperial eagles, led the Zubov family and their guest down a long, curving corridor, decorated with garlands and medallions, pushed open a door and stood aside respectfully while the ladies entered what seemed to be a jewel-case of purple cloth. Tatiana Sergeyevna and Helen attended to their hair in a mirror in the little room before taking their seats at the front of the box. Their lorgnettes were at once directed at the pit. Every face in the orchestra stalls and the ground-floor boxes was known to them. They flirted with their fans and commented in an undertone on the dresses and hair-styles of other women. Standing behind them, Russell gazed with a slight feeling of dizziness at the swelling tiers of balconies, with their fine arabesques and their velvet-covered fronts on which were boxes of sweets, programmes, a naked elbow, or fingers clutching a handkerchief. Both below and above, people were turning in all directions, and smile answered smile across the bays. Above the gulf hung an enormous crystal chandelier. Facing the stage, the imperial box was empty, but the canopy and blazons and the two-headed eagle witnessed to the omnipresence of Nikolas II. All this luxury had a crushing effect on Russell. He was no longer surprised that a box at the Grand Theatre should cost at least fifteen roubles, but he could not understand how it was that in Moscow so many people could afford such luxurious entertainment.

In the orchestra pit that was filled with musicians in evening-dress, white shirt-fronts were leaning over the white scores. Violins, hautbois and clarinets were playing an unobtrusive prelude. Alexander Vassilievitch explained the subject of the ballet they were going to see in a few minutes. The auditorium grew dark, the conductor emerged, tapped the edge of his rostrum with his baton, and soft music rose towards the crimson curtains that were lit by the footlights.

Russell was not a balletomane. Nevertheless he admired the aerial evolutions of the dancers, the imposing dimensions of the stage and the rustic scene of the ballet. In the interval Alexander Vassilievitch had champagne and chocolates brought into the little room adjoining the box. Glass in hand, he told Russell that the Russians had a passion for dancing and that the rivalry of Moscow and St Petersburg in this sphere had the appearance of open warfare. In St Petersburg it was held that Moscow's artistes sacrificed tradition to facile effects, while in Moscow the artistes of St Petersburg were criticized for pushing technique too far to the detriment of feeling.

Each of the two cities had a dancing-school under the Emperor's patronage. The pupils at these illustrious establishments received a general education, of course, but most of their time was devoted to choreographic studies. Apprenticed to a cult which absorbed them completely, they were unaware of the events that took place beyond the walls of the institution; they wore clothes of antiquated cut, slept, ate, worked and dreamed together, and for their rare outings crowded together into big carriages with the windows screened, so that no gaze could fall upon their faces during the journey from school to theatre. After the final examination they became in effect dancing officials, with a salary that began at 600 roubles ($309) a year, and for the principals was 720 roubles ($371) a year. Then began a brilliant and exciting life, punctuated with homage, intrigues, success and disappointments. In Russia the craze for ballerinas was so great that those without a rich patron were rare. It was even whispered that certain members of the Imperial Family set the example in this matter. But beyond the sentimental considerations, the balletomanes constituted an educated, exacting and fiercely dogmatic public. They knew all the ballets by heart, followed the careers of the dancers, were indignant at the least deviation from the established rules, awaited tensely the moment when their idol started upon a difficult dance, and counted the beats with anxiety in their breasts.... It would have taken a catastrophe or a mortal illness to make any of them miss a gala performance. When Matilda Kchessinskaya came to dance in Moscow, all the front rows of the orchestra stalls in the Maria Theatre at St Petersburg were empty, for the incomparable dancer's devotees had followed her to Moscow.

With this information Russell watched the rest of the performance with added interest. The flying skirts so absorbed him that unconsciously he nodded his head in time with the music, and when the curtain fell upon the last vision of the star standing between two baskets of roses and blowing kisses to the crowd, he had not the least doubt that he would remember this performance always.

The audience streamed towards the exit. The snow swirled among the tall white columns. The attendants were shouting for carriages. The carriage lanterns swung around in the darkness. In the centre of the square a few coachmen were still warming themselves at the big braziers that had been lit in the iron-roofed shelters, while they waited for their masters.

❊   ❊   ❊   ❊

The next evening, Alexander Vassilievitch and his wife decided to take Russell to the Moscow Arts Theatre. This theatre, recently founded by Stanislavsky and Nemirovitch-Danchenko with the aid of a subsidy from the Russian merchant, Sava Moroxov, was reckoned to have revolutionized the aesthetic ideas of all nations and all ages. Reacting against declamatory styles and papier mâché décors, this new group claimed that it could recreate life on the stage. Stanislavsky demanded absolute devotion from his colleagues, tireless patience and the desire to purify themselves through work. The company rehearsed for months in the country, and if an actor gave evidence of doubtful morality his master did not hesitate to dismiss him, whatever his talent, in order to preserve his colleagues' peace of mind. The smallest details of the performance were handled with a fanatical concern for realism. In historical pieces the costumes were copied exactly from those of the period. The actors wore them for a long time before the first performance so as to get used to them, and so to shape them to their bodies that they would feel as much at home in them as in their own clothes. In open-air scenes painted trees were replaced by real trees. In indoor scenes the rooms had real walls, real ceilings, real furniture and real lamps; real chickens were served at table, real tea was poured from the teapots, and real fires burned in the grates. Everything was conceived so that the public should not have the impression of being present at a theatrical performance, but of looking in on the intimate life of the persons of the plays as if by a ruse.

Exacting as he was towards his actors, Stanislavsky was no less so towards the spectators. They had to enter the theatre religiously. At eight o'clock precisely the doors were closed and latecomers were driven away relentlessly. To avoid such a contretemps, the Zubovs and their guest had dined quickly and in an unusually frugal fashion. 'After the performance we'll make up for it at the Strelnya Restaurant,' Alexander Vassilievitch had said as he rose from the table with his mouth still full.

They arrived ten minutes before the curtain rose. What a contrast to the sumptuous decoration of the Grand Theatre! Here the colours and the lines were deliberately simple. The walls and stalls were done in the same grey material. The stage curtain was also grey, with a seagull pattern amongst its folds. 'That's because the theatre's first great success was Chekhov's *The Seagull*,' said Alexander Vassilievitch in an undertone. His normal exuberance had given way to a sort of timidity. The whole audience, moreover was as quiet as in the precincts of a temple.

'But this is nothing!' Alexander Vassilievitch went on. 'You'll be surprised by the silence after the curtain goes up. Silence is indispensable if the spectator is to catch the smallest stage effect arranged by Stanislavsky: the murmur of the wind, the patter of rain, the hammer of horses' hoofs, the ticking of a clock, the shrilling of crickets ... Chekhov made a little joke about this craze of Stanislavsky's when he said to a friend in Stanislavsky's presence: "I'm going to write a new play, which will begin like this: 'How nice it is! How quiet! Not a bird to be heard, not a dog, not a cuckoo, not an owl, not a nightingale, not a clock, not a bell, not a single cricket ...'" The joke went all over Moscow ...'

He stopped speaking and held his breath. There was not an empty seat in the theatre. The lights dimmed. The doors were closed hermetically, like those of a safe. The curtain quivered and then opened gently. Without leaving his seat, Russell found himself tossed headlong into a noisy boyar feast. Servants were carrying enormous plates laden with geese and pigs, and piles of fruit and vegetables. Others were rolling barrels of wine. This motley throng recreated the very disorder of reality. They were playing *Tsar Fedor*.

Although he did not understand a word of the retorts that were tossed to and fro across the stage, Russell followed the performance enthusiastically. Each interval was a dead period, for which his friends' gossip could not console him. 'This is the real theatre!' he stammered. 'We ought to follow its example. If I could only take them home with me, show them . . .' At the end of the performance it was in a half-conscious state that he let himself be carried by the crowd towards the doors.

❀   ❀   ❀   ❀

To get to the Strelnya Restaurant, Alexander Vassilievitch had ordered a troika from the livery-stable keeper Echkin,[1] and it was the owner's son who drove them. Bundled up in his overcoat, he could not even get down from his seat to welcome his customers. The horses pawed the ground and pranced. Alexander Vassilievitch, his wife and Russell settled down upon their luxurious seats and muffled themselves up to the chest in woollen blankets and bear-skins.

Echkin Junior started off. The little bells tinkled gently. In Tverskaya Street dry snow lashed their faces and there was not even the shadow of a passer-by on the white pavements. A few steamy windows were lit, showing dark silhouettes against the diffused light of a chandelier. A servant stood at a palace gate. The plumed helmet of a policeman was visible. Sleighs passed with their loads of muffled-up revellers. A coachman sang at the top of his voice. Another shouted: 'Heh! *Grabyat!*'

'What's he shouting?' Russell asked.

'He's shouting: "We are being robbed!"' said Alexander Vassilievitch.

'But why?'

'It's an old Moscow coachman's cry from the days when the roads were not safe. . . . The danger has gone, but the cry survives. . . .'

Beyond the Tverskaya Gate all the teams speeded up. One sleigh, drawn by a single horse, caught up with the Echkin troika.

'That's Gusev, the best *likatch* in Moscow,' said Alexander Vassilievitch.

'The best what?' asked Russell, swallowing a mouthful of frozen air.

'The best *likatch*. The *likatch* are the aristocracy of Russian coachmen. Their horses are half-breeds, former race-

---

[1] Echkin, like Ukharsky, had one of the best livery-stables in Moscow.

horses, which cost a lot. No one can compete with them for speed. The most famous *likatch* are Gusev and Spitzin, but their charges are very high. Gusev has another string to his bow! He has an admirable voice and sings all through the journey. Very often, when he takes his customers to the Strelnya or the Yar, they take him into their private room so that they can go on listening to him.'

At that moment Gusev was not singing but yelling in a terrible voice:

'*Beregis! . . . Kuda edesh! . . . Gusev pravit. . . .*'

'He's saying: "Look out! . . . Where are you going? . . . It's Gusev driving!"' Alexander Vassilievitch explained, and he tapped on the coachman's back to suggest that he should slow down. Echkin docilely drew in to the right and Gusev passed him in a whirlwind. His passenger was an officer.

'As a rule, officers are not allowed to use ordinary hired carriages,' said Alexander Vassilievitch. 'They always take the *likatch*, or half-*likatch*, never the wretched little sleigh with its rawboned horse and tattered driver, whom we call a *vanka*, *Vanka* being the diminutive of Ivan – begging your pardon, my dear Ivan Pavlovitch. And here's another kind of equipage, the *golubki*, with a wheel-horse and another on a breast-harness. They are quick and pleasant. . . . You see a lot of them outside the Merchants' Club for the big Tuesday dinners. . . .'

'Oh! those Tuesday dinners,' sighed Tatiana Sergeyevna. 'My husband always comes back from them at impossible hours with his smoke-inflamed eyes and a headache. . . .'

'I *must* go there from time to time, angel,' said Alexander Vassilievitch. 'It's a matter of great business interest. I meet important and influential men there. . . . Every headache's worth a fortune. . . . This one's in scrap metal, and that one in cloth, in the oil trade or in railways. Their pockets are bursting with roubles. And what meals! My mouth waters even when I think of them! You will never eat better sucking-pigs, Ivan Pavlovitch, than at the Merchants' Club. It comes straight from Testov's farm, where the pigs are fed in pens where they can scarcely move their feet. Another remarkable speciality is *kulibyaki* in a dozen layers, each layer being composed of a different filling: meat, fish, mushrooms, chicken, game, and I don't know what else. And the champagne, and the fruit drink! The club treasurer is a specialist in fruit drinks.... Stepan Ryabov's orchestra plays during meals. Hungarian and Russian tzigane choirs take turns in singing....'

'Yes,' said Tatiana Sergeyevna, 'and afterwards these men invite the chorus girls to their tables!'

'So what?' asked Alexander Vassilievitch. 'Russian merchants have a mania for singing. The choruses are those from the Yar or the Strelnya. Pretty girls, too! From the Russian chorus it is the director, Anna Zakharovna, who chooses the singer for each client. She knows everyone's taste. But obviously, the soloists, like the violent Polia or the beautiful Alexandra Nikolayevna, can do as they please. Generally the Muscovite merchants prefer the Russian chorus girls, who are gentler than the tziganes and more approachable than the Hungarians, whose lingo is disconcerting. However, the "rape of the Sabines", as we say, is strictly prohibited in the environs of the club. All the chorus girls, after singing and eating, have to return to the Yar and the Strelnya. Their admirers follow in their wake in sleighs. They will wait until the girls have finished their work before dealing with them. You will see these professional charmers at the restaurant very soon!'

Russell did not reply. He was only mildly interested by the prospect of these musical and amorous pleasures. Without daring to admit it to anyone, he was sorry that Helen had not accompanied her parents to the Strelnya, but it was regarded as unseemly for a young girl to appear in a place where ladies of easy virtue were on show.

Beside the road the trees of the Petrovsky Park hung their white tracery branches, and the troika sped along under the frosty lacework. Other troikas followed. In the darkness the tinkle of the little bells mingled with bursts of singing and gusts of laughter. Lights were shining in the distance.

'We're there!' said Alexander Vassilievitch.

Beyond the snowy shadows appeared something like an enormous block of ice, lit from within. The roof and walls of the restaurant were of glass. Beside it were a *traktir* for the coachman and a stable for the horses. The sleigh slowed down and then stopped. A braided porter hurried up to the travellers, helped them to descend and brushed the snow from their clothes. In the entrance other servants relieved them of their fur-lined coats, their galoshes and boots. Coming out of the arctic night, Russell was plunged into an immense and overheated room where the penetrating odours of caviar and fine sauces prevailed. In the middle of winter, tropical plants spread amongst the guests. Palm-trees raised their scaly and hairy trunks to the ceiling. On the periphery, within the stony jaws of artificial caves, were little white tables surrounded by pink faces. Fountains splashed into basins and cascades ran down the sides of the rocks. A Hungarian orchestra was playing on a raised platform.

A head waiter hurried up to Alexander Vassilievitch, greeted him with all the deference due to a distinguished habitué and led the new-comers to the table reserved for them. Still dazed by the sleigh-ride, Russell gazed with stupefaction upon the crowd of diners with cheerful faces and clattering forks. Alexander Vassilievitch drew his attention to a big and bearded person, a merchant in his own trade, who on a gala occasion had payed an exorbitant sum to have one of the finest palm-trees in the room cut down because, he said, it hid the orchestra.

Two waiters were politely leading away a man in evening dress who was obviously drunk; they were going to revive him and bring him to his senses in the lavatory. Tziganes with motley shawls and glittering trinkets were seated here and there amongst the customers: these were the charmers of whom Alexander Vassilievitch had spoken. Meanwhile some little Hungarians, very young and very pretty, dressed in frogged waistcoats and wearing soft leather boots, were unenthusiastically playing a potpourri from a Viennese operetta. The violinist, the pianist and the flautist each had an admirer who, alone at his table, was impatiently waiting for the music to end.

Alexander Vassilievitch was scarcely seated before he decided that they would be better in a private room, and once again the head waiter and the waiters made themselves obsequiously busy. The private room opened out on the main room through a glazed bay and was furnished with a table,

1 *Left:* Workers' quarter in Moscow, with an ikon above the street

Right: Railway police on the Trans-Siberian line

Left: Second-class carriage at the end of a train on the Trans-Siberian railway

2 *Above:* The Kremlin and the Moskvaretzky Bridge at the end of the century

Left: The Spass Gate of the Kremlin at the end of the century

chairs, a sofa and a piano draped with a fringed shawl. Of course, they were served at once with iced champagne, 'with icicles'. Fresh caviar, liver *au madère*, sterlets, partridges *à la crème*. . . . Over dessert, Alexander Vassilievitch called in a group of Russian singers with their balalaikas. After the regulation five songs they gave way to a tzigane chorus, and girls with the dark faces of wild creatures slipped into the room. Alexander Vassilievitch knew them all. As he explained to Russell, they were not ordinary gipsies, but women of great talent, fawned upon by Moscow's high society, who, as a result of the princely tips received from their admirers, had amassed fortunes. Their jewels were authentic and their adventures were numerous.

'A true Russian,' said Alexander Vassilievitch, 'is prepared to spend heedlessly in order to listen to good tzigane songs. These songs arouse his melancholy as well as his gaiety. They take him out of himself. That's what's important. A man who does not know how to get out of himself from time to time is as much to be pitied as a prisoner in a cell.'

Behind the chorus girls three musicians entered, dressed in red tunics with split sleeves thrown over the back. The soloist, a mature woman with black eyes and prominent cheekbones, placed a glass of champagne on an upturned plate, advanced upon Tatiana Sergeyevna and sang a drinking song. Russell was surprised to see the respectable Tatiana Sergeyevna empty her glass at a draught. 'Are they now going to attack me?' he wondered apprehensively. And he was right. Directed by Alexander Vassilievitch, the chorus begged 'Ivan Pavlovitch' to oblige too. He swallowed an enormous bumper of champagne and a shout of delight greeted his performance. The ceremony was repeated with Alexander Vassilievitch, who, with his moustache askew and his eyes bright, was bursting with satisfaction. Afterwards the soloist sang in a harsh voice a chant that brought the tears to Russell's eyes. He did not know whence had come this desire to be sad. The more he listened to the tziganes, the more he wanted to drink, as if to prepare the substance of his body for a wonderful revelation. The bottles of champagne – both for the chorus girls and for the guests – followed one another on to the table. Suddenly Russell felt that he was drunk, but with an intoxication infinitely noble and poetic. Alexander Vassilievitch and Tatiana Sergeyevna were his brother and sister. He would never leave them. He was going to live with them till the end of his days. The singers' gaudy finery fascinated him. He beat time with his hands and no longer heard what his neighbours were saying.

He never understood how it was that he found himself, at about three in the morning, in complete darkness in a snowy landscape. A troika was bearing him and his friends along. As far as he could make out, they could not go home until they had eaten an omelette at a local inn.

CHAPTER V

BATHS, *TRAKTIRS* AND NIGHT SHELTERS

Russian bath-houses and how their attendants were recruited –
Their duties – Life in the 'traktirs' – The underworld of Mos-
cow: the Khitrov market, its shelters, taverns, and dens of
thieves, criminals and beggars

Russell had read in his Baedeker that a conscientious
tourist must visit the Russian steam baths. Some were
in the luxury class, with private rooms, which cost three
or four roubles to enter, but there were others for the masses
costing from five kopecks per person, where there was only a
communal room for the men and another for the women. As
soon as he had made his intentions known to Alexander
Vassilievitch, the latter proposed to take him to an establishment of the better class. They asked for a private room for
two, which embarrassed Russell, for he was hardly prepared
for the idea of undressing in front of his host. But they were
scarcely in the little room before Alexander Vassilievitch had
stripped himself quite naked with evident pleasure. He
laughed and slapped his belly. His baptismal cross shone on
his flabby chest.

The robust simplicity of his attitude encouraged Russell to
undress also. He had just pulled off his shirt when two strap-
ping fellows came into the room flexing their shoulders. These
were the bathers whom Alexander Vassilievitch had engaged
at the entrance. They were dressed very lightly in linen
trousers, tied at the waist, with a mountain of muscles above.
Russell's distrust increased. They passed into the next room,
which was tiled, overheated and full of steam, in which a
slight odour of damp flesh persisted. In a trice the customers
became as clay on a white marble table. Russell's bather
sprinkled him from head to foot with boiling water, lathered
him with a fibre sponge and violently rubbed his ears, neck,
arms, and the whole of his anatomy. Beside him, Alexander
Vassilievitch groaned under the efforts of the other fanatic,
whose head was shaven and who wore a scapular over his

hairy chest. Turned over and over, sat up forcibly, stretched
out on his stomach, kneaded, beaten, massaged, scraped and
washed, Russell had no time to recover his wits before he had
been pushed through a little door into a suffocating cloud of
steam. Plunged not far from him into the same cloud, Alexander Vassilievitch was furiously beating his own body with a
broom made of twigs to stimulate the circulation of the blood.
His red face, glistening with perspiration, hovered in the
murky emanations of the stove. He beat himself, punished
himself, and delightedly expiated the sin of being a man with
dirty skin.

'Try it, Ivan Pavlovitch, it's marvellous!' he cried in a
breathless voice.

About to give up the ghost, Ivan Pavlovitch declined.
When he was no longer a piece of overheated and enervated
flesh, a cold shower fell upon his shoulders. He then found
himself in the changing-room again with a chiropodist seated
before him on a stool. Alexander Vassilievitch, stretched out
on a bench, had lit a cigar and was savouring, with half-
closed eyes, the pleasure of being as clean as a new kopeck.

'You will never get as clean in a bathroom as in one of our
bath-houses,' he said. 'Here the pores open up, the flesh
breathes, the smallest bits of dirt run away. Believe me,
having a modern bathroom would not stop anyone in Russia
from going to have a good sweat in the hands of experts.
Ordinary folk go up to the bath-houses every Saturday. For
them it's a holiday. People of the upper classes meet in a
private room like us. They relax, idle and gossip. The most
famous bath-houses in Moscow are the Sandunovsky. But
there are easily a hundred others in the city. The Tsentralnye
baths, the Poltavskie baths ... I will show you some of
them. . . .'

He kept his word. During eight consecutive days, Russell
visited the bathing-establishments with him: some were very
modest, while others were astonishingly luxurious. At the
end of this investigation, the life of the 'bathers' or *banshchiki*
held no more secrets from him. Alexander Vassilievitch explained that the staff of each bath-house came from the same
commune, or at least from the same region. Apprenticeship
began when very young.

A fully qualified 'bather' would return to his native village to spend a few days' holiday. His closest friends admired his new boots, his cap with its patent-leather peak, and his watch, which he wore on a chain round his neck, hanging down as far as his stomach. Relatives who had a son of ten or twelve years would beg this splendid citizen to take the boy with him when he returned to the city. The boy would learn the craft among men who were not really strangers. The 'bather' agreed. A passport had to be obtained in the boy's name by faking his age, for the law forbade the employment of children under twelve years in any kind of labour, or fifteen years in activities detrimental to their health. Of course a tip had to be passed to the official who would add a few years to the document. The boy scarcely knew how to read, but he had learned to sign his name. He was given a pair of *lapti* – footwear of plaited bark – a little linen and an old coat, and he went off to work and to make his fortune.

At the baths where he ended up, all confused, his hair was cut, he was scoured, and he was taught to bow very low to important visitors. On the days when the baths were closed, either on Monday or Tuesday, he ran errands for the master, cleaned the rooms with water, and helped his elders to put kvass into bottles; on all the other days, he prepared the little twig brooms, of which the consumption was enormous. On the days before holidays, in the larger bath-houses, close on three thousand were distributed, which quickly softened and came to pieces in the hands of the flagellants. The soldiers who came from their barracks in complete platoons had the right to one broom between ten men. The trees of neighbouring forests provided these thin and supple branches. They were brought into the city in convoys. The firewood for heating came down the Moscow River from Mojaisk as rafts.

The baths always comprised a changing-room, a soaping-room and the bathroom properly so called. The soaping-room was warmed by a Dutch stove and the steam-room by a stove of stone or cast iron on which an attendant threw buckets of water to produce the steam. The temperature rose to over 160° F. All day long men leapt about in the smelly steam, beat themselves, and sprinkled one another with water. The same thing went on in the women's section. To sweat better, the real enthusiasts climbed up some steps, for the heat was even greater nearer the ceiling than it was at floor level.

Meanwhile, our little boy, naked to the navel, an apron round his hips, rapidly made scrubbing-cloths from sacking. From five in the morning till midnight he suffocated in the heat, among the crowd. Cuffs rained upon him. His profession was thrust into his head and back with blows. Sometimes a small coin was dropped into his hand by some pink and damp personage with a glistening beard. By fifteen or sixteen he had learnt to cut toe-nails, and to pare corns and callouses. At seventeen he was no longer regarded as an apprentice, but as a bathing-attendant. His earnings increased with his experience, and the time came to think of marriage. Now, marriage was not possible without new clothes, a *tulup* and a pair of boots. The *tulup* and clothes would be ordered from Ioan Pavlov, who lived at the far end of a court in Marosseyka Street. The bath attendants patronized no other tailor, and he had no other customers but the bath attendants. Payment was made in two parts, the first half at Easter and the other half at Christmas. From Ivan Pavlov one went to Peter Kirsanytch, who lived in Karetnaya Street and likewise worked for none but the bath-house staff.

When the measurements had been taken, Peter Kirsanytch asked: 'Do you want these boots with or without a squeak?' And received the answer, 'With!'

The answer was correct, for everyone knows that new boots must squeak when one walks, so that passers-by may notice and covet them. Thus clothed and shod the man went back to his village and chose a wife, and afterwards the young couple returned to settle in Moscow close to the bath-house. So good a profession could not be abandoned. With time this man grew in importance. He had regular clients. On some of them he even attempted a little massage. His fame grew. He bought a watch. And one day, when he paid a visit to his family in the country, a neighbour brought his son to him, a boy of ten, who could not read or write but would like to work with him in Moscow at the steam baths, where one could earn so good a living.

However, there was one situation for small peasants that was even more desirable, provided that they were not totally illiterate; that of a waiter at a *traktir*. The majority of waiters in baggy trousers and white shirts whom Russell had seen in restaurants had been brought to the city by their parents when very young. If they were from Iaroslav they had a strong chance of being engaged, for it was this province which by tradition provided the staff for the best houses. Every father's dream was that his son might be taken on at the Hermitage or at Testov's. But to begin with he had to be content with second-rank establishments. The apprentice exchange was held in a *traktir* near Tverskaya Street. The *restaurateur* concluded a five-year contract with the parents, and the boy followed his new master, who housed and fed him, and taught him his profession. To begin with he would help the dish-washers, and then, if he had the inclination, he would be allowed into the kitchens, where he would be instructed in the preparation of the dishes, and when he knew 'all the sauces', he would be launched into the dining-room amongst the customers. But it would only be after five years of obscure labour that he received the insignia of his profession: a silk sash and a purse of black patent leather for his counters. He always kept the purse in his sash; as for the counters, he was given them at the cash-desk every morning, to the value of twenty-five roubles, and they served to pay for the dishes ordered at the 'buffet'. Thereafter he would exchange the money he received from customers for further counters. Tips were put into a pool and at the end of the day were shared by the staff. They were paid no wages and even had to pay their employer up to 20 per cent of their earnings; in some fashionable restaurants, moreover, they had to provide themselves with an outfit comprising half a dozen white calico or holland shirts and trousers.[1]

Running continually between the office and the restaurant, they worked from fourteen to sixteen hours a day. It was the tea service which took the most time and brought in the smallest tips. Five kopecks a glass with two sugars! And customers would ask for boiling water to add to the pot. Certainly, in the big *traktirs* one made it up on the food, but in the *traktirs* for coachmen, for example, one slaved for almost

---

[1] It should be noted that in the few restaurants of European style the frock coat was *de rigueur* for waiters.

nothing. In Moscow these *traktirs* for coachmen were innumerable. A courtyard with a drinking-trough for the horses, and a shack with a food-counter for the men. Frozen by long waiting in the street, they entered and sat at a table in a corner, nibbled a salted gherkin or a crust of black bread, drank a glass of tea and stayed there, weary and stupefied, enjoying the warmth, the smell and the darkness. On fast days they did not take sugar with their tea, but lime honey instead.

In the famous Egorov *traktir* in the Okhotny Ryad Square, customers had the choice of tea with lemon or tea with a serviette. Those who prefered the former received two glasses of tea with lemon and sugar. Those who preferred the latter received a cup, a little pot for the preparation of concentrated tea, a large pot full of boiling water and a clean serviette which they tied round their necks. Drinking their boiling hot infusion they sweated abundantly and sponged their foreheads, necks and beards with the linen. When they had emptied three or four pots and sweated in this fashion, the linen serviettes were no more than sodden rags which were then proudly abandoned on the edge of the table.

In every *traktir* an ikon, lit by a night-light, hung on three little silver chains. The customers bowed and crossed themselves before it as they passed the threshold. The luxury *traktirs*, the restaurants of European style, also had their ikons, but they did not receive the same veneration from the visitors. Among these *traktirs* de luxe there were some that specialized in Siberian dishes, like Lopachev's; others, like Testov's, were famous for their sucking-pig with horseradish; the big merchants preferred to frequent the Hermitage Restaurant, or the Slavyansky-Bazar, the Yar or the Strelnya; and the lovers of cock-fighting went secretly to the Golubiatnia. In all these establishments the staff found a good living. Even the little apprentices were relatively well treated. In any case their fate was more enviable than that of the children who worked in the bathhouses, or with the shoemakers, tailors, carpenters or masons. Among these boys, who were taken into the crafts while very young, some were so famished and beaten that they fled back to their villages or joined the bands of ragamuffins that hung about the Khitrov market.

According to Alexander Vassilievitch, the Khitrov market

was a resort of brigands, and he refused to take Russell there
although the latter very much wanted to go. More courageous
than his father-in-law, Paul Egorovitch Sychkin volunteered
to accompany their friend to the Muscovite Court of
Miracles. Paul Egorovitch Sychkin was a progressive; he believed that man would be set free by machines and told himself that in his heart he was very close to the people. Nevertheless he asked Russell to dress in a modest fashion and not
to carry much money in his pockets.

The Khitrov market spread over a vast square in the centre
of the city near the Iauza River. Tortuous alleyways ran down
into a sort of basin, surrounded by low houses with façades
of rotted and flaking plaster.[1] Was it the closeness of the
water that seemed to keep a blanket of mist over the area?
In these murky vapours swarmed pale-faced phantoms in
ragged and filthy garments. Innumerable stalls, rooted in the
snow, offered sausages, herrings and cucumbers for sale. Soup
was steaming in saucepans. When they were opened, the
doors of the *traktirs* gave out thick and nauseating odours.
Russell halted in front of a row of matrons seated, like
bundles of rags, on great earthenware or iron pots. Hunched,
and with blue noses and toothless mouths, they were shouting
in throaty voices to draw the attention of passers-by.

'What are they doing?' Russell asked.

'They're keeping their wares warm.'

'What?'

'Yes, indeed! There are *lapsha*[2] in those pots. The food
stays warm for a long time under their skirts. When a customer turns up these women lift the lids of their seats in order
to serve them. It isn't very appetizing, but quite ingenious.'

Russell felt uneasy in his clean clothes and holeless shoes.
Menacing shadows surrounded him and barged into him. The
whole Khitrov market seemed to be watching him and him
alone.

'And these houses around the square,' he went on timidly.
'What are they for?'

[1] Gorki was inspired by the customs of this quarter to write *The Lower
Depths*. In the interests of realism the actors of Stanislavsky's company went
to these places to study the language, dress and behaviour of the degraded
population from nature in order to present it on the stage afterwards.

[2] Dishes made of vermicelli.

'They are night-shelters.'

'All of them?'

'Yes. More than ten thousand destitute persons can stay in them for five kopecks each.'

'How do you know?'

'I made inquiries, purely out of social curiosity,' said Paul Egorovitch.

He told Russell that every morning entire groups of workers came straight from the station to the Khitrov market, lined up in a shelter and with their bundles in their hands waited to be hired by the overseers for work in the city. In the afternoon it was in the same shelter that the ragmen settled down to do business with the tramps. The latter undressed or took off their boots on the spot, sold their boots or *tulups* and went off half-naked with a few kopecks in their pockets. By stripping themselves they acquired the means to spend two or three more nights under a roof. Moreover, each shelter had its own kind of customer.[1] The Rumiantsov shelter comprised two *traktirs*, the Siberian and the Stage. To the Yaroshenko shelter there was only one: the Convict Prison. At the Stage the homeless, the beggars and the ragmen mainly gathered; at the Siberian the pickpockets and receivers; at the Convict Prison those who had deserted from forced labour or had escaped from municipal prisons, all men of noisy and violent temper who could be roused to madness by raw vodka. Two policemen of giant stature ruled over this labyrinth of alleyways. Even the boldest of the malefactors feared their fists, which were as heavy as stone. They knew everyone, but they made an arrest only in the event of a brawl or on the express instruction of the authorities. When Paul Egorovitch asked him about this, one of these representatives of order answered with a great laugh:

'It's because I close my eyes to these fellows' pasts that I have stayed on the job for twenty years. Otherwise I should have been rotting underground for a long time. You see, I am here to guarantee order and not to denounce those who have disturbed it at some other time.'

These words, which Paul Egorovitch translated for Russell,

[1] Shelters were known by the names of their proprietors: Rumyanstov, Bunin, Kulakov, etc.

still further increased his feeling of uneasiness in a hostile world.

'Let's make a tour of the Convict Prison,' Paul Egorovitch suggested with an engaging smile.

'What Convict Prison?'

'The *traktir* I spoke about just now.'

'Do you think it's necessary?'

'Yes, of course. Don't be afraid. The habitués of the Khitrovka don't attack well-meaning visitors like you or me. Anyway the policeman is at the door. . . .'

They entered a low, dark room, foul with the smell of boots and *makhorka*.[1] Thick smoke obscured the light of a petrol-lamp standing on the counter. Hideous faces floated in the half-light like jelly-fish on the surface of the sea. The sound of voices was deafening. The men were quarrelling. A dishevelled woman with a bleeding nose and a crazed look barged into Russell and rushed towards the door. A drunkard followed her with raised fists, staggering. After a few seconds of hesitation, Paul Egorovitch and Russell left also. In front of the *traktir*, the drunkard had collapsed in the snow and was sleeping off his vodka. The woman was in flight along an alleyway, screaming. The policeman had seen it all and had not moved.

'Now,' said Paul Egorovitch, 'let's take a look at the sleeping-rooms.'

Russell did not dare to say that he would have preferred to go home. He forced a smile, but fear seized his limbs. Following Paul Egorovitch he penetrated into a leprous two-floored building, climbed a staircase that stank of latrines, and came out into a big room in which some sleeping men lay like corpses on litters. Curled up under their rags they were steeped in a nauseous odour of rotten meat, vermin and human excrement. The majority of the bunks were of slightly sloping planks of wood on supports, a yard above the floor. Ten men were snoring upon them side by side, but a slat had only to be moved to disclose a second layer of customers, stretched out below, on the bare floor.

'Above, they pay six kopecks a night,' said Paul Egorovitch. 'But below, as they have less air, the price is only five

---

[1] Bad tobacco in use amongst the people.

kopecks. The whole place is full by nine in the evening. But during the day it is only the lazy ones and the sick who stay here. This shelter is regarded as the intellectual centre of the Khitrovka. You will find the unsuccessful actors here, writers who have never published a thing in their lives, drunken poets, and penniless geniuses.... Among them are the copiers.'

'The copiers?'

'Yes. Come this way and you'll see.'

In the next room about a dozen men in rags were seated around a table, with their heads bent, pen in hand. Not one raised his eyes to look at the visitors.

'They are copying plays,' said Paul Egorovitch. 'The job is always urgent and seldom well paid. Those you see will work all night. Then, before daylight, they will elect one to deliver the goods. One man will lend him his boots, another his coat and another his hat in order to give him a presentable appearance. Thus attired he will go to the theatrical agent and return with the money. Fifty kopecks an act!'

The pens squeaked and the backs remained bent. The old scholars laboured elbow to elbow over their task.

'Another remarkable shelter is the Bunin,' said Paul Egorovitch, drawing Russell out into the street again. 'It is the refuge of professional beggars and especially tailors. The latter are called "crabs" here because they never stick their noses outside. In the middle of the night the thieves arrive and tumble into the room. They carry bundles of fur-lined coats, lined overcoats and elegant capes. Then the tailors share out the task at once. All the garments are transformed. How could a policeman recognize a sable cloak, which he had been told had disappeared, in these fur caps and slippers? What connection could there be between this well-cut waist-coat and the overcoat which some gentleman has complained of having lost in a bath-house cloakroom? The next morning the dealers will carry away armfuls of all these articles, which have been made by half-naked tailors in a few hours by the light of a wretched petrol-lamp. The profits are shared equit-ably. There's no trickery between comrades in such a busi-ness as this. Khitrovka law is merciless. Anyone who cheats ends some day with a knife in his back.'

A woman with a dirty furrowed face and wrapped in sordid rags, passed with a shivering baby in her arms.

'That's a professional beggar-woman,' said Paul Egorovitch. 'She hires the baby by the day.'

'You can hire babies in the Khitrovka?' Russell asked.

'Of course! They are very much in demand among the shrews who live by public charity. With that sodden and scabby bundle they are sure to soften the hearts of the crowd. During the last week of Lent a rather peevish infant will bring in twenty-five kopecks a day, and a child of three will bring in ten. They trail them through the cold and the mud and take their shoes off so that they will be more pitiful. If they are still at the breast they are deprived of milk so that they will whimper more. In many cases the baby dies in the arms of the hirer, who will continue to carry it until it is dark so as not to miss any alms.'

'It's abominable,' Russell stammered.

'Yes, my dear fellow,' said Paul Egorovitch. 'The Khitrovka children have a lot to complain of. Those who survive learn to keep watch very young, to steal from window displays, or simply to beg. They specialize. They join groups. From time to time there's a round-up in the shelters. A few bad types go to prison. But when they've served their sentence, they slip back into the same surroundings and resume their old habits. As to the girls, they all end up as prostitutes, either on the streets or in brothels. In the Khitrovka a virgin of fourteen is something rare. Don't you have districts of ill-fame in your own cities too?'

'Certainly,' said Russell. 'But it is my impression that the poverty and decay are less horrible than here.'

'Yes, yes!' Paul Egorovitch conceded. 'In Russia everything is big: riches, poverty, faith. . . . There is no such thing, so to speak, as a middle class. On one side are the high aristocracy and the opulent society of merchants, industrialists and landlords; and on the other are the immense masses, illiterate and superstitious, who were perhaps better adapted to serfdom than to this false freedom of destitution. Between these two extremes is a thin layer of skilled workers, technicians, lesser officials and intellectuals who are struggling to defend their taste for progress and independence. They are the modern and active element of the country and cannot draw the inert mass of the nation along with them. They are constantly in danger of being crushed by the rest or swallowed up. My father-in-law, who is an optimist, believes that things will turn out all right in time. For myself, I fear the worst. There is too much social inequality in Russia, so the stability of the régime must be endangered at some time or another. When I leave the Khitrov market and see the fine shops in Tverskaya Street, I wonder with anguish how the two worlds can exist together.'

The sky was growing dark. Faint lights were appearing behind the dirty windows. Snow began to fall.

'This is the time when the Khitrovka becomes dangerous,' Paul Egorovitch went on. 'I don't advise staying here after twilight. Let's go quickly!'

A steep and narrow road lay before them. Creatures with grimacing features turned as they passed. A few jeers rang out. Russell drew his head down between his shoulders. Paul Egorovitch took his hand and drew him on, like Virgil leading Dante amongst the damned. When they got back, Russell found that someone had stolen his watch.

CHAPTER VI

THE ORTHODOX CHURCH

*Ikons and their mystic meaning; their place in everyday life –
Prosfors, holy water and fasts – White Clergy and black
clergy; the supremacy of the monks; the ordinary priests – The
Orthodox Church as distinct from other religions – Differences
between the Orthodox Church and the Catholic Church – The
piety of the Russian people – The sects – Pilgrims – The
Orthodox saints – Religious and other festivals – The Russian
liturgical chants – Rites and creeds*

RUSSELL, though a freethinker, found it natural to accompany the Zubov family each Sunday when they went to Orthodox mass. He felt that he would have betrayed his duty as a tourist had he refused to participate in these collective acts of devotion which reveal a nation's heart. Moreover, all philosophical considerations excluded, he appreciated the stately ostentation of the Russian liturgy. His only regret was that the congregation had to stand throughout the service. There was not a bench in the whole vast nave of the Church of the Saviour where the Zubovs customarily went. This church, which was built to commemorate the deliverance of Moscow in 1812, was in the form of the Greek cross. Four enormous pillars supported the central dome where the picture of the Sabaoth God hung. All around, in a gallery, marble plaques bore the names of the heroes who were killed by the French and the list of battles won against Napoleon. The several levels of the ikonostasis were also of marble, of unreal and dazzling whiteness. Gold was everywhere, in the niches, in the little balconies and down the columns. Hundreds of chandeliers hung their flaming constellations under the painted vaults.

Russell had been surprised at first by the absence of sculptures, but Alexander Vassilievitch explained that, contrary to the Roman Catholics, the Orthodox had kept the biblical prohibition against idols of stone, wood or metal: 'Thou shalt not make unto thee any graven image, or any likeness of any thing that is in heaven above...' But they considered that this prohibition applied only to works of art which, by their size and shape, were likely to be confused with the person represented. They therefore barred any statues or figures in the round from the sanctuary, but permitted painted images, which in their flatness could not affect the minds of the faithful.[1] For did not the heathen of earlier days burn incense and immolate their victims before the statues of their gods and goddesses? The Russian clergy went even further in discouraging the suspect forms of devotion by not reserving chapels to the principal Church saints. These saints almost always had their effigies on the pillars in the naves, on the walls of the ikonostasis, but rarely in any place where they could be the object of exclusive worship. Moreover, at the end of the last century the believers were still opposed to giving the colours of living flesh to the faces of the blessed and insisted that artists should continue to colour them with a sepia tint that was as far from natural as possible, a tradition which went back to the legendary madonnas of St Luke.

Ikon-worship in the Eastern Church had been sanctioned by the Seventh Oecumenical Council (at Nicaea in 787). According to this high assembly's definition, there was a mystical relation between the picture and the model. The copy shared in the essence of what had inspired it. The saint on whom the artist was concentrating entered into the artist's work and transfigured it – vivified it, so to speak. If the subject himself was present in the ikon, his divine power lay therein. St John of Damascus said that an ikon was 'a substance full of divine energy, power and grace.' When performing the rite of consecrating an ikon, the Orthodox Church asked God to cause the light of the Holy Ghost to descend upon the picture which had been painted by human hands, so as to confer on it the miraculous power of curing sickness and expelling demons. 'It is not before powerless images that we prostrate ourselves. . . . When engraving the features of the likeness, we uphold it, we adore it . . . we draw

---

[1] It is interesting to note that, although the Orthodox clergy did not permit statues in the sanctuary, they sometimes allowed them as ornaments to the outside of a church. Thus the façade of the Church of the Saviour itself was decorated with forty-eight high reliefs, and at St Petersburg the French architect, Richard de Monferrand, was able to place kneeling bronze angels on the roof of the Cathedral of St Isaac.

from it the grace of salvation.' The ikon being a mystery, the art of painting it was a holy undertaking. 'Sanctify and illumine the soul of Thy servant,' the artist asked, 'guide his hand so that it may produce the holy ikon worthily and perfectly.' (*The Painter's Guide*, Mount Athos.) In this ideal state of mind, he did not seek to flatter the eye by the beauty of the lines and colours, but to effect as complete an incorporation as possible of the supernatural essence in forms perceptible to the senses. He complied with very old graphic rules, handed down from generation to generation. He became an anonymous person, a hand detached from the body, the instrument of a higher will. The colours he used were mixed with holy water and with tiny particles of the relics of saints. When the picture was completed, the idea of signing it never entered the artist's head; for, properly speaking, it was not he who had directed its creation, but the entire Church. According to Alexander Vassilievitch, ikon-worship had nothing in common with neo-fetichism, since the veneration of the faithful was not directed to the picture itself but to what it represented. The Russian bishops, when consecrated, took an oath to prevent the people from giving the ikons an adoration which was due to God alone. However, their vigilance could not stop the superstitious impulses of lowly people towards the dark Byzantine paintings. To be convinced of this, Russell had only to watch the genuflexions and the impassioned signs of the cross which men and women made before some smoke-blackened Virgin or white-bearded saint with a fixed stare. Forests of candles burned before them. The bottoms of the pictures were worn and obscured by the kisses of the multitude. Of most of the saints, male or female, only the feet, hands or faces could be seen through gaps in a carapace of goldsmith's work. Wrapped in chasubles of silver and gold, brown faces with deep black eyes and closed lips showed their hieratical indifference to the mumbled prayers.

Miraculous ikons were legion. That of the Iberian Virgin, studded with pearls and diamonds, was particularly venerated by the Muscovites. Not a day passed but it was taken in a carriage, at a high fee, to the bedside of a sick person, or to a newly installed apartment, or to a family feast. The carriage

was drawn by four trotters, accompanied by four postilions on horseback. Behind, and under an awning which pro-
longed the roof of the vehicle, were two valets in faded livery.
Coachman, postilions and valets were always bareheaded.
Inside the carriage was a priest in his sacerdotal habit and an
assistant. The ikon was placed before them on a seat. All
along the road the passers-by uncovered and crossed themselves, and when the carriage stopped in front of a 'client's'
house a crowd formed to witness the 'descent' of the image.
The faithful followed it to the door, while others devotedly
kissed the seat on which the ikon had rested. During its
absence from the Iberian Chapel (until six in the evening, at
the latest), it was replaced by a copy.

In war, the Russians always carried a few holy ikons into
the field and any success was attributed to them. The Virgin
of Smolensk was dear to the whole Orthodox West after the
victory of Poltava. Our Lady of Kazan owed her fame to the
capture of Kazan under Ivan the Terrible, but it was also
thanks to her that Minin and Pozharsky had driven the Poles
from Moscow and that Alexander I had halted the French
invasion of 1812. On the eve of the battle of Borodino,
Marshal Kutuzov went in person to beg the help of the
miraculous Virgin. Reproductions of the most famous ikons
kept watch over all Russian homes, and there had to be at
least one in every dining-room and every bedroom. In certain,
particularly pious, households there was a real oratory in
miniature. The holy pictures by their infinite multiplication,
were integrated into domestic life. No important action was
taken without their intervention. They were taken down from
their corners to watch over the sick and the dying, to follow
the dead to the cemetery, to keep an eye on a birth, and to
serve as witnesses to big business affairs and small oaths.
When a young man asked for the hand of a young girl, the
parents blessed the betrothal with the house ikon. This same
ikon, held by a boy, accompanied the girl when she went by
carriage to church on her wedding day. When some member
of the family was about to leave on a long journey, everyone
gathered before the ikon, sat down together in silence, then
rose, crossed themselves and kissed the traveller to wish him
bon voyage.

Other practices of a religious nature surprised Russell

when Alexander Vassilievitch told him about them. Russians crossed not only themselves (by taking the right hand to the forehead, breast, right shoulder and finally left shoulder); they also made the sign upon those who were dear to them, as well as upon various articles and food, to drive the powers of evil away from them, after the custom of the early Christians. Parents crossed their children in their beds at night. A wife crossed her husband when he left for work, saying 'God be with thee!'

In Russia, everything that had been blessed by the priest took on a sacred and, so to speak, a magical value. Holy water was very often given to the sick to drink. Tatiana Sergeyevna brought back from the church little bread rolls that had been blessed, and she shared them with her husband and children after making the sign of the cross over them. Russell tasted these blessed Orthodox rolls one day; they were round, bigger and closer than the Roman hosts and they were leavened. Widows of the lesser clergy, the *prosforni*, had the job of making them. To celebrate mass, the priest took several *prosfors* and with liturgical lance cut them into five lots: the pieces of the first *prosfor* were dedicated to Christ, those of the second to the Virgin, those of the third to the Apostles, the Prophets and the Martyrs, those of the fourth to the living and those of the fifth to the dead. After Mass, the unused pieces of bread were distributed among the congregation. To eat a piece was to perform an act of faith and an inner purification. For Palm Sunday, the consecrated box-trees were replaced by willow branches with silvery and woolly buds. At Easter the faithful had their coloured eggs, their *kulich* and their *paskha* blessed by the parish priest. In Russia there were no registers of births, marriages and deaths other than those of the Church; therefore, since all certificates of birth were drawn up by the priests, it was impossible to exist officially without having been baptized. The natural consequence of this legislation was that the annulment of a marriage could only be carried out, in rare and well-defined cases, by an ecclesiastical tribunal, subordinate to the Most Holy Synod.[1]

---

[1] The divorced wife continued to bear her husband's name legally and a special decision was necessary to authorize her or to force her, as the case may be, to resume her maiden name.

Contrarily to the Catholic Church, the Orthodox Church had not evolved with the centuries. An archaic austerity continued to rule over the practices it imposed upon the faithful. When Alexander Vassilievitch enumerated all the fasts and abstinences of the Orthodox, Russell was staggered by their number. Instead of a single Lent, the Russian Church had four: the first, corresponding to Advent, preceded Christmas (from November 15 till December 24), the second, the principal Lent, lasted for the seven weeks before Easter; a third preceded St Peter's day (lasting from June 7 till June 28); and the fourth preceded Assumption (from August 1 till August 14). Apart from the lents and the feast-day vigils, there were two days of abstinence each week: Wednesday, the day of Judas's betrayal of Christ, and Friday, the day of the Saviour's death. The total number of fast-days was a third of the days in a year. During the four lents, meat, milk, butter and eggs were prohibited. Alexander Vassilievitch, although a strong believer, thought that this was excessive, and he was not the only one. The majority of enlightened people took great liberties with the rules and only fasted during the first and last week of the principal lent, for which it was not necessary to obtain a dispensation from the priest. If Catholics regarded abstinence as an obligation to the Church, the Russians regarded it as chastening and as a preparation for the fast-days. Thus they relied on their own consciences for a decision.

'Amongst Catholics,' said Alexander Vassilievitch, 'timid people go to the curé to ask for a privilege, or a dispensation, or for advice. With us, most of the time, we follow our own inspiration. If we sin, the word of the "pope" will not efface our guilt. We may confess it, but we do not think we are forgiven. We are alone with our own souls. Take my wife, for example: ought she to ask a priest for permission not to fast when, by giving her a delicate constitution, God has prohibited her from fasting?'

These words left Russell pensive: evidently the Orthodox priests did not enjoy the same respect from their flocks as did the Catholic priests. The Russians did not see them as spiritual guides able to free them from their sins and to enlighten them as to the path they should follow, but rather as simple custodians of ritual, leaders of prayer, dispensers of the sacraments. So much was this the case that in the churches there were no pulpits from which a priest could preach to his flock.[1] Sermons were rare and were mostly restricted to the upper clergy. Commentary on the Gospels by the priest was replaced by readings from the Fathers or from a few treatises approved by the Most Holy Synod. These books, studded with Slav expressions, were often unintelligible to the masses. Then, even when he took the floor to address the throng, the priest did not enter into close communication with them, but remained a reciter of a sacred text. Dressed in his rich sacerdotal habit, he was too far from humble mortals to arouse their friendly confidence, and in everyday life he was too close for anyone to think of treating him with veneration. Had he not a wife and child like other men? His long, neglected beard, poverty and domestic worries made one smile. The whole misunderstanding derived perhaps from the division of the Orthodox clergy into secular (or white) clergy, and monastic (or black) clergy. The monastic clergy were vowed to celibacy and it was from them that the high dignitaries of the Church were recruited; but the secular clergy provided the parish priests who were all subject to the obligation of marriage.

There were three degrees of monastic clergy: monks, priest-monks, and bishops. The monks and priest-monks spent their lives in the monasteries and were subject to a very austere régime: notably, they were forbidden to eat meat except in case of illness. They began as *poslushniki* (lay brothers), and after a long period of waiting and study they took their final vows and became *monakhi* (monks). Of course, there were several echelons in the monastic priesthood: first of all one was a deacon (*ierodyakon*), then one became a priest-monk (*ieromonakh*), and finally an archimandrite (a rank intermediate between a bishop and a monk). One was only ordained archimandrite after acquiring an academic degree: Master or Doctor of Theology. But even to be a simple *ierodyakon* one had to complete one's studies at a seminary.

[1] Dostoyevsky wrote: 'The Russian people were educated in the churches where, throughout the centuries, they had heard hymns that were worth more than sermons.'

At the highest levels of the Orthodox ecclesiastical pyramid were the bishops, archbishops and metropolitans. The whole of Russia was divided into eparchies, or dioceses, administered by an archbishop (*arkhiepiskop*) or a bishop (*episkop*). Three of these eparchies, the most important ones, had metropolitans: Novgorod and St Petersburg, Moscow, and Kiev. In each eparchy there was a consistory presided over by the bishop. The secular clergy of the country and the towns were in absolute dependence upon this high prelate of the monastic clergy.

As for the secular (or white) parochial clergy, it was subdivided into: *protoierei* (archpriests), some of whom wore the episcopal mitre during services; *hierei* (priests, or commonly 'popes'); *protodyakony* (archdeacons, attached generally to the service of a bishop); and *diakone* (deacons). All the members of this clergy had to marry, and to wear beards and long hair. If their wives died, they had no right to marry again and usually retired into a monastery. They were therefore careful of their partners. The parochial clergy was subordinate hierarchically to the bishop of the diocese. The bishop's directives were passed to the priests through the consistory. Each parish had its church, served by a 'pope' and a deacon, himself assisted by a psalter-reader (*psalom-shchik*) and a sacristan (*ponomar*).

The parochial clergy was recruited from the pupils in the seminaries and theological schools or academies. There was a seminary in every diocese and four theological academies in the whole Empire.[1] To be ordained as priest one had to have completed the whole seminary course with the degree of Bachelor of Theology. In general the function of the academies was to create future high ecclesiastical dignitaries, in other words monks.

While these monks could as celibates aspire to a brilliant career, the ordinary and married priests abandoned all personal ambitions when accepting their charges.[2] It was the rule that they should remain attached throughout their lives

[1] St Petersburg, Moscow, Kazan, Kiev.

[2] Their lot was so unenviable that recruitment to the seminaries was exclusively from the sons of priests. The clergy thus became a caste, a great family, in which, from generation to generation, the same names were to be found.

to one church, without expecting either advancement or transfer to a pleasanter or richer region. The sum allotted them by the Holy Synod was starvation pay: 60 roubles (less than £7) a year! From this pay they had to provide for the maintenance of their numerous family, to busy themselves after a fashion with the village school, to look after the peasants in the absence of a doctor and to go hither and thither performing baptismal, burial and marriage services. As there were no fixed fees for such religious ceremonies, everyone paid what he liked, that is to say the least possible! Kept in such a low state by their ecclesiastical superior, the priests could acquire the respect of their parishioners only with difficulty. Their flock only asked that they should have a majestic manner, a fine beard, and a strong and solemn voice.

The monks, on the other hand, were deeply revered by the people. They were learned, remote and mysterious; they led an ascetic and contemplative life. They were thought capable of performing miracles, and people went to the monasteries to seek their advice. The biggest monasteries were called *lavra*, and the smallest *skit* or *pustyn* (hermitage or retreat), but there were no religious orders like those of the Roman Church and nothing comparable with the powerful communities of other parts of Europe, with their diverse habits, their strict rules and their international missions. The Russian monk had no other desire in retiring from the world than to expiate the sins of the age by prayer.

Alexander Vassilievitch Zubov spoke with wonder of a certain monastery, Optina Pustyn, which he had visited about fifteen years earlier. It was situated in the heart of Russia, in the province of Kaluga on the banks of the peaceful Jisdra River. The white boundary walls and the blue church domes and golden crosses stood out from the green forest, and there was no sound but birdsong and the murmur of running water. To cross the threshold of this establishment was to turn one's back on the futile turmoil of the age. In the middle of the night, according to the rules, the monks assembled to sing matins. Communal prayers were numerous and were said punctually. In the refectory, the silence was disturbed only by the voice of a monk or a novice reading the life of the saint who was being venerated that day. Thanks to subsidies from merchants, industrialists and well-to-do peasants, the monastery maintained a school, a hospital and an orphanage. Close to the monastery, in the forest, was a small group of buildings, a *skit*, where a very limited number of monks, wishing to devote themselves to asceticism, lived in solitude and peace. A palisade, and a gate decorated with ikons, surrounded this refuge of intense spirituality. The white cells, flower borders, cedar avenues, the pond, church, beehives and cemetery: all seemed made peaceful by the daily orisons. Yet it was neither the beauty of the landscape nor the fervour with which the services in this place were celebrated that attracted so many pilgrims, but the unusual fame of its *starets*.[1]

The Russian word *starets* means 'an old man', but, contrary to the current expression *starik*, it conjured up an idea of moral dignity and serene experience. The *starets* was generally an elderly monk who by meditation and prayer had acquired the power to understand and to guide those who came to him in trouble. Whether he was the superior of the monastery or whether he assisted the superior in his task, he was the brotherhood's spiritual guide. But there was one strange fact: the *starets* was not necessarily a priest; in that event, the faithful asked his advice as spontaneously and as humbly as if he had been a minister of God, but confessed regularly to another.

In Russia the renown of these *starets* was so great that from morning till night the most famous of them received crowds of sinners in search of truth in their cells or visiting-rooms. The sick in body or soul, dull-witted illiterates or tormented intellectuals, rich merchants or half-starved pilgrims, they all wished to enlighten or right themselves by contact with the admirable old man. They would ask him for his advice on whether to accept or decline a job, on a love affair gone wrong, on a secret crime. . . . Sometimes, even before a newcomer had unbosomed himself, the *starets* guessed his problem and responded with a pacifying word, an inspired look or a smile.

At one time, at Optina Pustyn, Father Leonid used to

[1] See the admirable portrait of the *starets* Zosima in Dostoyevsky's *The Brothers Karamazov*.

receive the pilgrims seated on his bed, dressed in a white smock and wearing a cap, and while he talked spiritedly he plaited girdles. His visitors knelt or squatted on the floor around him. His successor, Father Macaire, had received and advised Nikolas Gogol and the slavophil publicist Kireyevsky, whose conversion caused such a stir at that time. After Father Macaire came Father Ambrose, who had continued the brilliant tradition of the *starets* of Optina Pustyn. His teaching had led Constantin Leontiev, the philosopher and man of letters, to turn away from the world and enter the priesthood. Other eminent personalities had come to him seeking lessons in wisdom: officers of the Guard, savants, high officials, the famous critic Strakhov, the publicists and philosophers Khomiakov and Vladimir Soloviov, the Grand Duke Constantin and the two most famous novelists of their time, Dostoyevsky and Tolstoy.[1] The *starets* Ambrose had died in 1891.

'He was already very old when I saw him for the last time,' Alexander Vassilievitch Zubov said. 'Imagine a tall, thin, stooping man with a bright eye, a deeply furrowed face and a little beard. He looked at me with penetrating gentleness and I felt that everything in my head was becoming clear. If there were a few more *starets* of his kind, even misfortune might become for us a source of joy!'

'Are there many monasteries in Russia?' Russell asked.

'About five hundred and fifty, with eleven thousand monks and eighteen thousand nuns. That's not enormous!'

'And to what authority is the Monastic clergy responsible?'

'Only the Holy Synod and the Tsar are above them.'

❋ ❋ ❋ ❋

The association of the Tsar and the Church was of relatively recent origin.

Evangelized by Greek monks in 988, during the reign of Vladimir Svyatoslavitch, the Russian nation remained Orthodox even under the Mongol occupation. When the invaders

[1] In 1910, when Leo Tolstoy finally resolved to leave his family, it was to Optina Pustyn that he finally made his way with the intention of seeing the *starets* Joseph, Ambrose's successor.

had at last been driven from the country, the supremacy of the Patriarch of Constantinople had not been recognized by the Russians for a long time. Attempts by the Popes to reconcile the Orthodox and Roman Catholic Churches remained unproductive. In 1591 the Metropolitan of Moscow was recognized as Fifth Patriarch, leader of the Russian ecclesiastical hierarchy. In the middle of the seventeenth century, under Tsar Alexis Mikhailovitch, the Patriarch Nikhon ordered the liturgy to be revised, but his innovations infuriated people and caused several sects to be created, the most important of which was that of the *Staroveri* (Old Believers). This schism, the *raskol*, was accentuated when Peter the Great united the spiritual and temporal powers by not appointing a new holder to the vacant seat of Patriarch (1700) and by founding the Most Holy Synod, a body entrusted with the direction of religious matters (1721). The Most Holy Synod was composed of the highest dignitaries of the regular clergy nominated by the Tsar. He was himself represented in this assembly by the Procurator-General, a lay official who made known what questions were to be debated. No decision of the Most Holy Synod was valid without his approval, and, therefore, the Emperor's.

The State religion was the Orthodox faith,[1] but according to the last census the Roman Catholic faith had 11,420,000 followers (mainly in Poland and in neighbouring governments), the Armenian-Gregorian Church 1,600,000, Protestants 3,743,000 (mainly in Finland, the Baltic provinces and in the German colonies in southern Russia), Mohammedans 14,000,000 (mainly in the Caucasus and eastern provinces), with heathen among the Finnish tribes and the Asiatic followers of Brahma.

From the doctrinal point of view, the principal difference between the Orthodox and the Catholic Churches turned upon the Latin formula of *filioque*. This formula is part of the creed which the Catholic Church recites at Mass: 'I believe too in the Holy Ghost ... which proceeds from the Father and the Son.' Now this statement is not to be found in the

---

[1] Foreign cults evidently escaped the competence of the Most Holy Synod, but were equally subordinate to Imperial authority, since they were controlled by the Ministry of the Interior.

Gospel according to St John,[1] nor in the text of the Council of Nicaea, where it was said simply that 'I believe in the Holy Ghost which proceeds from the Father.' Having added the *filioque* to the formula of the traditional faith, the Catholic Church had refused to submit to the orders of Photius, Patriarch of Constantinople, who regarded the Latins as heretics. The Orthodox repudiated the *filioque* with horror. For them the Holy Ghost did not proceed from the Father and from the Son, as for the Catholics, but came from the Father 'through the Son'. More precisely, the Orthodox distinguished between eternal emission of the Holy Ghost issuing from the Father, and the emission of the Holy Ghost at a point in time, in other words the temporal sending of the Holy Ghost into the world by the Son, through the Son, in the features of the Son.[2]

Other divergences between the two churches were these: obviously, the Orthodox did not recognize the primacy and infallibility of the Pope and they rejected the western ideas of indulgences and purgatory. According to them, immediately after death the soul went from stage to stage acknowledging its sins and suffering agony while awaiting the last judgement. For the righteous this agony was, however, mitigated by the awareness that they were close to God. But even the Saints did not share in perfect felicity, since final judgement had not yet been given. Thus there was no such place as purgatory where purification might be obtained through suffering; there was no possibility of expiation before the great awakening; all the dead, the good and the evil, were in an intermediate state in which joy and despair balanced one another.

Finally, as to discipline, the Orthodox Church permitted the marriage of priests but not of bishops, condemned the use of unleavened bread in the celebration of mass, and baptized by triple immersion and not by sprinkling water on the

---

[1] 'But when the Comforter is come, whom I will send unto you from the Father, even the Spirit of truth, which proceedeth from the Father, he shall testify of me' (John xv, 26).

[2] The idea of the temporal emission of the Holy Ghost through the Son in the features of the Son was so subtle that certain western theologians were able to accuse Photius of no longer distinguishing between the Son and the Holy Ghost, contrary to the Evangelical and Nicaean faith.

head of the person as amongst the Latins. Moreover the baptismal formula differed in the two churches: with the Orthodox it was God Himself and not the priest, the minister of God, who carried out the baptism; and while the Catholic priest declares: '*I baptize you* in the name of the Father, and of the Son and of the Holy Ghost', the Orthodox priest was content to declare: '*So-and-so is baptized* in the name of the Father,' etc. Finally, and contrary to the Catholics who, since the thirteenth century, partook of the sacrament kneeling and in one kind, the Orthodox, according to the rites of the primitive Christian Church, took communion standing and in two kinds: a piece of consecrated bread, soaked in wine, was offered them by the priest in a silver spoon. With his hands crossed on his breast, each communicant spoke his forename. Having placed the fragment of wine-soaked *prosfor* on the tongue of the faithful, the priest announced: 'The Servant of God, So-and-so, has taken communion.' Thereafter the communicant withdrew from the altar, drinking a little wine from a cup and eating a morsel of consecrated bread which was offered him on a plate.

❖   ❖   ❖   ❖

Without doubt, the Orthodox Russian people were unstintingly pious, as in the early days of Christianity. The forms of worship, sacraments, benedictions, relics, candles, chants, signs of the cross, and the genuflexions all played a great role in their expression of faith. They were sensitive to the beauty of the ceremonies, but their instincts forced them to find a very deep and very simple evangelical truth behind these ceremonies. Its religion drew its inspiration chiefly from the Sermon on the Mount: 'Blessed are the poor in spirit, for theirs is the Kingdom of Heaven. Blessed are the meek, for they shall inherit the earth. . . . Blessed are those who weep, for they shall be comforted. . . . Blessed are the merciful, for they shall obtain mercy. . . .' Touched by the Galilean's predictions, the most humble moujik had infinite compassion for his brothers in distress. But, lavish with mercy for others, he ardently hoped that he would receive it himself. Around Russell the large congregation crossed themselves and murmured: '*Gospodi pomilui* (Lord, have mercy on us). This phrase, which constantly recurred in the prayers, was, according to Alexander Vassilievitch, very characteristic of the spiritual torment of his fellow citizens.

'Russia,' he said, 'is haunted by the idea of sin and punishment. In Christ it sees the One who came on earth to save souls in peril and to promise the repentant sinners a better heavenly future than the righteous who thought themselves at peace with their consciences. Is there a crime that cannot be redeemed by a sincere impulse of the whole being towards the All-Highest? We do not think so. We do not hate the thief, the depraved or the murderer; we are sorry for him, we call him *neschastnyi*, the unfortunate. Always in our minds is the memory of Christ granting the Kingdom of God to the thief who was crucified beside him on Calvary. This is a very pure, very ancient Christianity, stripped of all metaphysics, a reverie on suffering, death and future justice, a vague and childish love of everything that breathes, a confused desire for brotherhood, a step towards indefinable felicities. . . .'

Russell wondered if this evangelical idealism, this search after a personal religion, was not at the origin of the numerous sects that existed in Russia. Alexander Vassilievitch had enumerated them.

In the first place there were the Old Believers (*Staroveri*), who were not properly speaking sectarians but schismatics. They did not forgive the Patriarch Nikhon for having corrected copying errors in the religious books. For them these very errors were sacred, since the faith of their elders had rested upon them. They forbade their followers to attend worship according to the new texts, to shave their beards, to make the sign of the cross with three fingers (instead of only two fingers as their ancestors did), and to say *Iissus* (Jesus) like everyone else, when the copiers of the old manuscripts wrote the name *Issus*.

During the eighteenth century the central power had increased its persecution of the elements hostile to Peter the Great's 'European innovations'. Excommunicated, and pursued by troops and police, the *Staroveri* defended themselves with arms, perished by hundreds or found refuge in the forests and deserts of the Empire. Great schismatic communities were gradually formed in this way, which were

closely united within themselves. These communities cultivated the arid lands, succoured the poor of the neighbourhood, opened monasteries and shelters for pilgrims, and
absorbed numerous peasants, attracted by the solid economic
and religious organization of the brotherhood. With time the
pursuit of the Old Believers weakened, but the *Staroveri*
clung no less tenaciously to the customs and beliefs of earlier
times. In 1886 the Holy Synod declared that the Orthodox
Church was not opposed to the old texts so dear to the *Staroveri* so much as to the spirit of rebellion of which these texts
were the symbol. The Metropolitan Platon had even authorized the ordination of priests who would officiate according
to the old rites. The adepts of this new cult, or rather of this
archaic liturgy, called themselves *Edinovertsy*. Throughout
the Empire special churches, under the protection of the
Holy Synod, were opened to receive them.[1] But the *Staroveri*
scorned returning to religious legality and preferred to elect
and to pay their own priests in conformity with a secular
tradition.

According to Alexander Vassilievitch Zubov, Moscow was
the *Staroveri*'s capital. Whether they were peasants, writers
or merchants, the *Staroveri* were distinguished by their
piety, sobriety, economic sense and the patriarchal structure
of their homes. Severe as they were to themselves and to
others, certain of these Old Believers had amassed considerable fortunes. Their prosperity was yet another means of
imposing a respect of the schism on the ecclesiastical authorities and the police. At the Nijny-Novgorod fair, which for
many business men was only an occasion for pleasure, the
Staroveri behaved with decency and dignity. The long per-
secutions they had suffered had developed in them the spirit
of mutual aid. Their association was a sort of freemasonry, in
which the members knew each other by various signs (rings,
rosaries, wooden spoons painted according to a special design). There were towns and regions almost entirely subject
to the economic domination of the *Staroveri*. Some small
industries were monopolized and controlled by them to such
an extent that the workers and moujiks joined the schism in
order to obtain work. This was especially so with the manu-

[1] There were already 224 in 1886.

facture of wooden spoons. A good half of the Russian peasantry used wooden spoons for their soup, and these were made by the enemies of the official church!

Side by side with this strong, virtuous and rich organization innumerable sects with the most disquieting peculiarities developed: the *Dukhobory*, who recognized only one source of faith, inner inspiration, and refused to do their military service so as not to have to shed blood; the *Molokany*, milk-drinkers who devoted themselves to realizing the Galilean life in its original purity; the *Stranniki*, the wanderers, who, in order to escape 'the Church's demoniacal servitude', travelled endlessly in the steppes and forests of Siberia; the *Nemolyakhi*, who claimed to dispense with priests and sacraments in order to join with God outside the formalities of worship; the *Khlisty*, who, in their erotic ecstasies, felt that the Divine Master was reincarnated in them; the *Skoptsy*, who castrated themselves in order to be free of fleshly temptations; the *Beloriztsy*, who dressed themselves in white 'like heavenly angels' and went from village to village preaching innocence; the *Skakuny*, who prayed while jumping . . .

All these sects, and many others, expressed the need to do without the official mediation of the clergy and to establish a direct relation between man and God. Was it not this propensity to judge everything by himself which explained the violence into which the normally so peaceful moujik allowed himself to be drawn? Assassinations, tortures, fines, pillage . . . These terroristic flare-ups were by no means rare in the country. To such primitive beings the idea that 'everything will be pardoned' was very close to an assurance that 'everything is permissible'. Worn out by poverty, they suddenly gave themselves up to their basest instincts, but repented immediately afterwards, confessed their crimes and accepted their punishment. According to Alexander Vassilievitch, the Siberian prisons were stuffed with men who, having paid the forfeit, continued to pray to God with the most Christian humility. Had they not been told that the last should be first?

Another religious phenomenon peculiar to Russia was the incalculable number of pilgrims who trod the roads. There were few peasants without an ambition to visit the Petchersk catacombs at Kiev or the laura of the St Serge Trinity. In Moscow Russell had met several of these *bogomoltsy*, distinguishable by their dirtiness, their weary air and the bundles they carried over their shoulders. Almost all of the pilgrims were of advanced age, for the young people were kept back by work in the fields. Having left their distant villages with a few kopecks in their pockets, they travelled on foot for weeks or months, begging as they went, sleeping under the stars or in a shed beside a monastery door. Distance did not frighten them. Some of them crossed the whole Empire, from the western frontiers to the heart of Siberia, or from the banks of the Dnieper to the shores of the Baltic. The most courageous of them went down to Odessa and embarked in the hold of some old tub sailing for the Holy Land. Their faces were dirty and haggard, their clothes hung in rags, their *lapti* were no more than scraps of mud and blood, but a gentle bewilderment lit their eyes. Men or women, most of them were realizing a long-cherished dream and did not doubt that they would be recompensed at the end of the journey. On their way they collected alms for the construction of a church or for themselves; the mystical nature of their approach incited men of means to come to their aid. Alexander Vassilievitch had read in the newspapers that the flow of pilgrims to Kiev far exceeded a million a year. As to the monks of the St Serge Trinity laura, they had scarcely enough candles, small ikons or consecrated bread to satisfy their clientele. The pilgrims slept in huge barrack-rooms, ate at the common table, heard mass, drank the holy water from a fountain, visited the caves, went into ecstasies before the extraordinary richness of the treasure in the sacristy, yawned in the library, leaned trembling with fear over the sarcophagus in which the remains of St Serge lay, covered with a sheet of red velvet, kissed the golden cross which was placed on these remains, and went away lit to the depths of their souls.

Before his journey to Russia, Russell had imagined there were no specifically Orthodox saints. His Moscow friends were not slow to disillusion him. In fact the Russian Church reckoned its saints, its blessed and its venerable (*Prepodo-*

bnye) in great number.[1] In the catacombs at Kiev alone there were a hundred of them. Even monasteries of secondary importance had relics of which they were very proud. Among these were national heroes like Alexander Nevsky, tireless converters like St Serge, and anchorites and ascetics like those monks of Kiev who for years had lived motionless in subterranean darkness. But, turned by preference towards its origins, the Orthodox Church was reluctant to record new miracles. In the previous century a vast movement of opinion was required to make the Church recognize Bishops Mitrofan and Tikhon as saints. In Russia, moreover, canonization was not preceded by the long inquiries and costly proceedings of the Roman Church. Here, as in primitive times, it was the voice of the people that designated the elect of God. For the faithful and for the Church the great sign of sanctity was the incorruptibility of the bodies of the blessed. If, in addition, one could point to a few miracles achieved over their tombs, the Holy Synod proceeded to a rapid investigation of the remains and in irrefutable cases submitted a decree of canonization to the Emperor.

However, it was not the multiplicity of Orthodox saints that explained the number of holidays in Russia. Besides the religious festivals there were the days of national celebration; the patron saint's day of the Empress (April 23), the birth of the Emperor (May 6), the Emperor's coronation (May 14), the Empress's Birthday (May 25), the Dowager Empress's birthday (November 14), the birthday of the Crown Prince Mikhail Alexandrovitch (November 22),[2] and the Emperor's patron saint's day (December 6). Taking Sundays and the Church festivals into account, the total of non-working days was as many as 100 a year. Moreover, in Russia the word 'feast-day' derived from the word 'idle' (*prazdnik*, feast-day; *prazdnyi*, idle). But were the Russian people truly idle? Yes, if one thinks of Alexander Vassilievitch, no, if one thinks of his son-in-law.

Russell struggled to put some order into his ideas, but did not succeed, carried away as he was by the singing of the

[1] The number of canonized Russian saints was about 385.
[2] The son of the Emperor and Empress, the Tsarevitch Alexis, was not born until the following year, July 30, 1904.

choir which echoed in the vaulting. Never would he have believed that a vocal ensemble could give such an impression of profound harmony. The choir was composed exclusively of men and children.[1] Their voices were so well blended that the melody seemed to come from a single mouth, from a single inexhaustible and majestic breath. The number of the bass voices made the bowels of the earth tremble, when suddenly sounds of heavenly purity mingled with the storm and rose, ever clearer, shriller and more joyful, to evoke the Christian faith. No keyboard, wind or stringed instrument was used to accompany these canticles. In fact the Orthodox Church would tolerate only the most natural instrument of all, the voice, for sacred music. Had not God given man a voice so that he could sing His praises for ever? In the most sumptuous cathedrals and also in the most humble village churches the choirs played a preponderant part. It was incontestably in Russia that the plainsong, inherited from ancient Greece, had best preserved its nobility. But to the plainsong the anonymous masters of the Middle Ages had added original chants, called *raspievy*, sad in design, which belonged to the old popular plaints. Great importance was given to the musical education of priests and deacons in the seminaries, for they too had to have fine voices to command the attention of the faithful. The lowliest moujiks would have despised a 'pope' with defective diction or a nasal voice.

Without exactly understanding the significance of the different phases of the Orthodox mass, Russell followed it with sustained artistic interest. Alexander Vassilievitch had told him that the Orthodox clergy had retained the usages of the early Christians, and according to these usages the Russians never sat down during the service. Moreover, they never carried prayer-books or rituals to mass, for they would have thought it unsuitable to turn the pages in the sanctuary of the Lord. In order to follow the liturgy better, pious people read the service before going to church. There were no church officers to regulate the order of the great ceremonies, no hand-bell to call the faithful to meditation, no confessional where the priest could conveniently isolate himself in order

[1] In the women's convents, on the other hand, it was the nuns alone who formed the choir.

to hear the confessions of sinners.[1] Always careful to change nothing of the ancient ritual, the Orthodox Church forbade shortening mass. There was nothing analogous to the Catholic low mass, in which the priest conducts a dialogue with a server only, who responds in the name of the absent congregation. In Russia the services had all to be public. They were directed at the congregation. Faced with an empty nave, the priest could pray, but he could not conduct a service. The greater number of innovations introduced by Rome to revive and stimulate the piety of the faithful were looked upon by the Orthodox clergy with a distrustful eye. The most widespread Catholic services, like that of the Sacred Heart, for example, remained foreign to it. The austerity of its worship was visible in the scenes of the sacred drama. To the east, at the back of the apse, stood a single altar, since there was but one God and one Saviour. Between the altar and the nave, the enormous barrier of the iconostasis, gilded and decorated with pictures, represented the temple veil. Of the three gates of the ikonostasis, the middle one, with two doors, was called the Imperial Gate, while the two others were known as the deacons' gates. Only the priest had the right to pass through the Imperial Gate, or the Tsar himself, to receive communion on the day of his coronation. This gate was closed during the mystery of the consecration. A curtain was drawn behind it: the symbol of the fleshly condition of human beings which prevented them from seeing heaven. But at the solemn moments of worship the curtain was drawn aside and the gate opened; heaven was revealed to the faithful and the very throne of God became visible. From the left side of the altar, properly so called, towards the north-east part, was a table like an altar, the *zhertvennik*, or offertory. The entrance and exit of the priest in his heavy gilded chasuble, the carrying of the sacrificial items from the offertory to the altar, the progress of the deacon with the gospel or the chalice, the closing or the reopening of the doors of the ikonostasis, were the different stages of a mystical performance.[2] The incense

[1] The confessionals were not allowed by the Catholic Church until the sixteenth century.

[2] The costume of the Orthodox priests consisted of a *stikharion* (the Catholic priest's alb), a long sleeveless tunic, of the scarf, the sleeveless

rose from a silver-chained censer which the *dyakony* swung at knee level. All these slow solemnities harmonized with the severe luxury of the old Byzantine churches. This antiquity was apparent even in the liturgical furniture. Among these were the flabellum,[1] a metal fan which the deacon waves before the tabernacle, the golden spoon for the communion wine, the holy spear and sponge,[2] reminiscent of Calvary, and other sacred articles which have long been in disuse in western countries.

The great Orthodox ceremonies drew their inspiration from the same simple symbolism as those of the early Christian Church. For example, the marriage rites, as described to Russell by Alexander Vassilievitch, were very strange indeed to a European mind. Throughout the service groomsmen took turns in holding two heavy gilded crowns at arms' length above the heads of the couple. After the couple had exchanged rings and kissed before the tabernacle, the officiating priest offered them a cup of wine, from which they drank thrice in turn, for everything henceforth would be held in common; then, having tied their hands together with a silk handkerchief, the priest made them follow him three times round the altar, so that they should be imbued with the idea that from that day hence they would walk through life closely united.

A ceremony no less picturesque was that of Easter, undoubtedly the most beautiful festival in the whole Orthodox liturgy. In Russia midnight mass took place on the very night of the Ressurrection. At the given hour, after the psalms had been sung, the priest approached the sepulchre, symbolically raised the shroud and saw that the Saviour was no longer in the tomb. Then, instead of announcing the resurrection, he hesitated, like the disciples of the Gospel, and went out into the square with all the clergy to make a circuit of the church

chasuble (*phelonion* or *risa*) with an opening for the head, and a tall cylindrical headdress (*kamilaukhion*). The Bishop wore a *sakkos* instead of the chasuble, a mitre instead of the *kamilaukhion*, and finally the crucifix.

[1] The Catholic Church had suppressed the use of the flabellum in the fourteenth century. But it is still carried today, in certain ceremonies, before the Pope.

[2] The holy spear is used to cut into pieces, or *dolabs*, the bread intended for consecration; the liturgical sponge is used by the deacon to purify the paten.

in search of the vanished Christ. Finally, convinced of the miracle, he re-entered the temple and, facing the crowd, proclaimed: 'Christ is risen.' The congregation replied in an outburst of joy: 'Truly, He is risen.' In every hand a little taper burned. Friends, kinsmen and strangers then exchanged the triple Easter kiss, and none might refuse this sign of brotherly affection. The sombre liturgy of the days of sorrow gave place to wildly joyful singing. All the bells of Moscow rang together above the city. In the houses coloured eggs and ritual cakes appeared, the *pashkha* and the *kulich*, decorated with the letters XB, the Russian initials of the words 'Christ' and 'Risen'.

In the country, after the night service, the congregation, with the lighted tapers still in their hands, moved to the cemetery to take the Easter greeting to their dead. Little eggs of coloured porcelain were hung upon the arms of the crosses, so that the dead should not be excluded from Christian rejoicing. Russell wanted very much to attend the Easter festivals in Moscow. But would he still be the Zubovs' guest at that time? As he pondered the question he inhaled the odour of incense which had strengthened in the nave, and in the end he found the sweetish oriental odour rather sickly. His limbs grew numb. His gaze floated over the compact mass of faces. All classes of society intermingled in the precincts of the cathedral. The coarsest and the most refined faces had the same air of abandon. Heads were bowed. Lips were murmuring. Signs of the cross, the wrong way round, were made upon every breast. The crowd prostrated itself, bowing like a cornfield at the passing of the wind. The common people touched the earth with their brows; the rest were content with a more discreet genuflexion.

Russell was ill at ease standing alone beside a pillar, but no one paid attention to him. The congregation rose. Alexander Vassilievitch lightly dusted his trousers with the tips of his fingers. How did Tatiana Sergeyevna and her daughters endure the fatigue of these long services? Russell watched Helen out of the corner of his eye and found her singularly pale and beautiful in the exaltation of her prayers. Young Nikolas, wearing the grey uniform of a gymnasium pupil, began to show signs of restlessness. He turned towards the doors; he sighed. There, beside the altar, surrounded by a cloud of incense, the priest proclaimed some glad truth. He was superb, mitred in oriental fashion, leonine, with his hair falling over his shoulders, his flowing beard and his shining chasuble with folds as neat as joints in armour. At last came the ceremony of 'dismissal', corresponding to the *Ite missa est* of the Catholic Church, and the congregation began to move. Everyone went in turn to kiss the crucifix and the hand of the priest held out to them. Russell stood aside while his friends carried out the rite. 'How unhygienic!' he thought. 'Thousands of people going to put their lips, one after the other, to this cross. Among them there are certainly some who are diseased. Here is a dirty, slobbery old man. Behind him a woman carrying her child in her arms, and the infant kisses the cross after the old man. And we are in the twentieth century!' But Alexander Vassilievitch and Tatiana Sergeyevna explained to him that the strength of the Orthodox faith was such that no case of contagion had ever resulted from this practice. But Russell was still distrustful. The procession seemed to him very long.

Out in the open air again he was dazzled by the sunshine and the fresh odour of the snow. In the church square some nuns, collecting alms, were seated at little tables in their long black veils. Each little table bore a tin plate filled with kopecks. The faces of these women were shrunken and blue with cold. They had the lips of corpses. Where did they come from, from what faraway convent, where the roof was threatening to collapse or the ikons needed regilding? Farther off were ragged beggars, some of whom were genuine pilgrims, while others were 'specialists' from the Khitrov. Alexander Vassilievitch distributed some money, rather at random, into the frozen hands that were held out to him.

The Church of the Saviour stood above the Moskva. On the great snow-covered square the crowd flowed between the masters' sleighs. The Zubovs' equipage was in the front row. The horses snorted. Up on his seat the driver growled into his beard and pulled on the reins. Before getting into the sleigh Helen smiled at Russell and murmured: 'Did you like our Sunday mass, Monsieur?'

'Enormously,' he replied, gazing at her gratefully.

CHAPTER VII

THE WORKERS

Russian factories, working conditions, pay – The new social laws – The role of factory inspectors – Free medical aid – The housing problem: factory dormitories, kamorki, *rooms in the city – Visit to a swingling shop: workers sleeping by their machines – Workers' food – Educational establishments subsidized by manufacturers – Movements for social improvement – Workers' budgets –* Artels *– State monopoly of alcoholic drinks – Public and private assistance in Russia – The foundling hospital in Moscow.*

IT WAS the obliging Paul Egorovitch Sychin, again, who undertook to take Russell to the workers' suburbs of Moscow. Zubov's son-in-law had acquaintances among the leading industrialists and their doors were open to him. Cloth-factories, tanneries, foundries, sawmills, giant iron-works, and workshops, where nails, leaden objects and samovars were made – Russell lived for weeks on end among gear-wheels, driving-belts, the smell of warm grease, the hiss of steam, the glare of flames, the vibration of machines and the shouts of overseers. At first sight nothing distinguished Russian factories from those of other countries in the same field. But it could be seen that the machines were of British or German make, that the workers were more poorly dressed than in England, and that the roofs of the workshops were seldom glazed because of the climate and heavy snowfalls.

In accordance with the law of June 2, 1897, a working day must not exceed eleven and a half hours, excluding rest time. On Saturdays and on the eve of feast-days, this was reduced to ten hours.[1] It was forbidden to employ night workers for more than ten continuous hours. Whenever the day exceeded ten hours it had to be broken by one hour's rest at least. But, for sure, these regulations were often broken and it was not uncommon for a worker to labour for thirteen or fourteen hours a day just as in the days before the law was

[1] Day work could not begin before five in the morning nor finish later than nine at night.

promulgated. The great number of holidays compensated for the excessive effort imposed on employees during the rest of the year.[1]

As to pay, it obviously varied according to the work and where it was done, and the sex and age of the worker. In the Moscow region an adult male earned on the average 14 to 15 roubles per month, a female 10 roubles, a young male (15 to 17 years old) 7 roubles, and a child (less than 15 years) 5 roubles. According to the exchange rates at that time (100 roubles = $51.50) the monthly salary of a Russian worker came to about $7.35. But certain skilled workers received very much higher pay. Thus in Moscow cotton-spinners were paid up to 20 roubles ($10.30) a month, wool-spinners 22 roubles ($11.33), skilled pottery or porcelain workers 17 roubles ($8.76), those in the silk industry 22 roubles ($11.33), and in engineering or construction works 40 to 50 roubles ($20.60 to $25.75). These figures increased for workers close to the western frontier of the Empire (Lodz or Warsaw) or in St Petersburg; they decreased (by 20 per cent) in the eastern regions, and fell to an absurdly low level beyond the Urals.

Whatever his occupation, every worker when engaged received a booklet from his employer, in which the conditions of his employment, the payment of wages, deductions in the form of fines, rents and various liabilities were recorded, and, should the occasion arise, the reason for his dismissal. In brief, it was a sort of professional passport which, together with his official passport, ended by fixing an individual's capabilities and predisposed him to accept his inferior status. Though an employer had no right to dismiss an employee without a fortnight's notice, he could inflict penalties for certain mistakes which were provided for in the rules. In former times the sums collected in this way went into the owner's pocket, but since the new law they had gone into a special account and were used as a rule to improve the lot of necessitous workers. Factory inspectors[2] watched over the application of the laws in the Empire's industries and mines. Estab-

[1] According to the official statistics from Demetriev (1897), more than 80 per cent. of factories were subject to 89 to 99 holidays a year.

[2] They numbered about 300.

lished by the law of July 7, 1899, they were attached directly to the Ministry of Finance. Their powers were even further extended as Russian industrial legislation was subsequently enlarged by numerous decisions relating to the hygiene of premises, conditions of juvenile and female labour, compulsory education, accidents, free medical care, etc.

Russell, who thought his own country a century ahead of Russia in social progress, was surprised to learn that the employment of children of less than twelve years and the employment of women at night had been forbidden in Russia (by the laws of July 1, 1882, and July 3, 1896[1]) and that in Russia there was a medical service at large factories (of more than 100 workers), and that employers' responsibility in the matter of working accidents was constantly recognized.[2] Since 1888 there had been a system of workers' insurance against this kind of accident. Six large companies shared the industrial custom of the Empire. But the new law, the promulgation of which was awaited impatiently, would introduce the idea of professional risk into Russian law. The employer would be personally and directly responsible for accidents at work without the victim having to prove that the owner or his manager was at fault, and instead of hoping for redress the worker would be certain that payment would be made to him for temporary or permanent disablement, that should he die his funeral expenses would be covered by his employer up to thirty roubles, and that his widow and children would receive, in the same event, a pension representing two-thirds of his last annual wages.

As to free medical aid, the methods differed from one factory to another. Certain employers quietly ignored the law

[1] At the beginning of the twentieth century, juvenile, adolescent and female labour was controlled in Russia as follows: it was forbidden to engage children of less than twelve years in factories; further the Ministry of Finance reserved the right to prohibit the employment of children from twelve to fifteen years old in industries injurious to their health; night work (from 9 p.m. till 5 a.m.) was forbidden for children in all industries (except glassworks, in which they could be employed for six continuous hours at most) as well as for women and adolescents in textile industries or phosphorus match manufacture. Finally, neither women nor children could be employed in mines.

[2] The Russian law on accidents at work was promulgated on June 2, 1903, and entered into effect on January 1, 1904.

of 1866,[1] others only maintained an ambulance or an infirmary at their works, from which the sick man was sent if necessary to a public institution; and others (mainly the big businesses) had real hospitals at their disposal where they cared not only for their workers but also for their families and even for the neighbouring population. As an example, Sychkin told Russell of the Ramensk cotton-mill, which employed 6,500 workers and boasted of a hospital with 90 beds and a maternity home with 16 beds; also the Bogorodsko-Glukhovsky factory (8,210 workers) with a modern clinic in which, in a single year, nearly 20,000 persons had been cared for and nearly 2,000 had been hospitalized. While listening to his guide, Russell realized that the laws were interpreted and adapted by each firm in its own way. But Paul Egorovitch Sychkin seemed less concerned with this incoherence than with the practical problem of workers' dwellings.

'In your country the workers live where they like and usually quite a long way from the factory. Even when they are settled in dwellings specially built by their employer, they pay rent in exchange. In short, they forget the factory atmosphere when they go home. In Russia, on the contrary, half the workers live gratuitously, either in the workshops themselves or in huge buildings attached to the factories. This is explained by the fact that in Russia the majority of the population is rural and the peasant who comes to town to seek employment is obviously unable to find a room at a low cost. Moreover, in their *izba* they have acquired the habit of living six, eight or ten together in a smoky room. Why should they be more refined now? If you want to understand the life of the Russian worker you must visit a few of these houses, exclusively occupied by the workers and their families. . . .'

Under the guidance of Paul Egorovitch Sychkin, it did not take Russell long to see that all the large factories were flanked by grey and dejected buildings of several stories, which were simply warehouses of labour. The same architectural style was recognizable in all: they were civilian barracks. Inside, a dark and narrow corridor was flanked by thin plank doors, which opened into dormitories for twenty

[1] By a law of August 26, 1866, the owners of factories were obliged to install a hospital for their workers near the works.

or thirty workers or into minute rooms (*kamorki*) each shelter-
ing several families. Each family strove to mark off its modest
domain in the *kamorka* with hangings made of old pieces of
cloth and plaited mats. But these flimsy partitions were not
enough to ensure the privacy of couples. The beds (simple
plank bunks) touched one another. One chair and one table
served ten persons. Men, women and children mingled their
voices, odours, illnesses, quarrels and reconciliations. Yet the
tenants of a *kamorka* were envied by those who lived in the
dormitories. There the bunks stood side by side without the
least separation. Often they were placed one above the other,
the highest being about two feet below the ceiling. The
workers did their washing in the room and dried it on lines
strung from wall to wall. A sour odour came from these rags
as they dripped upon the muddy floor. The casement windows were clearly too small to permit the ventilation of the
premises. In any case, they were carefully nailed up and
blocked in.

This kind of dormitory was generally reserved for single
men. Nevertheless, Paul Egorovitch Sychkin showed Russell
some communal rooms in which, as a result of overpopulation
at the factory, women, couples and complete families lived
among the bachelors. The beds were separated by wooden
partitions fixed to their frames and rising to a height of about
three feet six inches. Thus each household had its compartment and the room resembled a stable. According to Sychkin,
in certain workers' houses the tenants had on the average
only two square yards of space and three or four cubic yards
of air per person. And these figures took account only of the
number of occupants at a given moment. Now, all the big
factories worked continuously, and quite often the same beds
were occupied turn and turn about by two workers, one on
day shift and the other on night shift. Because of this relief
system the dormitory was never empty. In such conditions
the quantity of breathable air calculated by Sychkin must be
reduced again by half. Appalled by these details, Russell
wondered why the Russian worker, himself so badly housed,
was not content till he had made his family leave the village
to join him.

'It's very simple,' said Paul Egorovitch Sychkin. 'Having

left his own people to work in the town, a man soon sees that he doesn't get money enough to keep both himself and those whom he has left in the country. In forcing his wife and children to join him, he reckons that they will be hired at the factory for a fair wage and that their housing will raise no problem. Doubtless to encourage this kind of family migration, the big manufacturers have built such barracks on their factory land. The Russian peasant has a robust constitution. Comfort and hygiene do not interest him. He almost distrusts them. What he wants is a corner in which to lie down on bare boards for not too much money. Now the dormitory is always free of charge, and the *kamorki*, at the very most, are let for a deduction of one per cent of the wage, or virtually nothing, so the worker writes home. His wife and children arrive, and the whole lot pile up in some stifling den, already overcrowded with two families, or in the communal room with worn-out bodies strewn upon their litters all around them. With the help of bits of cardboard and cloth hung from nails, the women try to make a refuge in which to protect themselves against indiscreet glances. But no one pays any attention to them. The men are too worn out during the week and on Sundays most of them are drunk. According to statistics which I have consulted, the proportion of women working in the factories in 1855 was 33 per cent. and today it has risen to 44 per cent. In the textile industries they represent as much as 77 per cent. of the staff. We are watching a strange phenomenon. So long as the worker's family lives far away from him in the country, he keeps his ties with the soil and with the patriarchal customs of former times. He returns to the village from time to time in order to share in the work in the fields. He knows that there he has his roof, his friends, his graves, his memories. This nostalgic attraction ends abruptly as soon as our man has been able to make his wife and children come and settle in the great barrack. All are employed in the same factory. They have sold their little shanty. They are no longer peasants. And they are proud of it! Gradually a new class is born, homeless, without regrets and without traditions, who have no possessions of their own and live from day to day, lost in an anonymous mass of people just like themselves. As a result of living so close together, they acquire a vague awareness of their strength. Just consider that at the present moment there are no more than two and a half million workers in Russia for a total population of 129 millions.[1] Nevertheless, one can already speak of a "workers' will", while the Russian peasants, many times more numerous, are far from showing the same cohesion in defending their interests.'

Having inspected the dormitories of three factories, Russell was sure that nowhere in Russia were workers worse housed. To destroy his illusions, Paul Egorovitch Sychkin showed him what went on at a small factory specializing in the swingling of flax and hemp. The master, a big man with a fiery beard and eyes of forget-me-not blue, gave the two visitors an enthusiastic welcome and opened the great workshop door.

As he crossed the threshold, Russell thought he was entering a tropical forest of damp and discoloured foliage. Bundles of fibres hung from the ceiling and intercepted the daylight. To move forward, Sychkin had to push the damp and woody beards apart with his hands. The floor was covered with a thick layer of sticky nauseating filth, with here and there a pool of black water in front of a steaming bucket. Along the wall, close to the windows, stood the machines for breaking the fibres, which consisted of two pieces of wood, held together at one end by a strong pin. The lower piece was mounted on four feet. The whole thing formed a sort of cage, about three yards long and two yards wide. Paul Egorovitch Sychkin explained to Russell that the restricted space served both as a work place and a lodging for the worker's family. They lived there for twenty-four hours a day. At meal-times the whole little tribe sat on the ground between the piles of hemp and the bowls of dirty water; to sleep they stretched out on planks with bundles of fibre as pillows.

'Living together, these poor people have lost all sense of modesty,' Sychkin whispered. 'They have no embarrassment in promiscuity. The women even give birth here in front of everybody.'

[1] Of these 2,500,000 workers the textile industry alone employed nearly 700,000, mines and metallurgy 600,000, food production 250,000, and metal goods 225,000. In the textile industry, cotton manufacture led with 325,000 workers, followed by woollens (150,000), linen (60,000) and silk (40,000).

Russell perceived a child of about fifteen years on a bed of
rags at the foot of a machine. His eyes were closed and he
seemed to be sleeping deeply. But the sweat ran down his
livid face and his nostrils were pinched. In fact, he was
shivering with fever. Above him a robust fellow with dishevelled fair hair, undoubtedly the boy's father, mechanically
raised and lowered the jaws of the machine for breaking the
stems. Seated on an upturned bucket, a mother suckled her
baby, who was wrapped in dirty rags. As the heat and moisture were necessary to the processing of the fibres, a wash-
house atmosphere prevailed. The walls were cracked and
eaten away by brownish mould. The ceiling dripped. A grey
film covered the windows. At each step Russell's feet sank into
the black mud on the floor.

'In this kind of factory,' said Paul Egorovitch Sychkin, 'it
is usual to scrape the floor only once a year, in July.'

'And do these miserable people live like this in the filth for
a whole year?' asked Russell.

'Alas! Yes.'

'Is it only in these mills that the workers and their families
sleep, eat, procreate and die beside their machines?'

'No,' Sychkin admitted, 'it's the same in almost all the
smaller factories, where the work is still done by hand or at
least by simple mechanical means. I mean particularly the
small silk and woollen factories, and the textile printing
works. In these workshops they sleep on the floor, under the
benches, or on looms covered with planks. The weavers'
babies lie in cradles hooked up to the ceiling and are lulled to
sleep by the rhythmic beat of the lays. . . .'

As he left the mill, Russell was so appalled that Paul Egorovitch Sychkin regretted having shown things in such a bad
light.

'The housing problem is much in the minds of the public
authorities,' he said. 'Many societies have already been
formed for building hygienic houses at a low price. Don't
forget that the cloth-factory at Ramensk, together with the
Krupp factories in Germany, got the highest award at the
Brussels Exhibition of 1876 for the comfortable furnishing of
its workers' dwellings. Other Russian factories have followed
that example, including some of the biggest. In many respects

other parts of Europe, like France, are behind us, I have been told, with their slums and their leprous areas. Poverty is frightening everywhere. But with time and goodwill we will bring it to an end.'

Russell was not easy to convince.

'I suppose,' he said, 'that there are Russian workers housed elsewhere than in the workshops and barracks.'

'Of course,' cried Paul Egorovitch Sychkin. 'Although more than 60 per cent of the workers in the Government of Moscow live in such places, the proportion is less in other industrial centres, such as St Petersburg, Lodz, Warsaw, Riga, Odessa. . . . Actually, the workers who fix up their own living-quarters are scarcely better off than those in the communal room or *kamorki*. The "apartment" in the city usually consists of a dark and tiny room, furnished with a bed, two chairs and a table. All the doors of these "apartments" open into the same corridor. The rent depends on the area of the room. On the average it is 5 roubles 50 kopecks a month for a room of from 30 to 40 cubic yards. For this sum the proprietor also provides the wood for heating. Of course, only workers living with their families can afford the luxury of such a dwelling. With their women and children they crowd together into one room. Then, to lower the cost, another worker, by preference a bachelor, is taken in as sub-tenant. At night a folding screen separates him from the rest of the brood. He pays his host 1 rouble 50 kopecks a month. In exchange he has the right to a bed, a lamp, boiling water for tea, and sometimes even sauerkraut and kvas. It is always the tenant who buys the provisions and does the cooking for the sub-tenant. . . . In fact, their food is very plain for them all: black bread, sauerkraut, cabbage soup, boiled buckwheat with bacon, fresh cucumbers in summer and salted cucumbers in winter, and kvass. Morning and evening it is the same menu. Meat almost never appears. On fast-days the bacon is replaced by sunflower-seed oil with a penetrating odour. From this point of view, the workers who sleep and eat at the factory are infinitely better treated, for, in addition to the items I have just mentioned, they get meat at midday. The "pension" in the refectory costs about 3 roubles 75 per month. The employer deducts this sum from the wages. For everyday purchases, there are special shops near the factory authorized to sell to the workers on credit, guaranteed by their wages. The prices of the most essential articles are controlled and approved by the factory inspector. For example, women's footwear costs 1 rouble 65, cotton material 8 kopecks an arsheen, printed calico 10 kopecks. . . . In the end, the workers living in the buildings attached to the factory, like those who live in a room in the town, find themselves at the end of the month with empty pockets!

'There's another important fact: Russian law does not oblige the factory proprietor to open schools for teaching the children they employ, nor to send those children to schools which already exist. But it stipulates that children not provided with certificates of primary education must have the "opportunity" to attend school three hours a day and eighteen hours a week. Although they might not be compelled, the majority of big Russian firms have created educational establishments near their factories, under the control of the Ministry of Public Education. On January 1, 1899, there were 446 schools of this kind in Russia, attended by nearly 50,000 adolescents.[1] The maintenance of these centres costs 787,000 roubles a year, of which 732,000 roubles are exclusively at the cost of the employers. It seems to me that this proves that the manufacturers have become aware of the wretched state in which their employees still vegetate and that, in the interests even of their business, they are trying to create a new generation of workers, developed, literate and ambitious. . . .'

While they talked the two men had left the workers' quarter of Presnia and were walking along streets that looked quieter and more prosperous. They stopped for tea at a *traktir*, but they were scarcely seated at a table before Russell asked the question which had been on the tip of his tongue:

'These various social laws of which you have been speaking. Were they enacted spontaneously or under pressure?'

'I am sorry to have to say,' Sychkin replied, 'that the workers only secured this quite relative improvement of their

[1] To be exact, 46,973. Of this total, 4,307 were children who worked in factories, 32,958 children whose parents worked in the factories, and 9,708 children who were not associated with the factories.

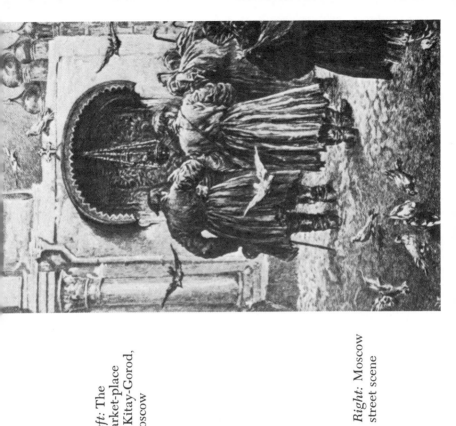

3 *Left*: The
market-place
of Kitay-Gorod,
Moscow

Right: Moscow
street scene

4   Moscow shops

Moscow street scene

lot by recourse to social agitation. It was following the strikes organized between 1870 and 1880 that the government promulgated the law of June 1, 1882, forbidding the employment of children of less than twelve years in factories and restricting the employment of adolescents and women. In January 1885 the strike at the Morozov factories (11,000 workers) was provoked by the abuse of fines, which the management inflicted under the most varied pretexts in order to reduce the wage-earners' pay. The outburst was put down by the military and ended in the disbanding of 800 workers. Thirty-three rioters were brought before the court. The jury acquitted them, and the following year, on June 3, 1886, a law regulating the system of fines fixed their rates and specified that the sums thus collected must not under any circumstances benefit the employer. Meanwhile, this same law laid down the penalties which would be incurred thereafter by instigators of strikes; from four to eight months in prison. Of course, strikes began again and were more serious. In 1896, 35,000 workers in the cotton-mills of St Petersburg ceased work. In 1897 there was a further strike of all textile workers. The Government at once instituted the 11½-hour day by the law of June 2, 1897. At the present time it seems that the Tsar's policy is now to give way gradually to the legitimate demands of the workers, but also to strengthen the repressive apparatus in order to prevent any further outbreak. The number of factory inspectors has been increased, and the number of police agents, charged with watching the industrial suburbs, has been augmented considerably. Thus the struggle promises to be increasingly harsh. The workers are organizing themselves. Obviously there exists as yet only a single kind of authorized professional association: the mutual assistance funds. They are multiplying throughout the land: mutual assistance funds for shoemakers, weavers, papermakers, domestic servants ... Their activities are limited to handing out money to the sick, widows, orphans and necessitous persons, but although devoid of any political significance, these groupings give the labouring masses the impression that they are not absolutely defenceless. Add to this that, for close on ten years, clandestine circles have proliferated in St Petersburg and Moscow, and all the big cities, and that the intellectuals – students, engineers, journalists – fed on the doctrines of Karl Max, are elaborating the programme of the 'future democratic Russia.' According to them, it is necessary to free labour from the capitalist yoke, to bring the workers to power, to turn the bourgeois order of things upside down. . . . You know as much as I do about their ideas! The party theoreticians are already mingling with the factory workers to prepare them for the revolt. In 1897 a new organization was created: the Bund, a general league of Jewish workers of Poland, Lithuania and Russia, directed by a central executive committee. Thus the workers are uniting, no longer in isolated centres but from city to city, in order to cover Russia with a network of branches with a common inspiration. The result of this campaign was the first Social-Democratic Congress at Minsk in March 1898. I have read the party's manifesto: "The proletariat will shake off the Tsarist yoke!" It makes one tremble. I simply hope that here, as elsewhere, liberal measures will disarm the fanatics of disorder. You are looking at me anxiously. Do you really believe that the Russian worker has more to complain about than others?'

Russell was slow in answering. 'I think,' he murmured at last, 'that your workers haven't a lot of reason to envy others. But poverty in Western Europe is less obvious, perhaps less aggressive, than what I have just seen. One might say that here poverty, squalor and shame are ostentatious. People here display their wounds and glory in their misfortunes!'

'Don't be too quick to generalize,' said Sychkin. 'Have you anything in your country like our *artels*?'

Russell confessed that he did not know what the word meant, so Paul Egorovitch Sychkin told him that side by side with the ordinary workers, there existed in Russia a large class of artisans, grouped in communities, or *artels*. These *artels* were of very ancient origin[1] and were founded on the principle of the co-operative: the members all had to be of the same trade, to work with their own hands, to have equal rights, and to be jointly responsible for the actions of any member of the brotherhood. There were *artels* of porters, of bank and commercial messengers (*bankirskie* or *kupechie artelshchiki*), etc. All the *artels* had registered capital, deriving

[1] There were *artels* in Russia in the twelfth century.

from payments made by the *artelshchiki* on their joining the community: the *vkup*, the gift on admission, and the *novizna*, the gift on being received. This capital served as the members' guarantee when they assumed responsibility in some work or service. Thus united in common interest, the *artelshchiki* therefore did not tolerate lazy, unscrupulous or unskilful individuals within their group. They all kept watch upon one another, and the public never had cause for complaint. Once a year, early in the autumn, they met to hear their delegates' report, approve accounts, settle the portion of the receipts to be put to reserve, determine each member's share of the benefits and decide the pensions for widows and orphans. Afterwards they elected their president, *starosta*, or old one, and a secretary, the *pisar*, entrusted with the *artel's* correspondence and accounts. To be a member of an *artel* was for a Russian worker a certificate of excellence. Paul Egorovitch Sychkin even claimed that there was no such thing as a really poor or intemperate *artelshchik*.

'Anyway,' he concluded, 'intemperance is decreasing in our country. All the statistics agree upon this.'

Here again Russell asked for clarification. What miracle had cured the Russian people of intemperance? But the reply was disappointing: there was no miracle, only a law, dated 1894, which made the sale of spirits a State monopoly.

'Before this law,' Sychkin went on, 'drunkenness was a chronic vice among the lower orders. Private industry manufactured poorly refined alcoholic liquor embellished with injurious ingredients. Every *traktir* had its thirsty clientele, ready to hand over their shirts and boots for a small glass. The law of 1894 has almost completely suppressed the sale of drinks. It is the State which now distils and sells vodka. Whoever wants to drink it can only buy it by the bottle in special shops. . . .'

When they left the *traktir*, Paul Egorovitch Sychkin led Russell to the door of one of these shops. Workers and moujiks entered the shop soberly, one by one. Each reappeared shortly afterwards clasping a bottle of ordinary vodka with a red seal. The better vodka had a white seal. Once in the street the man went off for about fifty yards and stopped, for by the regulations he was forbidden to consume the alcohol within fifty yards of the shop or ninety yards of a church. There was an infallible technique for opening the bottle. The customer applied a sharp and powerful blow to the bottom of the bottle with the palm of his hand and the cork sprang out. Standing in the middle of the pavement, the man thrust the neck of the bottle into his mouth, threw back his head, swallowed the spirits in two or three gulps, grimaced, drew a scrap of black bread from his pocket, broke it, chewed it and returned to the shop with a sigh. There he acquired a few kopecks for the empty bottle. With this money he bought another but smaller bottle, which was known as a *merzavchik*, 'a little rascal', and went off to empty it fifty paces away, thinking sadly that the operation could not be repeated a third time. Mostly the vodka-lovers had not the wherewithal for a bite of food and swallowed their doses of alcohol without eating a thing. This practice was dangerous when it was very cold. In winter it was not uncommon for a drinker to fall, dead drunk, into the snow. The police gathered up the strays and took them off to the police station.

Sychkin and Russell wanted to take a cab home, so they went over to a line of *isvoschiks* that were freezing in a little snow-covered square, and there was at once a chorus of shouts from the bearded drivers, with their tall hats and filthy greatcoats. After much bargaining Sychkin at last agreed a price for the journey with one of the drivers and all the rest fell silent. The happy chosen one took off his hat to invite his customers to be seated. Russell hauled himself up into the carriage beside his companion and they curled their legs up under a great blanket. In front of them the *isvostchik* sat as if impaled upon his tiny seat. He clicked his tongue. The carriage set off. Fed on cabbage-stalks and putrid peelings, the horse trotted along, breaking wind at every jolt.

The outer parts of Moscow, with their little wooden houses, little bare gardens and shops with painted metal signs, were like large villages, and the passers-by resembled moujiks. Men, women and children nibbled sunflower seeds all day long. They would take a handful from their pockets, put them into their mouths, shell them with their teeth and tongues, spit out the skin and eat the little kernel. The pavements were strewn with the small black husks, almost like a carpet of crushed insects. As the two men drew closer to the centre of the city, the roads became cleaner, the shop-fronts more pleasing, and the faces of the pedestrians more European. Every time he passed a church the coachman took off his hat and crossed himself. Snow gleamed on the roofs. Bells were ringing. Gradually, Russell forgot the factories and the dormitories, and was no longer ashamed to be happy in his wadded greatcoat and astrakan hat, with his residence permit in his pocket.

＊　　＊　　＊　　＊

Having introduced Russell to the poverty of the Russian working masses, Paul Egorovitch Sychkin wanted to show him also the efforts of the State and of private persons in matters of assistance. In Russia there was no general plan fixing the organization and limits of public or private charity. Such chaos prevailed among the laws in force that the Senate had lately thought it necessary even to make clear that aid for the poor was a *right* and not an *obligation* for towns and *zemstvos*. Despite the confusion of the various official regulations, benevolence was keen from top to bottom of the social scale. The merchant class, the *petit bourgeois*, the parish guardians, *zemstvos* and municipalities, all had their own ways of bringing help to the needy. Even the peasants were not outside the movement. According to official figures, every moujik of a certain degree of comfort gave three or four pounds of cereals a year to the poor, to a value of three or four roubles. Mendicancy was not regarded as shameful in Russia, and to refuse bread to a beggar was a great sin. But the most widespread aid was given by private charitable societies. There were many such societies in the Empire: about 2,500, of which 360 at least were in the Government of St Petersburg and 125 in that of Moscow. The biggest of these organizations was certainly the Administration of the Institutions of the Empress Marie, created in 1797 and placed under the protection of Her Majesty the Dowager Empress Marie Fedorovna. Asylums for the blind, deaf and dumb and aged, hospitals, foundling hospitals in St Petersburg (33,000 people assisted every year) and in Moscow, which was even bigger

(39,000 a year), depended upon this administration. According to Paul Egorovitch Sychkin, the generosity of the Russian spirit could not be understood without visiting the Moscow Foundling Hospital. It was, he said, the biggest charitable establishment in the world. The State paid an annual subvention of more than a million roubles (£100,000), deriving mainly from the sale of playing-cards, towards the foundlings. Visiting-days were Thursdays and Sundays.

Russell at first thought that such a home must necessarily be in the suburbs of Moscow, but he was quite surprised when Paul Egorovitch Sychkin led him to the centre of the city, not far from the Kremlin, and showed him an enormous building, with five floors towering above the Moskva. In its anonymity, frigidity and cleanliness, this endless plaster-white façade was the symbol of officially assisted poverty. At the entrance, in Solianka Street, two allegorical sculptured groups represented childhood and education. From the entrance one passed into a square with flowers and green plants. The hospital, built under Catherine II, had 2,000 identical windows.

A young doctor, a friend of Sychkin, undertook to conduct the visitors into the temple of abandoned childhood. As soon as he was in the building, Russell was surprised by the size of the corridors, 140 yards long! Immense rooms opened up on either side of them, each lit by thirty windows and warmed by Dutch stoves. Floors, ceilings and walls were painted. Dirty linen never remained in the room: it was dropped direct to the basement, where it was disinfected on the spot in high-pressure steam-baths. Despite the hygienic precautions, a stale and sour odour prevailed in the dormitories. The doctor who accompanied Russell and Sychkin explained that it was fruitless to combat this odour because the rooms were over-populated and the cubic air-space inadequate.

The cast-iron cots were lined up along the main axis of the room, each being draped with a white muslin veil. Blue gauze veils were reserved for ophthalmic cases. For premature infants there were forty-five warmed cots, made of two metal bath-tubs fitted one into the other, the space between them being filled with warm water. The doctor called this apparatus an 'incubator-bath' or 'samovar' and thought it preferable to the eight Tarnier incubators which the establishment had at its disposal.

The nurses scarcely ever left the infants entrusted to them. They slept at the foot of the cradles on straw mattresses which, during the day, were piled in a corner of the room, covered with a grey sheet to hide them from the eyes of visitors. Russell was amazed by this opulent troop of milch-women, the *kormilitsy*. They were all dressed in blouses with puffed sleeves, bodices with shoulder-straps, and heavily embroidered red skirts. Their round white bosoms stretched the cloth. A diadem, or *kakoshnik*, crowned each head, and the colour varied according to the wing to which the nurse was attached. All were peasant women who had abandoned their own infants in the villages in order to earn some money by nursing other people's babies. The majority of the *kor-militsy*, however, had insufficient milk. Those who had plenty took on two or even three nurslings, which secured them extra food, a litre of beer and fifteen additional kopecks a day. The doctor told how some of them had begun, very ingeniously, by leaving their own babies with the hospital; knowing the numbers by which they had been registered, they searched for their own infants and suckled them secretly at the expense of the management, which was an unprotesting party to this little fraud.

Sick infants were isolated in an infirmary, where a special section was given over to syphilitic cases, which were very numerous. These were suckled by some fifty nurses who were themselves syphilitic. Mortality in this service was higher than anywhere else.

According to the new rule, dating from December 18, 1890, the hospital accepted infants of less than one year, illegitimate, deprived of their mothers or with mothers too poor to care for them, foundlings, legitimate children whose mothers were dead (or who could not feed them at the breast), etc. The persons who brought the infants had, as a rule, to provide certificates of birth and baptism. As to the babies collected from the public highway, they were admitted on a mere report from the superintendent of police. With illegitimate children the regulations provided further that the management could, in certain cases, make do with a statement by the almoner or the principal maternity doctor, declaring under oath that it was preferable to keep the baby's birth secret so as not to harm the mother's social position. Such a statement had to be accompanied by the payment of fifteen roubles.

The office for abandoned children was on the ground floor, and in it day and night two inspectresses resolutely awaited the living bundles which women brought in from the street. It was almost never the mothers themselves who undertook this painful step, but neighbours or friends. They had to show the infants' certificates of birth and baptism as well as their own passports. As soon as a child was admitted, the inspectress established its identity, entered it in the great register of the house and gave it a number. This number was reproduced on an oval bone medallion which was hung round the neck of the little inmate. The person who had brought the nursling to the office received a form (pink for girls, blue for boys) bearing the same number and the date of deposit. It was by this form that the child's mother or family could, if the occasion arose, find it again after it had been placed in the country.[1]

When these first formalities were completed, the child was stripped of its rags, washed, measured, cared for, swaddled, directed to a 'waiting section' and handed over to one of 30 nurses who, until the next day's medical examination, were charged with suckling the newcomers. The rules of the house did not limit the number of admissions, and their daily average was 60, with 'peaks' of 80 to 100! On certain days, said the doctor, the infants were brought in by dozens, in baskets, from the boundaries of the Government of Moscow, or even from Asia and Caucasia. The majority were half-dead with hunger and cold. Of more than 20,000 nurslings who entered the hospital every year, 4 per cent died within a few hours of admission, 20 per cent were seriously ill, 32 per cent showed congenital weakness. In good or poor health, they formed a daily total of 2,000 mouths to feed. The number of nurses was almost equal to that of the consumers.

The majority of them were girls from the environs of

[1] According to statistics for the year 1900, there were 108 illegitimate births in every thousand in the towns of Russia.

Moscow. On arrival they were examined by a doctor and, if the quality of their milk was regarded as satisfactory, they were entered in a register, plunged into a bath, and were given the linen and uniform of the establishment. After a final examination by the chief doctor, each took a nursling from among the infants brought in the day before to the office of abandoned children. At that moment the priest baptized the few newly born who had been taken in without baptismal certificate and gave them the name of the day's saint. The nurses received a monthly wage of seven roubles ($3.61) if engaged for six months, or five roubles ($2.58) if engaged for a shorter time. Those who suckled more than one nursling at a time received supplements of food, drink and pay (15 kopecks = 8 cents a day).

With the doctor's complicity, Russell and Sychkin were able to watch these women at their meal. They made their way to the refectory in compact groups of 350 to 400. With diadems on their heads, their bosoms thrust out, their red dresses rustling, a heavy-breasted regiment flowed down the corridor. There was something rather odd about these living sources of nourishment going to feed themselves. Each held her wooden spoon in her hand. At the refectory door each received an enormous piece of black bread. Having bowed several times to the Virgin's altar, which stood at the far end of the hall with candles that stayed alight throughout the meal, they took their places at the table and the meal began. The menu normally comprised meat *shchi* and boiled buckwheat. The soup was served in a dish big enough for six persons, into which each dipped her spoon in turn. There was no rationing. Servants refilled the plate as many times as necessary until the company was satisfied. However, the doctor made clear to Russell that the nurses had to follow the rules of the Orthodox Church and to fast for 29 Wednesdays and Fridays and for the whole duration of the four great Russian lents: the great Easter Lent (7 weeks), the great Christmas Lent (39 days), the great St Peter Lent (21 days), and the Assumption Lent (14 days). In all, a nurse's year contained almost as many meat-days as fast-days, the fast-day being placed under the austere sign of the herring!

The medical staff comprised 30 to 40 doctors and more

than 200 sick-nurses. But, despite their knowledge and devotion, the mortality rate at the hospital was very high. The young doctor admitted that an average of 25 infants died each day, and it was during the months of April, May, June and July that the figures were highest. During these months, in fact, there was a shortage of wet-nurses for the foundlings, because the village women were kept at home by the work in the fields.

Once admitted to the home, the healthy children did not remain there for more than three or four weeks. As soon as the umbilical wound had healed, the infants were vaccinated with cow-pox and sent in groups to the provinces. The journey by train, and then in a wretched carriage over rutted roads, often covered 250 or 300 miles, and often in winter the infants, who had left Moscow in good health, arrived sick, exhausted and frozen at the end of the expedition. There a village nurse welcomed them and they shared the life of the moujiks. In the majority of cases, the young doctor said, there was not even a bed for the infant to sleep in. The nurse put several into a basket hanging by ropes from the ceiling. No supervision was possible, for the villages were very far from the central administration. Half these abandoned children who swarmed in the *izbas* died while still very young.

Though Russell was saddened by such misery, he was pleasantly surprised to learn of the liberal organization of the maternity annexe to the hospital. In this model establishment, the pregnant girls had no need to fear interrogation about the reasons for their distress, nor even that they would be reproached for it. They could, without difficulty, abandon their babies by conforming to the rules. There was even a section for secret confinements, comprising 13 paying rooms (75, 60 and 50 roubles a month, according to the size of the room). Any woman wanting to be delivered secretly entered the maternity section in the last month of her pregnancy. On arrival she gave her name and address in a sealed envelope to the doctor in charge. A nurse, always the same, was attached to her. Only the doctor in charge visited the patient, delivered her and gave her all necessary care. Her child, if she so wished, was admitted officially to the foundling hospital. In that event, the doctor in charge handed the mother a certificate stating that she had been delivered secretly in the maternity section. As soon as she had recovered, she left the establishment without any questions at all. Before her departure, the doctor in charge handed her back the sealed envelope which contained her identity.

'Our organization has many shortcomings,' said the young doctor, 'but has its origin incontestably in a generous idea. We strive to spare the woman's honour; we respect her even in her weaknesses.'

Two wet-nurses passed along the corridor, each holding a baby to her breast. Russell followed them with a glance that was touched with emotion and said:

'In this field we are a little less broadminded than you, doctor.'

CHAPTER VIII

THE ARMY

The officer cadets (or 'junkers') at school: traditions, ragging, studies, examinations, promotion – The Corps of Pages – The Kammerpages – General organization of the Army – Recruitment – Grades – Service to the Regiment – Relatives of officers and men – Officers' pay – Distinctions – Discipline, uniforms – The barracks – Soldiers' pay, food and equipment – The Cossacks: 'the dzhigitovka' and the lava technique

RUSSELL would certainly have learned nothing about the Russian Army if Alexander Vassilievitch had not introduced him to his nephew, Cornet Vassili Fedorovitch Kapytov, then on leave in Moscow. This young man was fresh from the Elizavetgrad Cavalry School and very proud of his new uniform and his fair waxed moustache. Having been invited to dinner by his uncle, he lent a willing ear to the questions which Russell put to him about his military training. During the meal, it is true, the conversation was disjointed, but when they left the table Vassili Fedorovitch had no difficulty in holding everyone's attention. Leaning against the chimney-piece with a glass of kümmel in his left hand, a cigar in his right, he smiled as he recalled his astonishment when faced as a novice with the strict discipline of the school. For pupils from the gymnasia who, like himself, could produce a qualifying certificate, the course lasted only two years. At the end of these two years the junkers who had satisfied their examiners were incorporated in the regiments with the rank of cornet. But before this promotion what a lot of study they had to do and what ragging they suffered!

The 'seniors', who called themselves 'honorary cornets', led the new-comers (who were called 'second-rate animals') a hard life. An 'honorary cornet' was always right in his dealings with a 'second-rate animal' and spared him neither punishments nor public humiliations. Both in school and in the street the latter had to march upright, with his arms stretched and his little finger down the seam of his trousers. Whenever

he saw a second-year junker he had to salute him respectfully, turning his head towards him as if he were a hierarchical superior. The cadets' assembly-room, known pompously
as a smoking-room, was divided in two by a deep line drawn
with a white-hot poker in the asphalt floor. The 'second-rate
animals' were kept beyond this frontier and could only cross
it on the invitation of an 'honorary cornet'. At seven in the
morning the trumpeters sounded the reveille at the four corners of the barracks and the 'second-rate animals' sprang
out of bed and fled to the washrooms in order to leave them
free for the arrival of the 'seniors'. But they had to be quick
before they were deafened by cries of 'Get out! Vermin! Lazy
dogs! The last three will get extra guard duty!'

After roll-call came common prayers and breakfast, which
consisted of tea, black bread and butter. Then studies began.
The instructors were all officers. The school was under the
direction of a colonel with two majors under his orders. Each
squadron numbered 140 junkers. The very full curriculum
comprised equitation, jumping, fencing, gymnastics and foot-
drill as outdoor exercises. In the classroom they learned military history, the art of fortification, ballistics, topography,
administration, hippology, mechanics and chemistry. These
last two sciences were regarded by the pupils as unworthy of
a junker. It was traditional that 'second-rate animals' must
handle books on mechanics and chemistry only with gloved
hands, as a sign of contempt. The 'second-rate animal' who
got a zero for chemistry had the right to live for forty-eight
hours on terms of equality with the 'seniors'. He could lie on
a table, light a cigarette under the noses of the 'honorary
cornets' and walk before them with one hand in his pocket
and his collar undone.

Cavalry training took place in the school's riding-ring. The
'second-rate animals' began by mounting without spurs or
stirrups. When, after heaping his whole repertoire of abuse
upon them, the instructor reckoned they could keep more or
less in the saddle, spurs and stirrups were given them as a
reward. Then they learned to sabre cones of clay raised on
wooden frames. The supreme art consisted in cleaving the
obstacles with the point of the blade in such a way that the
cut part remained in its place despite the speed of the horse.

Often the clay cones were alternated with faggots, in which event the cadets asked the assistant instructors to soak the branches beforehand in salt water so that, dried and hardened, they might be easier to slice.

They lunched at midday in the large dining-hall and at half-past one, with their stomachs laden with meat, sauerkraut and plain water, the junkers returned to their classrooms until six in the evening. After supper, the cadets prepared their lessons and their duties in the study, which was decorated with commemorative plaques and military pictures blackened with age. The dormitories where they slept were meticulously clean. Mattresses and pillows were filled with horsehair, and blankets were made of grey wool. When he undressed, the junker had to fold his clothes in regulation fashion and place his socks on top of them 'in love', that is to say, in the form of a cross. The junker who was responsible for the squadron's night duties did his rounds, reprimanded any 'second-rate animal' who was slow in getting to bed, pushed over any badly arranged pack, handed out a few guard duties and retired. Lights out was sounded at ten. Each morning orderlies brushed the young gentlemen's uniforms and polished their boots. Regulations provided one orderly for ten cadets. The junkers gave them three roubles a month as a reward.

It was only when he had passed his preliminary examination that the 'second-rate animal' received permission from his major to go out. Trembling with pleasure, he dressed in an irreproachable fashion, drew on white gloves, made certain that his boots shone, that his cap was tilted over his brow, that the folds of his coat were correct, and finally presented himself to the guard-post. There the junker on duty, a 'senior', examined him from head to foot and asked him a ridiculous question at pointblank: 'What is the birthday of the colonel in command of the school?' or 'Since when have forts been used in Russia?' Astonished, the newcomer did not know what to reply and was pitilessly sent back to his dormitory. It was a rule, in fact, that a 'second-rate animal's' first outing should be stopped on any unexpected pretext. On his second outing, on the other hand, he no longer found the same obstacles. But in the town his martyrdom began. His

eyes searched the horizon in fear of seeing an officer's
uniform. Now the officers' uniforms were many and he must
not fail to salute with all the requisite stiffness. For a general
one had even to freeze to attention three paces in advance of
him and not to begin walking again until he was three paces
past. In the theatre junkers were not allowed in the first three
rows of the stalls. In all public places, before sitting down,
they had to ask permission of the officers present. If an officer
of high rank suddenly appeared before them, the junkers
rose, saluted him and repeated the request. To evade any
misunderstanding, therefore, the junkers avoided being
seated during the intervals. Moreover, they were strictly forbidden to enter music-halls and cafés with music. Kept away
from all the bright life, the junkers nevertheless discussed it
amongst themselves with assurance. On the whole their conversation was anything but intellectual. Three subjects excited both the 'second-rate animals' and 'honorary cornets':
wine, horses and women.

Though they drank only tea and water at school, the
junkers boasted amongst themselves of their knowledge of
champagne, bordeaux, burgundy and liqueurs. To hear them
one would think that at home they cleaned their teeth in
Veuve Clicquot! Of course, all of them claimed to be able to
drain a bottle of cognac without a tremor. To be a good
cornet, one had in fact to have a stomach that was proof
against the most diabolical of alcoholic drinks. As to horses,
they were an inexhaustible source of discussion among the
future centaurs of the Imperial Army. They weighed the
merits of one breed against the other. They expressed
opinions on the studs and on the trainers. They demonstrated
horsemanship seated astride a chair. But it was the subject of
women that aroused the liveliest feelings.

With an indulgent smile, Vassili Fedorovitch admitted that
many lies were told within the precincts of the school on this
subject. Every one of them sought to persuade the rest that
he had had adventures. But not sentimental adventures ('sentiment' was despised by the junkers). 'Passing adventures' or
'physical adventures'! No names were given, certainly, but
certain details brought a flush to the cheeks of the narrator
himself. The dream of all these young men was eventually to

have a comedienne, a dancer or a demi-mondaine for a mistress. Some of them were well known. The junkers who lived in Moscow and St Petersburg said that they cost fortunes. Moreover, the majority ended their careers with brilliant marriages. However, all the 'honorary cornets' were agreed that they would not marry a woman from the theatre, for she could be harmful to their careers. Officers of the Imperial Guard who married actresses were obliged to leave their regiment and to fall back upon some ordinary regiment. One would be mad to sacrifice one's future for creatures like that! With them one led a gay life, but it was the discreet and refined girls one chose when one wanted to start a home! As he spoke these words, Vassili Fedorovitch looked at his cousin Helen. She turned her head away. Russell felt suddenly irritated by this good-looking fellow's chatter, though he had asked for these confidences himself.

'I suppose,' said Alexander Vassilievitch, 'that your second year was not so hard as the first?'

'Of course not!' Vassili Fedorovitch replied as he shook the ash of his cigar into the fireplace: 'From a "second-rate animal" I became an "honorary cornet". It was now my job to train the new-comers! However, you can be sure that I was not too cruel. I only did what was necessary.... But how long and irritating that second year seemed! ... And then at last the exams! ... My average made me eighth in the first category of officer candidates. Quite a good result. Since one's choice of regiment depends upon the marks secured, I could expect not to be disappointed. As soon as the general rating was announced, a secret campaign was launched amongst my comrades. It was a case of everyone discouraging everyone else about the regiment he himself wanted to join. The strangest rumours circulated in the dormitories. Such and such a unit was not favoured by His Imperial Majesty. Service in some other unit cost an enormous amount. A third was well known for its colonel's strictness. But my own choice had long been made: I wanted to serve with the Alexandria Hussars.'

'Because of the uniform?' asked Paul Egorovitch Sychkin with a malicious gleam in his eye.

'Because of the unit's glorious past,' Vassili Fedorovitch

5 *Right:* Muscovite workers

Left: Workers' dwellings in Moscow; the proprietor's name (Volkov) can be seen on the lantern

Right: Artillerymen of the Guard

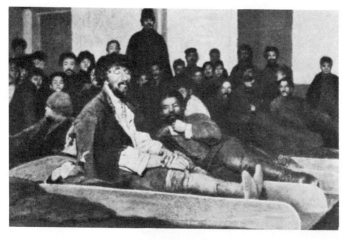

Left: Workers' dormitory at a transport undertaking in St Petersburg

Right: Interior of a St Petersburg traktir

Left: Interior of a shelter in the Khitrovka, Moscow

answered. 'Four days before we left on manœuvres, the colonel in command of the school received the list of vacancies in the cavalry regiments. The cadets were summoned one by one in order of their general rating to state their preferences. Being well placed I was able to get the regiment I wanted. Others, whose marks were lower than mine, had to make do with regiments that did not please them. . . . Laughter, shouts of joy, embraces, groans . . . the whole school was in a state of excitement. Immediately after the ceremony, tailors, bootmakers and saddlemakers invaded the common-room to solicit our orders. In all the dormitories measurements were taken, samples examined, prices discussed. Before leaving on manœuvres every junker had, according to tradition, to possess a cap of the regiment which he would afterwards join. Of course it was forbidden to wear the cap before the date of official appointment, but in the absence of superiors all the cadets strutted about the corridors with their new headgear set jauntily on their heads. There's no point in telling you that I found the September manœuvres, three versts from Elizavetgrad, wearisome. At last the "second-rate animals" left camp to go on leave to their respective families, and the officers-to-be remained alone in their barracks. No more exercises, no more courses, no more questions. Just waiting – waiting interminably for the telegram that meant freedom! One day, as I was walking beside the river, shouts rang out and I rushed towards the cantonment. Amongst a group of cadets stood a telegraph messenger, bare-headed, dripping with sweat. He was waving a dispatch at arm's length. Coins were raining into his cap, which was placed on the ground. At last he escaped the embraces of the junkers and ran to carry his message to the school's director. The bugle sounded assembly. The squadrons fell in. Then our colonel appeared, smiling and paternal, with the telegram in his hand. After the appointments were read, we rushed off to our barracks. Our new uniforms awaited us, stretched out on the beds. Until evening there was a gathering of varied uniforms in the camp: representatives of every cavalry regiment in the Empire walked up and down, side by side, smoking cigars and talking about their futures. The colonel assembled us for the last time in order to give us our leave passes for twenty-one days. . . . And there you are. . . . To you it means nothing, but for me it was like a fairy-tale. . . .'

A murmur of understanding greeted his words. Vassili Fedorovitch emptied his glass of kümmel.

'And is the life the same in all the Russian military schools?' Russell asked.

'Very nearly,' said Vassili Fedorovitch. 'Except in His Imperial Majesty's Corps of Pages, where the discipline is even more severe.'

The word 'page', as applied to military men, surprised Russell. But Alexander Vassilievitch explained that this term in Russia designated the officer-cadets of aristocratic birth. For a boy to be admitted to this institution, not only did his father and grandfather have to have been of incontestable nobility, but one or the other must have served in the Russian army with the rank of general. Children were mostly entered for the Corps of Pages at birth. They joined at twelve or thirteen years of age, and left it to join a Guards regiment only after five years in the middle classes and two years in the higher classes. In fact, any young man wishing to enter a Guards regiment was subjected beforehand to a very strict and secret scrutiny by the officers of that regiment. Priority was obviously accorded to the candidates whose forebears had served in the same unit. Thanks to this quasi-hereditary recruitment, the officers felt themselves bound to their regiment by genuine family traditions. For instance, one had only to glance at a list of Horse Guards Officers to see a considerable number of names of Baltic consonance. The Knights Guards, on the other hand, had on the whole specifically Russian names. Well before passing their final examinations, the pages knew the regiment to which they were destined by their origins. And they looked to this future with jealous pride.

The sumptuousness of the pages' full-dress uniforms was legendary: black or red cloth, with gold frogs, white gloves and a white-plumed helmet. In the preparatory courses the uniform was scarcely less showy, but the plumed helmet was replaced by a pointed one. The general and military teaching was intense in an establishment that was destined to create the Empire's warrior élite. Conscious of their privileged position, the cadets formed a caste, all the members of which were united by an oath of friendship unto death. Love for the Tsar and the Fatherland, respect for the regulations, and a thirst to prove their heroism burned in all of them. The Maltese Cross was their emblem, and their ideal was simple: to enforce respect by their valour, to treat women as objects of pleasure, and to accede rapidly to the highest ranks and to the most dazzling positions.

Meanwhile, within this nursery of future high officers were the *Kammerpages*, like an aristocracy within an aristocracy: the Pages of the Chamber. From among all the cadets the Imperial Family chose a dozen for Palace service. This selection was made less by the marks the young men secured than by their names and appearance. A tall stature, a fine face and a glorious genealogy were the best recommendations for this duty. Each *Kammerpage* was personally attached to the suite of a certain member of the Imperial Family. During dinners and banquets he stood motionless behind the seat of the Grand Duchess to whom he had the honour of being officially attached. In processions and ceremonials he bore her train. But no service was ever asked of him that was not prescribed by etiquette. After a few hours in the wake of the Tsar, he came back to earth, still dazed by his luck, returned to school and modestly resumed his studies. His comrades looked at him with envy, as if he were a messenger from some miraculous universe.

'Yes, yes,' said Russell, 'but these are exceptional cases. What is the composition of the Russian Army outside the Guards?'

The question seemed natural to Vassili Fedorovitch and he answered with all the assurance of his two years at the cavalry school. Overwhelmed by an avalanche of figures, Russell learned that since the reforms of 1874 military service was compulsory for everyone in Russia from twenty-one to forty-three years of age, without any possibility of buying out' or substitution. The men passed as 'fit' were registered either in the ranks of the regular army, or in the territorial reserve (*opolchenie*). Active army service was for eighteen years, five of which were with the colours and thirteen with the reserve or militia.[1] In view of the enormous size of the

[1] In the infantry or the foot artillery the men spent only four years with the colours.

population, only the young men selected by lot were incorporated into the regular army.[1] The rest were called up only in the event of war by the Emperor's edict. Further, there were among them a great number of persons exempted for reasons of health, studies or family.[2] Taking these special cases into account, each year 270,000 to 290,000 conscripts were recruited, which in peacetime assured a total permanent effective of a million men. This figure could easily be increased to 2,500,000 and only considerations of economy kept conscription within the limits named.

The officers of the reserve were recruited from volunteers who, according to their level of general education, spent a longer or shorter period with the colours and could be quickly promoted to the rank of non-commissioned officer, or to officer after examination. There were 52 infantry divisions, three of which were Guards, four of Grenadiers and 45 of the line; 19 cavalry divisions, four of which were of the Guards; 52 brigades of foot artillery, including three of Guards. Almost all the ranks corresponded to those of other armies, though they bore names that were difficult to remember, and were reminiscent of German influence: *unterofitser, feldfebel, feierverker, kornet, praporshchik, podporuchik, poruchik, shtabskapitan, kapitan, rotmistr, podpolkovnik, polkovnik* . . . And Vassili Fedorovitch, who was still only a *kornet*, would certainly end as a *polkovnik* (colonel).[3]

---

[1] Before the law of January 1, 1874, military service was for twenty-five years for those who, selected by lot, had no means with which to buy themselves out or have themselves replaced. Once called to the colours, the man became more or less a military man for life. When returned to civilian life after twenty-five years with the army, he remained a person apart, isolated, unadapted, no longer having the taste for the sort of life led by those around him.

[2] Thus, only sons supporting the family formed the second reserve of the *opoltchenie*, and could only be mobilized, in case of war, by an imperial manifesto.

[3] In the infantry, the hierarchy of non-commissioned officers comprised the four following grades: *mladshii unterofitser* (corporal), *vzvodnyi unterofitser* (sergeant), *feldfebel* (sergeant-major or adjutant), *portupei yunker* (acting officer). In the cavalry the corporal was known simply as *unterofitser*, the sergeant as *vzvodnyi unterofitser*, and the squadron sergeant-major or adjutant as *vakhmistr*. Among the Cossacks the corresponding grades were *mladshii uryadnik* and *starshii uryadnik*. In the artillery the corporal was known as *mladshii feierverker*, the sergeant as *vzvodnyi feierverker*, and the sergeant-major or adjutant as *feldfebel*.

'Will you tell us about your first contact with your men?'
Tatiana Sergeyevna asked him.

'Certainly. Are you really interested?' asked Vassili
Fedorovitch. 'I'm afraid that the moment which was so
moving for me would not be very interesting to others....
Anyway, here it is. When I arrived at Kalisz, where the Alex-
andriitsy were quartered, I was disappointed to learn that
the regiment was still on army manœuvres and would not
return for three days. Another cornet from the Nikolas
cavalry school was in the same position as myself. We spent
our leisure in looking for a room in the town and visiting the
restaurants and pleasure spots – which were, alas! wretched
– in that provincial Polish hole. At last the news spread in
the streets that the regiment was on its way back. Solemn
mass was to take place in the main square. My companion
and I hurriedly put on our parade uniforms and posted ourselves at the spot arranged for the assembly. A crowd of
sightseers had preceded us. I was filled with a sort of religious
anguish. Suddenly there was a sound which swelled and
drew nearer. A mob of urchins came along at a run to herald
the arrival of the hussars. The colonel's aide-de-camp led the
procession. Behind him came the trumpeters, blowing with
full cheeks and caracoling on their grey horses. Then a non-
commissioned officer, his chest covered with medals; he held
the regimental standard rolled up in its black oilcloth cover.
He was flanked by two officers. The colonel came next, quite
alone, on a superb chestnut. Then came the squadron in a
cloud of dust. The men were sunburnt, weary, happy....
They drew up in line in the square. The regimental chaplain
donned his priestly vestments and erected the field altar,

The officer hierarchy comprised the following: (1) *praporshchik*, ensign; (2)
podporuchik, second-lieutenant in all arms except the cavalry, where the
corresponding title was cornet; *khorunzhii* among the Cossacks; (3) *poruchik*,
lieutenant in all regular arms, *sotnik* among the Cossacks; (4) *shtabskapitan*,
second in command in the infantry, artillery, engineers and dragoons (*shtabs-
rotmistr* in the rest of the cavalry); (5) *kapitan*, captain in the infantry,
artillery, engineers and dragoons (*rotmistr* in the rest of the cavalry, and
esaul in the Cossacks); (6) *podpolkovnik*, lieutenant-colonel (the rank of
commandant had been suppressed in 1884), *voskovoi starshina* among the
Cossacks; (7) *polkovnik*, colonel, who was not necessarily regimental chief.

The hierarchy of general officers comprised four grades: (1) major-general,
or brigadier-general; (2) lieutenant-general, or general of division; (3) general
of infantry, cavalry, artillery or engineers; (4) field-marshal.

beside which the standard-bearer ranged himself at once. Orders rang out: "Dismount!... Caps off!" A few men assembled to form a choir and the prayers began. The priest spoke in a hurried indistinct voice, but the singing of the choir was wonderful.'

Russell observed that he found this practice of open-air mass very strange.

'The Russian Army is permeated by the religious spirit,' Vassili Fedorovitch replied. 'Morning and evening prayers are compulsory. Furthermore, in all important circumstances the priest intervenes to raise the soldier's spirit by celebrating divine service.'

'And every regiment has its own choir?'

'Yes. Some of them are famous. The art of singing is very widespread in Russia. In the infantry the men sing as they march. The choir leader is usually a tenor. He strikes up the first couplet and all the voices join in the refrain. Sometimes a dancer leaves the ranks and, with his knapsack on his back, jigs up and down, crouches down and flings out his legs to left and right with devilish agility. He is spurred on with shouts and whistles. The officers smile. Everyone forgets his cares and his weariness. Some of the soldiers' songs are spicy, others are plaintive ballads, and others still are marching-songs, and the repertoire is infinite. Every regiment is proud of its singers.... But I'm straying from my story! Where was I? Ah, yes! After the regiment returned to Kalisz, I was presented to the aide-de-camp. He welcomed me in a very friendly fashion and gave me a list of all those to whom I ought to pay a personal visit: the colonel in command of the regiment, the other officers, the chaplain, the military doctors.... When I had completed these formalities, our colonel assigned me to Squadron 2 because of my height and the colour of my hair. Among the hussars, they prefer to choose dark men for Squadron 1 and fair men for Squadron 2.... Each squadron has the same distinguishing hair colour....'

'What?' cried Russell. 'A cornet's physical appearance is of importance in his appointment?'

'Why not?' Vassili Fedorovitch answered. 'For officers this colour-matching is very approximate. But for the men it is the rule, especially in the Guards regiments. You ought to have seen the Grand Duke Vladimir sorting out the young recruits in the Mikhail riding-school. What an eye! What a sense of harmony! How quick! The bearded fellows and the tall ones are sent to the Preobrazhensky Regiment, the tall and fair ones go straight to the Semionovsky Regiment, those with pug noses are traditionally reserved for the Pavlovsky Regiment, in remembrance of the Emperor Paul who also had a flattened profile, those who are slender and thin have their appropriate place in the Knights Guards and the Horse Guards, and the small dark men join other small dark men in the Hussars. Believe me, it all looks very fine! But to return to myself, thanks to the friendliness which quickly grew up between my fellow-officers and myself, I have not felt in the least out of place in this new life. I have sixteen scouts under my orders. Instruction, foot-drill, physical exercises, galloping on varied terrain, target practice. . . . In the evening the officers get together in one or another's quarters to gossip or play cards. The colonel receives us often. He has a charming wife! As I have some talent as a pianist, there is no evening to which I am not invited. . . .'

Russell interrupted him to ask for other less personal details. He wanted to know how an officer's rank was identified. Vassili Fedorovitch launched into a very complex explanation, from which it became clear that the distinctions were shown only in the epaulettes. These epaulettes, which for officers were gilded, included stripes and stars that indicated the rank. In addition, they had different-coloured borders (red, blue, white, yellow) according to the regiment's number in the division. The same colours were on the soldiers' shoulder straps. The men never addressed a superior by his rank, but as 'Your Nobility' if he was a subaltern, 'Your High Nobility' if he was a colonel or lieutenant-colonel, 'Your Excellency' if he was a brigadier-general or divisional general, and 'Your High Excellency' if he was the general of an army corps. When he appeared before his troops the commander always addressed them in a familiar way by *'Zdorovo rebiaty!'* ('Hullo, children!'). And everyone, at attention, responded in chorus *'Zdravie zhelaem, vashe prevoskhoditelstvo!'* ('Good health, Your Excellency!'), or better, *'Rady startsya, vashe prevoskhodetelstvo!'* ('Happy to serve, Your Excellency!'

This exchange of friendly greetings was evidence, according to Vassili Fedorovitch, of the partriachal spirit which inspired the relations of officers and men. The men had no less respect for their superiors, but, thanks to a few benevolent words, the discipline was tinged with humanity and the regiment became a family.

Though they were held in high esteem by the people, Russian officers received relatively modest pay: 312 roubles a year for a second-lieutenant, 339 roubles a year for a lieutenant, 441 roubles for a captain, 1,017 roubles for a general of division. There were substantial allowances for food and lodging. The number of rooms assigned to each officer varied according to his grade and his family situation. In the mounted Guards a married lieutenant had five or six rooms, a cellar, an attic, a stable and a coach-house at his disposal. When quarters were not actually provided an officer received an allowance varying according to rank and station. At St Petersburg, Moscow, Kiev and Odessa this allowance was 200 roubles a year for second-lieutenants and rose to 800 roubles for regimental commanders. Table-money was 200 roubles for subalterns and 1,200 roubles for regimental commanders. Numerous secondary allowances were added to these basic allowances, so that in the end a second-lieutenant in a large city received 800 roubles a year. For Guards officers service was so expensive that their pay was insufficient to defray all their outgoings. The majority had considerable personal fortunes.

There was a great variety of medals and decorations in Russia. The most valued orders were those of St Andrei,[1] St Alexander Nevsky, St Vladimir and the Eagle. After these came the orders of St Anne and St Stanislas. As for the glorious order of St George, his cross was only awarded for deeds of war. According to class these decorations were worn on the breast, at the neck, or at the sword-knot.

Punishments normally inflicted on officers varied from open arrest to strict arrest. For serious lack of discipline or honour a tribunal of officers pronounced judgement on the

---

[1] The Order of St Andrei was restricted to members of the Imperial Family, to foreign sovereigns and crown princes and to a few heads of state.

guilty officer's case. There was a tribunal of this kind in every regiment.

The officers' uniform, except in a few Guards corps, was very simple: a dark green tunic, trousers of the same shade, boots and a cap with a wide crown and a varnished peak. The sabre hung at the side on a thin leather cross-belt. The full-dress uniform was more flattering: a shorter tunic with epaulettes. These epaulettes were fringed for senior officers, but not for subalterns. In winter the officers wore a grey cloth greatcoat over their tunics. In summer the dark green tunic was replaced for officers and men by one of white linen.

Of course, in the great Guards regiments the uniforms were more numerous, more varied and richer than those of the ordinary regiments. In the mounted Guards, for instance, every officer had five or six different outfits: the white dress, which consisted of a white tunic ornamented with gold; the red dress, a sort of red jerkin, decorated front and back with an enormous two-headed eagle; the field dress, a pleated tunic on which the service belt was worn; the parade dress, with gilded breastplate and a helmet surmounted by the imperial eagle with outspread wings; finally, the town dress, like that of other officers. Arms were just as varied: a mounted Guard carried a cuirassier's straight sword on parade, a dragoon's sabre on manœuvre and an épée for town wear. Furthermore, he had to equip himself at his own expense.[1] In other mounted troops, an officer up to and including lieutenant-colonel had the right since 1882 to a horse free of charge, but had to buy another at his own expense. The wearing of civilian clothes was strictly forbidden to officers, except when travelling abroad. In this respect there was nothing comparable to the tolerance allowed in England. Moreover, the Tsar set the example and never appeared except in general's uniform.

According to Vassili Fedorovitch, *esprit de corps*, very widespread throughout the Army, took on the character of real devotion in the élite regiments. A Russian officer could

---

[1] The Guards officers had superb horses costing as much as 2,000 roubles (over $530). Ordinary horses, reserved for the troops, were worth 150 to 300 roubles.

be a bad son, brother, father or husband, but never a bad comrade. In the gymnasium and afterwards in the military school, his instructors had already extolled the idea of sacrifice for friendship's sake. Later he learned to place the honour of the regiment above all other personal considerations. Among the Hussars of the Guard a mutual guarantee was the rule among officers. Many parents, who had accepted great sacrifices to see their sons in this becoming uniform, were afterwards obliged to sell horses, land and jewels in order to help pay the debts of a son's friend. Vassili Fedorovitch cited the case of Prince Paul Lobanov, who ran into debt to the extent of 800,000 roubles ($412,000). As he could not repay this fantastic sum in reasonable time, his comrades had got the necessary money together between them. As a result, numerous officers were completely ruined, had to leave the service and retire into the country.

In the cavalry the centre of military life was the riding-school. The mounted Guards had two: the big school was for exercises on horse and on foot, for reviews, inspections, horse-shows, and official celebrations which were honoured by the Emperor's presence.[1] The small school, on the other hand, was restricted to officers and was of a more intimate character. The second-lieutenants and lieutenants rode there every day; it was there, too, that the training of horses for the horse-show took place. In the evenings, during Lent, the officers organized tournaments and gymkhanas in the small school, at which their families and guests were present. When the competition was ended, they had supper there to the music of a brass band of the Horse Guards or its extraordinary balalaïka players. Every Thursday the officers of the Horse Guards were obliged to go to the mess for the grand weekly dinner. Only officers who were sick or who had the colonel's permission to be absent were exempt. Each officer had the right to invite a few friends, civilian or military, with the permission of the colonel or major, but women were not admitted to these military gatherings. The regimental commander presided at table and the officers took their places around it in order of seniority. The band wafted waves of music over all the tight uniforms. With dessert came the

[1] The Horse Guards' celebration was on March 25th, Annunciation Day.

balalaïka players and singers. To be invited to these meals was an honour, especially for civilians.

After dinner the officers played skittles in a specially furnished room, or gathered round the billiards-table, or made up a card-party in the green-room. Sometimes, at the request of those present, a cold supper was served at about midnight: it began traditionally with onion soup. However, whatever hour the officers left the mess, they had under severe penalty to be present in their squadrons at morning exercise.

The barracks, in the big Russian cities, were huge and well maintained. In the barrack-room, where the smell of boots, sweat and rifle-oil prevailed, there were rows of iron bedsteads, each provided with a palliasse. The packs were lined up on the floorboards. There was a rack for the rifles with their bayonets fixed.[1] The other furniture was a table, stools and parallel bars. From the walls hung pictures of the Imperial Family and instruction tables concerning the insignia of rank, firing positions and sentry duties. In a corner was the company's ikon with its red-glass lamp. The corporals and sergeants were quartered with their men. The sergeant-major had a separate room. The lavatories, refectory, disciplinary quarters, sick-bays, canteen, and workshops were comparable with those of other European armies. Every regiment had its own chapel.

A soldier's food was very copious and similar to normal peasant food: black bread, boiled buckwheat, meat soup, cabbage and beetroot. Potatoes were a luxury. On fast-days, meat soup was replaced by fish soup. Kvass was the drink, and on feast days a glass of vodka. Tea was not served to the troops, but each soldier had his personal tea-caddy and helped himself to boiling water from the kitchens. A soldier's pay was collected every four months only, amounting to 2 roubles 70 ($1.39) in line regiments, and to 4 roubles 95 ($2.55) in the Guards.

In winter the troops wore the grey greatcoat and the *bashlyk*, a sort of hood protecting the neck and ears. In summer the greatcoat was rolled up and slung round the body from shoulder to hip; the *bashlyk* disappeared and a flat

---

[1] The bayonet was always fixed to the rifle, even for shooting and drill. A soldier sheathed it only on marches.

cap (*furazhka*) took its place, with an engraved metal plate giving the regimental number. In the pack were two pairs of pants, two shirts, a linen smock, a pair of white summer trousers, and strips of material which were wrapped around the feet instead of socks. Handkerchiefs were unknown by Russian soldiers; they used their fingers dexterously. A Russian soldier's main qualities were endurance, obedience and good humour. During the four or five years he spent with the colours, he learnt not only to handle weapons, but also, very often, to read and write.

With the Cossacks things were quite different. One was a Cossack by heredity, regulated in certain areas by law. In exchange for lands which they cultivated, the Cossacks were all subject to personal military service and had to provide their own horses and equipment. There were eleven *voisko* or Cossack armies, established for the most part in the frontier regions: the Cossacks of the Don, Kuban, Terek, Astrakhan, Ural, Orenburg, Siberia, Semiretchie, Transbaikal, Amur, and Ussuri.[1] Each *voisko* had its chief, or *ataman*. But in peacetime only a third of the mobilizable effectives were with the colours. In fact every Cossack, after four years' active service in a first-time regiment, was enrolled for four years in a second-time regiment, then for four years in a third-time regiment. When they returned home after the first four years they were obliged to remain equipped and mounted to answer any mobilization measure at once. During the third four years, on the other hand, they were excused from maintaining a mount. In wartime, the Cossack troops could put 190,000 men into the line.

Their uniform consisted of a tight-waisted tunic (green for the Cossacks of the line, red for the Emperor's regiment, blue for the Hereditary Grand Duke's regiment), baggy trousers thrust into boots and a *papakha*, a fur cap with a cloth top, the colour of which varied according to the formation.[2] The Kuban and Terek Cossacks wore the black Circassian tunic (*chekmen*), without a collar, with sleeves that widened at the

---

[1] To this list one must add the Caucasian squadron of the Guard, the Tsar's private escort, and various regiments of irregular cavalry of Daghestan, Kutaïs, Kuban, Georgia, etc.

[2] In summer, the Cossacks wore a flat cap (*furazhka*).

ends, with a narrow leather belt around the waist and cart-
ridges to right and left of the chest; under the tunic was a
waistcoat of black, blue or red silk, the *beshmet*; they wore
also a coat of goat's or sheep's wool, the *burka*, which was
light and waterproof. A Cossack's arms consisted of a very
long lance (*pika*), a guardless sword (*shashka*) and a Berdan
carbine. The Terek and Kuban Cossacks had, in addition, a
dagger (*kinzhal*) and a pistol.

The Cossacks' horses were small, dark, strong in the leg
and inured to fatigue. Their saddles were like Arab saddles,
but with a cantle that was not turned up so far. The horses
were guided by a simple string in the mouth. The stirrups
were very short. In horsemanship the Cossacks feared no one.
They rode upright; when trotting the seat was raised and the
upper part of the body was forward; spurs were suppressed
on August 23, 1885 and the *nagaika*[1] became compulsory.
From their earliest years, the Cossack boys spent the better
part of their time astride their restive beasts. The distinctive
sign of these apprentice 'centaurs' was the tuft of hair, the
chub, which curled up on one side of their foreheads. Later
they learned the *dzhigitovka*, a group of equestrian acrobatics held in high esteem among the Cossacks of all provinces. A good *dzighit* must know how to fire in the most
difficult positions, to jump down and remount without slack-
ening speed, to pass from one mount to another at the gallop,
to stand upright in the saddle with the stirrups crossed on
the seat to form a point of support for the feet, to bend down
and pick up an object from the earth at top speed, and to
pivot under the horse's belly.

The great degree of freedom allowed the Cossacks, the
autonomy of their local administration, the material abundance in which they lived, all aroused in them a feeling of
dignity and courage. The Cossacks of the same formation
always came from the same *stanitsa*,[2] and the cohesion of the
body of the troops rested on the ancient customs of the population. However, the fact that each Cossack served with his
own horse, trained according to an original method, made
impossible the close-formation manœuvres usual to the

[1] Leather whip.
[2] Cossack village or small town.

regular cavalry whose animals were paired by height, strength and training. The regular cavalry were strong in mass onslaughts but weak in individual assaults. The Cossack cavalry, on the other hand, were strong in individual attack, and in pitched battles were hampered by the different speeds of their horses. It had therefore been necessary to devise a way of tackling the enemy in keeping with their capacities and defects. This very special form of charge was called the *lava*.[1] In the *lava* the Cossacks dispersed and prepared their attack by harassing actions so as to be able, when circumstances seemed favourable, to swoop upon the disorganized enemy and force him into a series of isolated fights with sidearms. In such cases, their address, their mobility, and their bravery were marvellous. They went in with lance and sabre, shouting their war-cry: '*Gik! Gik!* – an avalanche of demons, before whom the bravest sought safety in flight.

Enthused by Vassili Fedorovitch's account, Russell commented. 'The Russians are, I see, a very warlike people!'

'Yes,' said Alexander Vassilievitch, 'but only when attacked. The combative virtues of the race are only aroused if the enemy invades the soil of their fatherland. Otherwise, our men are rather calm and good-natured. Just think! In Russian the same word, *mir*, is used for "world" and for "peace"!'

[1] *Lava*, torrent.

CHAPTER IX

THE DIFFERENT SOCIAL CLASSES AND
THE ADMINISTRATIVE MACHINE

*The chin or table of ranks – The Russian nobility, titled and
untitled – The townspeople: citizens, notables, merchants,
artisans, and petits bourgeois – The peasants: the freeing of
the serfs and the modalities of repurchasing land from the
nobleman – Administration of the State: the Governor, the
zemstvos of a Government or district and the zemsky nachalnik; administration of the communes: the mir and the volost –
Supreme authority of the Tsar; the Council of Empire, the
Committee of Ministers, the Most Holy Synod and the Senate
– The regular police and the political police. Organization of
the Okhrana, its agents and methods – The Press – The censorship of periodicals and books*

INFORMED as he now was about the military hierarchy of
Russia, Russell was keen to know about the civil hierarchy.
In a travel book he had read that all Russian officials were
classed by categories according to the importance of the services they rendered the State, and that there were mysterious
connections between the army ranks and those of the bureau-
cracy. Alexander Vassilievitch confirmed this. It was Peter
the Great who, in order to discipline his people the better,
had created the *chin,* the table of ranks. This curious institution opened the ranks of nobility to persons not of noble
birth. Any servant of the State, whatever his birth, could rise
step by step until he had acquired a high honorary title. The
scale of human values thus established had fourteen *chin,*
ranging for civilians from that of college registrar to the all-
powerful Chancellor of the Empire, and for the military from
ensign or cornet to field-marshal. Between these two extremes
were the generals of infantry, cavalry or artillery, and privy
councillors in active capacity (second *chin*), with the right to
the title of 'Your High Excellency'; lieutenant-generals and
privy councillors (third *chin*), major-generals and state councillors in active capacity (fourth *chin*), with the right to the
title 'Your Excellency'; brigadier-generals and councillors of
state (fifth *chin*) with the right to the title 'Your High

Origin'; colonels and college counsellors (sixth *chin*), lieutenant-colonels and aulic councillors (seventh *chin*), majors and college assessors (eighth *chin*), with the right to the title 'Your High Nobility'; captains and titular councillors (ninth *chin*), seconds in command and college secretaries (tenth *chin*), lieutenants and Government secretaries (twelfth *chin*),[1] second-lieutenants and senate or synod registrars (thirteenth *chin*) with the right to the title 'Your Nobility'.[2] Thus in Russia an official was a *chinovnik*, a man with a rank, and not as in other countries a man with a function.

Thus, after some years of untiring labour in office, a young commoner could become the equal of a captain or a major without ever having served in the army. But although entered upon the hierarchical tables, he was only properly regarded as noble from the moment at which he entered the eighth class. Thanks to the mirage of this glorious ladder, the top of which was close to the throne, all the clerks in the Empire were obsessed by the race for honours. By distributing privileges and regulating the passage from one category to another, the Tsar made certain of his servants' obedience. From the most genuine prince to the lowliest peasant, everyone had his pigeon-hole and his serial number. Even the nobility itself was divided into two kinds: the hereditary and the acquired.

The so-called hereditary nobility, in some families, went back to the days of the very earliest sovereigns. The names of the oldest companions of the Tsar (or *boyars*[3]) were entered in a register known as the 'sixth book' (*shestaya kniga*) drawn up at the beginning of the eighteenth century. To weaken the power of these illustrious servants, who enriched and strengthened themselves with the years, Peter the Great had instituted the table of ranks and arrogated to himself the right to

---

[1] The eleventh *chin* had been suppressed.

[2] In Russian: Your High Excellency=*Vashe Vysoko Prevoskhoditelstvo*; Your Excellency=*Vashe Prevoskhoditelstvo*; Your High Origin=*Vashe Vysokorodie*; Your High Nobility=*Vashe Vysokoblagorodie;* Your Nobility =*Vashe Blagorodie*. There are no English equivalents of some of these forms of address, which are therefore rendered literally. For the latter three 'Sir' would normally be used in England.

[3] The Slav word *boyar* had become *boyarin* in old Russian, then, in popular parlance, as a result of deformation, *barin*, in other words, 'My Lord', or more simply, 'Sir'.

create princes, counts and barons at will.[1] His successors had continued the same policy by conferring nobility upon officials, both hereditary and personal. In the reign of Alexander II the emancipation of the serfs had shaken the position and wealth of the nobility. Alexander III had restored some of its importance by entrusting it, in the person of the marshals and district chiefs, with the administrative control of Districts and Provinces, and by establishing a State Bank of the Nobility, to help the landed proprietors by granting them credits at a low rate of interest. According to Alexander Vassilievitch, the Russian nobility no longer had any power as a caste, but its most eminent representatives had a certain influence on State affairs through the high positions they occupied in the administration. Thus the nobility in each Government constituted a corps, an autonomous noble society, which was itself divided into as many groups as there were Districts within the Government. Every third year the nobility of the Government met in an assembly of nobility. This assembly elected the person who would perform certain functions in the ensuing three-year period; it examined the list of members of the nobility in the Government (genealogical book); it financed the social treasury of the nobility of the Government by voluntary contributions; and when necessary it drafted the petitions addressed to His Imperial Majesty. A commission, known as the Assembly of the Delegates of the Nobility, instituted a permanent representation of the nobility of each Government, on the basis of one member per District and a president, the Marshal of the Nobility, elected for three years. Furthermore, a 'Chamber for the Protection of the Nobility' occupied itself with minors and disabled persons and looked after the administration of their property.

The official armorial of the Russian nobility comprised five ranks: princes, counts, barons, untitled gentlemen whose nobility antedated Peter I, and untitled gentlemen whose nobility postdated Peter I. There were no dukes, marquises, viscounts or knights. The title of Grand Duke (in Russian, *Velikii Knyaz*) may be literally translated as 'Grand Prince' and was reserved for members of the Imperial Family. As to the nobiliary particle, its use was unknown in Russia. One

[1] The last two titles did not exist in Russia before the eighteenth century.

was Prince Viasemsky or Count Vorontzov, but not Prince *of* Viasemsky or Count *of* Vorontzov, since the suffixes *sky, ov, iev, in,* which occurred in the majority of Russian family names, corresponded grammatically to the English word *of.*

In Russia the princely title was transmitted to the whole direct posterity of both sexes, and it was no exaggeration to say that there were at least two thousand princes (*knyaz*) in the Tsarist Empire. After the annexation of the Caucasus, the Georgian *tavads,* chiefs of small kingdoms, had been pompously recognized as 'princes' too. The same was done for the nomadic Khans and for the representatives of the greater Armenian and Tartar families.

The Russian counts were as numerous as the princes, the oldest families amongst the counts being the Golovins, the Cheremetevs and the Tolstoys.

The title of baron was conferred very rarely, and then mostly on bankers or great industrialists of foreign origin. Dimsdale, an English doctor, had acquired the rank of baron for having vaccinated the Empress Catherine and her son Paul. A few Jews of great merit were also barons, which was displeasing to the nobles of the Baltic provinces, where the title was very common among the descendants of the Teutonic Knights.

In addition to this titled nobility – princes, counts and barons – there was an untitled nobility, often more illustrious in its antiquity. Only the real experts knew how to settle the difference between the merits of a person ennobled through the rank of colonel or counsellor of State, and those without titles whose names had been inscribed for centuries in the book of the *boyars.* The old untitled families were almost innumerable.[1]

In the upper Russian aristocracy fortunes melted away in the sun. According to Alexander Vassilievitch, the richest persons were Counts Sheremetev and Stroganov, Prince Yussupov, Counts Orlov-Davydov and Orlov-Denisov, Princes Kochubei, Galitsin (both branches), Saltykov and Vasilchikov, Counts Bobrinsky, Vorontsov-Dachkov, Chu-

---

[1] According to Leroy-Beaulieu, the Russian nobility amounted to nearly two million.

valov, Tolstoy, Narychkin, Prince Bariatinsky, etc. But already, several of the great families had had to agree to mis-alliances in order to preserve their place in the world.

Parallel with the nobility were the clergy, about whom Russell had already been informed.

Next came the urban class, which in every town comprised the distinguished citizens, merchants, artisans and the *petits bourgeois*. Each corporation had its representative assemblies and its permanent institutions.

To become a merchant one had to be enrolled in one of two guilds, paying the corresponding levy to the State. The first of these guilds, heavily taxed, comprised the wholesalers; the second, less heavily taxed, the retailers. The artisans had to be enrolled in one of the professional bodies (*tsekh*[1]) in the towns. The *petits bourgeois*, 'without guilds', or *meshchani*, were those who were enabled by their means to live a regular life, but whose activities were not within the realms of commerce, industry or craft. The rank of 'distinguished citizen' was awarded for personal or hereditary reasons to merchants or manufacturers for services rendered to the economy of the Empire. Naturally, Alexander Vassilievitch, a merchant of the first guild, was an hereditary distinguished citizen of Moscow.

The most numerous of all Russian social classes were the peasants.[2] Before the emancipation of the serfs by Alexander II in 1861, all the peasants were tied to the land and belonged either to the State or to the landed proprietors. In giving freedom to the humblest of his subjects, Alexander II gave them the opportunity of purchasing a part of the land (*nadel*) which they formerly cultivated for their masters. The price (*obrok*) they had to pay the master in exchange for these plots was determined by the prosperity of the area and subject to revision every twenty years.[3] At first optional, the purchase became obligatory in 1881. After their first indignation at this measure, the landed proprietors themselves hastened its application, for almost all of them were deeply

[1] From the German *Zeche*, corporation.
[2] See Chapter XIII on the life of the peasants.
[3] There was one peculiarity about the *obrok*: it increased as the area of land diminished. It was not the cultivated lands that were valued highly but the enclosures on which the peasants' dwellings were built.

in debt.[1] But the peasants had not the money necessary to acquire the land immediately. If they wished it, the State came to their assistance by advancing them the amount needed to free themselves from the *obrok*. These advances were repayable annually over a period of forty-nine years, principal and interest amounting to 6 per cent included. Despite this generous credit, the scale of repayments was so exorbitant that the majority of the farmers could not face the payments demanded by the Treasury. Fortunately, in the closing years of the nineteenth century the Government had ordered a reduction in the price of the plots of land distributed to the freed serfs. It was just in time, for the whole rural population of the Empire was on the verge of ruin. According to Alexander Vassilievitch's calculations, based on a reading of the most recent economic documents published by the Press, the purchasing operation would be completed by 1931.

❋   ❋   ❋   ❋

From an administrative point of view, the Empire was divided into 78 Governments and 18 Provinces or Regions,[2] plus the Island of Sakhalin. Further, four cities – St Petersburg, Odessa, Sebastapol and Kerch-Ienikale – constituted 'prefectural cities' directly answerable to the central authority. Governments were subdivided into Districts (*uezd*) of varying size and number, which were themselves subdivided into towns and communes (*volost*).

At the head of each Government was a Governor representing the central power. Among his powers were the promulgation of the laws, control of their execution, supervision of all the administrative institutions and, as agent of the Ministry of the Interior, control of police and public assistance. In each District of the Government was an official at the head of the police: the *ispravnik* (High Commissioner of Police), having under his orders, in each subdivision or *stan*, a *stanvoi pristav* (*stan* commissioner), who himself commanded the policemen, known as *uryadniki*.

---

[1] When they were freed, seven-tenths of the serfs belonging to the landed proprietors were in debt to the State credit houses.

[2] Terms employed for territories which, by their remoteness or by the eccentricity of their institutions, were subject to special rule.

Side by side with the representatives of the central government there were, in each Province or Government and in each District, elected assemblies,[1] or *zemstvos*, concerned with the economic and agricultural interests of the area. The population of the District elected deputies (or *glasny*, deliberative members) entrusted with expressing the wishes of their principals by categories (nobles, tradespeople, moujiks). The District *zemstvo* usually met once a year and discussed local affairs under the presidency of the Marshal of the District nobility. Further, the assembly appointed from its members those who for three years would form the executive committee of the provincial estates; this executive committee of three sat permanently.

Each District having its *zemstvo*, the Province or Government had them also, with representatives who were elected for three years by the District *zemstvo*. The Government *zemstvo*, under the presidency of the Marshal of the Government nobility, dealt with questions of regional interest and from among its members appointed an executive committee of six, charged with expediting affairs between sessions.

These arrangements, which assured a semblance of autonomy to the provincial and communal administrations, had unfortunately been upset by the law of June 12, 1889, which created cantonal leaders (*zemsky nachalnik*). By the same law the Government and District *zemstvos* had seen their powers restricted and the number of representatives of the nobility increased in relation to that of other categories of deputies.

From 1870 administration of the towns was in the hands of a municipal council (*gorodskaya duma*), elected by the most important townsmen: property-owners, tradesmen or industrialists with large incomes. In Moscow, out of 1,173,000 inhabitants, including those of the suburbs, there were only 10,000 electors. Parallel with the *gorodskaya duma* there was an executive committee (*gorodskaya uprava*) and a mayor (*gorodskaya golova*).

The peasant class was divided into communities, with

---

[1] To be an elector one had to be of Russian nationality, twenty-five years old, and to represent a property qualification which varied with the three electoral categories: nobles, town-dwellers, peasants.

common lands in Great Russia, the East and the South, and with private properties in Western Russia. To administer their affairs, the peasants formed communal assemblies in the villages and, in the chief place of the canton, a cantonal assembly, the *volost*. The municipal authorities of the village commune were the council (*mir* or *skhod*) and its representative, the *starosta*, the elder. The *mir*, composed of all the heads of households in the commune, discussed the incidence of taxes, the admission of new members, the guardianship of minors, the organization of rural schools, assistance to the poor, and the distribution of lands in regions subject to the system of common assembly; the *volost* (one representative for every ten households), met under the presidency of its *starchina*, or senior, appointed for three years. This assembly had amongst its powers all affairs relating to the economic and social needs of the *volost*. It was completed by a permanent council and by a tribunal of three judges, who dealt with disputes to the value of less than one hundred roubles and with offences of no great seriousness. This apparently liberal measure of self-government was, in fact, from 1889, controlled and supervised by the *zemsky nachalnik*, the cantonal chief.

All the cantonal chiefs of the District formed a District assembly presided over by a Marshal of the nobility. The superior instance was the provincial committee, presided over by the Governor, who ruled with the co-operation of the officials of adminstrative and judicial rank. Thus in the end the control of the affairs of every Government was in the hands of the Governor, representing the Tsar. The Government and District *zemstvos* were placed under his control. The police, the promulgation of the laws, provincial administrative decisions, hygiene, public assistance, supervision of elected organs – in brief, the whole life of the area depended on him.[1]

Above this regional potentate were only those high personages who watched over the destinies of the Empire: the

[1] It should be noted that this organization was applied to the letter only in thirty-four governments, constituting, to some extent, the heart of Russia. For all the special racial territories and those of different cultures, a special form of government had been created to suit the special customs of the people.

Tsar, whose unlimited power was consecrated by the Church, the Council of Empire formed of all the ministers and of certain powerful dignitaries whose function was to sanction the laws, the Committee of Ministers, which prepared the legislative measures, the Most Holy Synod, charged with watching over the religious life of the nation, and the Senate, itself divided into eight departments, the competence of which extended to the publication of ukases, to the confirmation of the titles of nobility, to the settlement of the boundaries of landed property and to judgement on appeal of civil and criminal cases. All this political and administrative apparatus was backed by a strong police.

❁   ❁   ❁   ❁

During his walks with Alexander Vassilievitch, Russell had been struck by the great number of policemen (*gorodovoi*) who stood on guard in the streets. Usually they were men of heavy and uncouth appearance. They enjoyed no respect among the population. Their function was limited to ensuring the maintenance of order in the streets, preventing brawls, and taking drunkards and thieves to the nearest police station. The difficult tasks were reserved to gendarmes.

In Moscow, as in all large Russian cities, there was a High Chief of Police; under his orders were the Chiefs of Police, who themselves commanded police majors, one for every division. Next came the police officers, four or five to the ward, the 'aides', the copyists and finally the policemen properly so called. The porter (*dvornik*) of every house kept a daily list of the occupants and informed the local police station of departures and arrivals in the building. All the inhabitants of the quarter were thus checked in the police register. In Moscow,[1] furthermore, at the Gnezdikovsky Pereulok, in the police printing works, there was an office where private persons could take note of all the addresses by paying two kopecks per item.[2]

To Russell all this seemed scandalous; in it he saw official encouragement to indiscretion and the infringement of

---

[1] All Russian towns had their address bureau.
[2] One could also ask for the information in writing, by sending a special postcard to the address bureau of any town.

privacy. To him a man was free only if he was allowed to travel as he pleased, to think what he liked and to conceal the place where he lived from police and intruders alike. But Alexander Vassilievitch explained to him that in a land as vast and as diversely peopled as Russia, tolerance of that kind would have led the nation into disorder and ruin. The administration's control over citizens was not in the least tyrannical. The rules could always be modified by offering a tip to an understanding official, and the less well-paid the State's servants were the more widespread tipping became among the public. Meanwhile, one had to know when to give, how to give. . . .

'Sometimes it is enough to mention the name of a relative in governmental spheres for the trembling bureaucrat to give you the favour you require. Sometimes one has to slip a rouble, or two roubles, into the hand which is held carelessly open on the edge of the table. And sometimes, if it is an official of top rank, it is a good thing to prepare a well-filled envelope in advance. So you see, with us the law is rigid, but man is supple. That is the secret of our organization. Seen from outside it appears to be uncompromising, but from within you can see there are innumerable adjustments to the most terrible regulations.'

'What about the Okhrana?' Russell asked him point-blank.

Alexander Vassilievitch's face took on an expression of suspicious seriousness.

'What? . . . The Okhrana? . . .' he muttered.

'I've heard of it in England,' Russell went on. 'It's the political police, the secret police, isn't it?'

'It's very necessary,' sighed Alexander Vassilievitch, 'with all the revolutionaries and anarchists swarming on our soil! The strength and cunning of these fighting groups is disquieting. They are supported from abroad. Their object is to overthrow the imperial power and to bring chaos to Russia. To achieve that end any means are justifiable, murder especially. I will not remind you of the list of their crimes, but think for example of how Alexander II, the most liberal of our tsars, who suppressed serfdom, forbade corporal punishment, who granted municipal autonomy, reformed the law and public education, was the victim of six attacks before he succumbed in 1881 to a seventh attack organized by the People's Will Party. And the assassination last year of Sypyagin, the Minister of the Interior! And all the bomb factories, the clandestine printing works, that are discovered in the Empire! Believe me, to fight these people we need men better qualified than the *gorodovye*. We need a secret police, we need the Okhrana!'

'How does it function?' Russell asked.

At first Alexander Vassilievitch pretended that he knew nothing; then, plied with friendly questions, he agreed to give some information about the institution that was as mysterious as it was formidable. The Okhrana – a development of the Third Department – had its headquarters in St Petersburg. Like the police, it was answerable to the Police Department, itself subordinate to the Ministry of the Interior. The post of Director-General of the Police Department was often occupied by a judge with experience of political affairs. Sections of the police were spread throughout the Empire, but there were sections of the Okhrana in only a few centres. Moreover, control of investigations in the Okhrana sections, as with the police, was in the hands of a special body of officers. At the head of the investigation service was the chief of the Okhrana, surrounded by a constellation of officers and high officials. The office work was carried on by examiners who had at their disposal mountains of descriptive memoranda and fingerprints, as well as a library containing all the revolutionary publications of Russia and Europe.

The Okhrana's role was limited to tracking suspect individuals and frustrating the preparation of criminal attacks. Repression was not its job. When the observation of a group had produced adequate results, the Okhrana proceeded to 'liquidate' it, that is to say, after a search of the various 'conspiratorial premises',[1] the greatest possible number of conspirators were arrested. The law authorized the chiefs of Okhrana sections to keep the accused in custody for fifteen days. This delay could be extended to a month by the Governor's decision. Thereafter, the accused were freed if the evidence accumulated against them was insufficient, or they

[1] Term used amongst Russian police and revolutionaries to designate the place where the conspirators met clandestinely.

were handed over to the law for preliminary investigation. Representatives of the Public Prosecutor, attached to the various sections of the Okhrana, saw that the procedure was properly observed. The Okhrana never executed its prisoners. Sentences of death were all pronounced by regular courts, after indictment and pleading.[1] There was only one form of extra-judicial repression. The Minister of the Interior could, in certain cases, on his own authority decide to banish a suspect to a distant part of the Empire for a maximum of five years. As Russell showed astonishment at such arbitrary procedure, Alexander Vassilievitch assured him that the administration used it with discretion.

'Sometimes the culprit's preferences are taken into account. If he is a sick man, he is exiled to a region where the climate is suited to his state of health. At least, that is what was told me by one who is familiar with General Zavarzin. . . .'[2]

'Did he tell you at the same time how they set about shadowing suspects?' Russell asked.

'Oh! Everyone in Russia knows about that,' Alexander Vassilievitch replied. 'In the Okhrana there are "outside agents" charged with investigations, and "inside agents", or secret collaborators, charged with denunciation. The former are especially clever and courageous officials under various identities and disguises, whose task it is to watch suspects in the street, in trains, at the theatre and in restaurants. According to the circumstances, they disguise themselves as domestic servants, caretakers, newspaper-sellers, or railway workers. Their speech and gestures are appropriate to their disguise, which requires very thorough training. The Okhrana has a special store where clothing and uniforms of all kinds are piled up. It has a stable too, and a coach-house for carriages and sleighs. In the Okhrana building in Moscow, for example, there is a courtyard reserved for agents disguised as coachmen, who come and go continuously, according to the needs of the service.'

[1] Nevertheless, in provinces under martial law executions without trial could be ordered by the military commandant. Thus the Governor-General of Warsaw on several occasions condemned groups of terrorists to death.

[2] General Zavarzin (Chief of the Moscow Okhrana): *Memoirs of a Chief of the Okhrana.*

'Perhaps I've been driven by one of these coachmen without knowing it!' grumbled Russell.

'Perhaps,' said Alexander Vassilievitch. 'They do not refuse fares because that would arouse suspicion. But don't worry, they are not very many. A hundred at the most! Moreover, all the "outside" agents are well-bred fellows, of irreproachable honesty and morality. This work is for them a vocation. No descendant of a Pole or a Jew can join their ranks. They swear an oath before a priest before taking up their duties. All the information they report is centralized at the Okhrana. If a suspect shows anxiety by frequent changes of address, the agent breaks off his shadowing and a colleague takes his place. . . . But the Okhrana's trump card is its organization of "inside" agents. These are generally repentant revolutionaries, who, having kept their comrades' confidence, help us to unmask them. . . .'

'In other words, traitors!' Russell cried.

'That's a fine word!' Alexander Vassilievitch sighed. 'For me the end justifies the means. When the security of the State is at stake, patriotism obliges certain men to assume a role which in fact they find distasteful. . . .'

'Do you think it is patriotism which forces these men to change sides?'

'Yes, sometimes. But sometimes also, of course, the prospect of escaping punishment and sometimes the promise of reward. . . .'

'Are they paid a lot?'

'No. So far as I know, and quite confidentially, the inside agents rarely get more than twenty to thirty roubles a month. The Okhrana communicates with them with the greatest care. They all have false names. Their real identities are known only to the highest officials. Meetings between Okhrana chiefs and the secret collaborators take place in one of the innumerable apartments which the police keep in the city and its suburbs. . . .'

'And what about the censorship of correspondence?' Russell asked. 'Is it true that there is at the Okhrana a "black" room where letters and parcels are examined?'

'Yes,' Alexander Vassilievitch admitted. 'The service was begun by Alexander III. In the principal cities of the Empire polyglot officials work at examining the post on the basis of lists of suspects provided by the police. When a letter arouses the agents' suspicions, they open it by special means, or simply steam it open, take a copy and reseal the envelope so carefully that the recipient cannot believe, when he gets it, that it has been opened. Of course, if it happens to be a letter written in secret ink (lemon juice, milk or saliva) it has to be so treated that it is impossible to send it on. Letters of this kind are often written in cipher, and the Okhrana has expert decoders, able to unravel the cleverest of combinations! Think how useful such a censorship would be in wartime...!'

'Probably,' said Russell. 'But Russia is not at war, so far as I know.'

'It is at war against itself,' Alexander Vassilievitch cut in. 'It is forced to defend itself against those of its sons who, from fanaticism or aberration, would like to destroy it! Neither you, nor me, nor any one of our friends has anything to fear from the police. . . .'

'Because we're not involved in politics!'

'Just so!'

'In short, to live in peace in Russia, one must avoid politics or applaud the politics of the Government!'

'If you don't applaud the Government's politics, it is better to criticize them in a reasonable way and deferentially.'

Russell tossed his head. Accustomed to the maelstrom of public opinion at home and to violent parliamentary debates, attacks by the left-wing newspapers on those of the right and vice versa, he was astonished that in Russia discontent could only be expressed between reliable friends and by hints.

'Believe me,' Alexander Vassilievitch went on, 'it isn't good for the people to get mixed up in State affairs. Because they are badly informed, they get excited and lose their heads and see enemies everywhere. What I blame your own Press for is the abuse of cartoons. Why do you allow these wretched artists to make fun of leading statesmen? How can you expect honest citizens to respect a minister if he is pictured in the Press as a worm-eaten pear, a lame duck or a bearded goat? Government people should stand on a pedestal. Take the pedestal away and you have only a man like the rest, to whom only a fool would give his confidence.'

'So there are no caricatures in Russia?' Russell asked.

'Not of the Tsar or his entourage, at any rate, nor of ministers or high officials. . . . If a journalist has political views different from those of the Government, he expresses them in a serious, deferential and documented article. He weighs every word. In no country in the world has the art of insinuation been pushed as far as it has with us. Officially, our newspapers belong to no party, but they nevertheless reflect, very discreetly, the different opinions of society. Some tend to be liberal, others are rather conservative. . . . To the inexperienced eye all the papers seem to be written in the same spirit, but the regular readers know how to read between the lines. . . .'

'Are there many periodicals in Russia?'

'At the 1899 census there were about 1,000, of which 600 were dailies. Of course, St Petersburg and Moscow publish most. Taking weeklies and monthlies into account, St Petersburg leads with 300. Moscow accounts for only 100. Warsaw about 60. . . . Besides publications in the Russian language, these figures include regular publications in Polish, German, Lettish, Estonian, Georgian, Armenian, French. . . . The first Russian periodical, which saw daylight in 1703, was called *Military and other news worth knowing and remembering*. In 1728 it became the *St Petersburg News*. It was only in 1838 that His Imperial Majesty ordered the publication, in each Government, of a *Government Gazette*. The non-official part of these organs was devoted to writings on the history and geography of the various parts of the Empire. As to the first provincial newspapers published privately, they were the *Kiev Telegraph*, the *Kronstadt Gazette*, the *Novgorod Telegraph*, the *Voronezh Telegraph*[1]. . . Amongst the newspapers in the capitals, undoubtedly the illustrated paper *Niva* is the most successful. . . .'

Russell stopped this recital by asking in an evasive tone: 'What about the censorship, Alexander Vassilievitch? Is it as severe in Russia as they say?'

Alexander Vassilievitch began to laugh:

'Oh, you Englishmen! As soon as anyone mentions censorship you see red! In this matter, as in all the others, things

[1] Founded in 1858, 1861, 1869 and 1869 respectively.

are much less serious here than you think. In Moscow and St Petersburg, since 1865, every paper has been free to choose which way it will be censored: before or after publication. All the big newspapers have preferred to be exempt from censorship in advance by paying a surety of 2,500 roubles. As a result, they can print what seems best to them at their own risk and peril. If a newspaper abuses this privilege and supports subversive ideas it is suspended for a while, or even suppressed, after three ministerial warnings. In the Provinces the majority of newspapers work by prior authorization, which obviously complicates the task of the contributors. The unfortunate editor-in-chief must submit proofs of the articles to the censor day by day and sheet by sheet. The censor gets them late, after dinner, for the issue which will appear the next day. He spends his evening reading them and correcting them. The hours slip by. At the printing works the printers get impatient, the editor-in-chief gazes at his watch and gets desperate, wondering if his galleys will come back to him cut, disfigured and unusable, or whether the paper will go to press before dawn. At last the messenger appears, holding a bundle of papers in his hand. Everyone rushes up to him. Anxious faces bend over the grey print that smells of fresh ink. The censor has taken a favourable view: only a dozen insignificant changes. The editor mops his brow and heaves a sigh of relief. To work! The paper will be on sale at the proper time after all. Those who read it while they eat their breakfast have no idea of the anguish which has accompanied the birth of the paper. . . . Of course, it is tiresome that the expression of public opinion should be restricted in this way. But don't you think that by preventing writers from wasting their time in political quarrels and ephemeral articles, the imperial censorship has encouraged them to concentrate on eternal problems? Russian literature has benefited from all the talent which has not found employment in the superficial and urgent needs of the daily papers. The most brilliant epoch in Russian thought was that in which the Press had the least liberty. It was in the reign of the despotic Nikolas I that Pushkin, Lermontov, Gogol and many others displayed their genius. . . . Who knows if they would have given such poetic expression to their ideals in a country where their opinions could have been expressed in the papers? Who knows if, living in a Russian democracy, they would not have dissipated their creative energies in pointless polemics?'

Russell was not very receptive to this tortuous justification of censorship. Brought up on liberal ideas, he held that artistic success was inseparable from freedom of expression. But he had no wish to give offence to his host by contradicting him further, and he contented himself with asking if, in a land of absolute rule like Russia, the banality of the papers did not prompt the lovers of reading to fall back upon books.

'Of course,' said Alexander Vassilievitch. 'But don't forget that the cultured élite of Russia is only a minute part of the population. Yet I have read a well-documented article in which it is stated that last year nearly 20,000 works were published by the various Russian publishers. As to the subject treated by the authors, the largest section was of religious works (13·5 per cent); then came literary works (12 per cent), then various informative works, school books, medical books, science, morals and juvenile literature. . . . It was in the reign of Catherine II that the book trade was organized here by the publisher Novikov. Today we have some very large publishers: Suvarin, Sytin, Marx, Pavlenkov. . . . At the end of the last century there were 2,800 bookshops in Russia, 360 of them in St Petersburg, 220 in Moscow and 180 in Warsaw. . . . I think these figures have increased with progress in education. The general tendency of the publishers is to produce books at the lowest possible price in order to attract an ever wider public.'

'All these books are, of course, submitted to the censorship,' Russell interjected.

'Oh, yes!' answered Alexander Vassilievitch. 'In this connection I'll tell you something that happened to a young writer friend of mine, Gilyarovsky, a few years ago. He had got together about fifteen short stories of the life of the people treated in quite crude terms, and had given the collection the title: *The People of the Slums*. Having corrected the proofs, Gilyarovsky sent a hastily bound copy to the censor and awaited the response with anxiety. The next day, when he went to see Verner the publisher, he learned that in the night an inspector had appeared at the workshop, had confiscated all the volumes printed and had ordered the type to be broken up in his presence. As the final decision could only be taken by the censorship committee in St Petersburg, Gilyarovsky left for the capital, where he made innumerable representations, requests and entreaties on stamped paper. All in vain! He returned to Moscow hopeless. One day, when I was lunching with him at Testov's, the editor of the *Moscow Newssheet* came into the restaurant. Seeing Gilyarovsky, he cried: "What a coincidence! I have just learned, quite by accident, that they are just about to burn your book at the fire station in the Sushevskaya quarter. Hurry! You may arrive in time to enjoy the spectacle!" We rushed out. Indeed, in the barrack courtyard there was a pile of blackened, smoking sheets. The firemen were stirring the pile nonchalantly. Gilyarovsky rescued a charred page. It was the cover. On it one could read: *The People of the Slums, Studies from Nature.* My friend had difficulty in controlling his rage. This auto-da-fé was, I believe, the last of its kind. Today, when a book is condemned, all the copies are carefully torn up in a machine and sent as raw material to the pulp factories.[1] But don't put on that shocked expression! Since the accession of Nikolas II, it has been extremely rare for a book to be withdrawn from circulation by an administrative decision.'

At that point in the discussion Russell recalled the condemnation of Leo Tolstoy by the Holy Synod two years earlier. Excommunicated from the Orthodox Church on February 22, 1901, the great writer became a popular idol in a few days. Outside Russia the papers spoke enthusiastically of his courage. But in Russia? Alexander Vassilievitch admitted that the censorship was still very harsh towards the author of *Resurrection*. The publisher Suvarin was not able to publish in his journal, *The New Times*, two dispatches concerning Tolstoy's health because the police authorities had intercepted them. It was forbidden to show portraits of Tolstoy in the bookshops. This order must be obeyed, it was said, until the 'culprit's' death. Another scandal: the writer

---

[1] The last book to be burned was in fact Gilyarovsky's, in 1887. See Gilyarovsky's Memoirs: *Moscow and the Muscovites.*

Around the samovar

7   A colporteur

A rich Russian merchant,
by B. Konstodiev

The wife of a rich Russian
merchant, by B. Konstodiev

Children's nurse in
traditional clothing

8   Monks of the St Serge Monastery,
Moscow

A market in Moscow

Amphitheatrov had published in the paper *Russia* an article entitled 'Messrs. Obmanov',[1] which was clearly aimed at the Romanovs, the Imperial family.

'Of course, the paper was suspended and the author exiled from the capital,' said Alexander Vassilievitch. 'In earlier times they would have been more severe with him. But the Tsar is paying more and more attention to public opinion. The fashion in political matters tends towards tolerance. If that goes on we will one day have a parliament like yours, an empire Duma. A lot is being said about it in high circles.'

Russell remained meditative. The more he listened to Alexander Vassilievitch, the stronger grew his impression that the Tsarist administration was like a mailed fist plunged into a soft dough. The natural pleasantness of the people was at odds with the harshness of the laws which weighed upon them. It was difficult to imagine a gayer nation, a nation more hospitable, ingenuous and charming than the Russians, and a governmental apparatus more archaic and ponderous than that which held them captive.[2]

[1] The name Obmanov derives from the Russian word *obman*, a lie! The article was published on January 14, 1902.

[2] The principle of an empire Duma was only proclaimed on October 17, 1905, and the methods of election to this assembly were clarified by a law of December 14, 1905. The electors were divided into three groups or *curia*: landed proprietors (for the majority of the nobles), citizens and peasants. The electors of the first group (1,918 for the 51 Provinces of Russia) were elected by the district electoral assemblies; those of the second, numbering 1,344, by the town electoral assemblies; those of the third, numbering 2,476, by the peasants' electoral assemblies, themselves elected by the electors of the *volost*. All these electors met in the provincial (Government) assemblies. In each of these assemblies the peasant delegates, by themselves, elected first of all their deputy to the Duma. Then all the electors elected the rest of the deputies for the Province. The Duma comprised 412 deputies in all. To be an elector, one had to be 25 years old, to have property of some kind or a fixed residence, and to appear in the taxation lists. Workers had the right to vote in the *curia* separately, and their representatives also took part in the provincial assemblies in the election of deputies to the Duma. The legislative role of the Duma, which at first sight seemed very important, was considerably restricted by the later decisions of Nikolas II: the creation of an upper chamber, invested with a legislative competence equal to that of the Duma and entrusted with keeping the reformist activity of the Duma in check; retaining the Tsar's prerogatives in foreign affairs, military and religous regulations, and the Tsar's power to dissolve the Duma at will and to fix the date of new elections as he thought fit; also the Tsar's absolute right to legislate on his own between sessions of the Duma, etc. The first Duma, which met in 1906, showed its intentions to make wide reforms and was

dissolved the same year. The second Duma, which met in February 1907, showed itself more radical even than the first, and the Government ordered its dissolution after a few months' work. The third Duma, elected after a further law curtailing its powers, sat in apparent calm. But, misled by this trustful atmosphere, the Government wished to take advantage of the opportunity to revert to reactionary policies, and the assembly revolted openly against these subservient measures. The fourth Duma, which met in 1912, was no more than a symbolical organ where voices were still raised occasionally to protest against the excesses of the autocracy. This was the situation when war was declared in 1914.

CHAPTER X

THE LAW

The justices of the peace and the assembly of justices – Ordinary courts: appointment and competence of magistrates – The senate as court of appeal – The Zemsky Nachalnik – The cost of justice – Advocates – The examining magistrates – Composition and working of juries – The penal system in Russia: suppression of corporal punishment and of the death penalty – The condition of convicts and forced labour colonies in Siberia – A criminal trial in Moscow.

RUSSELL did not forget that at home he had studied law, and he questioned Alexander Vassilievitch about the working of the law in Russia. At first his host's answers seemed to be satisfactory. Out of the inextricable jumble of old written laws and customs, Speransky, in the reign of Nikolas I, had drawn up a chronological summary (*Polnoe sobranye zakonov*) of forty-eight quarto volumes. But one man's lifetime was not long enough to acquire a deep knowledge of this work, and in 1833 the statutes and contradictory ukases were summarized and co-ordinated in the form of a code (*Svod Zakonov*) divided into articles and chapters. There were fifteen volumes in all, treating civil, criminal, commercial and administrative affairs and procedure.

Later, Alexander II, son of Nikolas I, proceeded to re-organize the judicial system. Before the reforms imposed by this monarch, the courts had no independence, the procedure was secret and rigorously formalist, the judges were poorly trained, their decisions were too often dictated by venality and trials were protracted. But now the law was separated from the legislature and executive; proceedings were public, the more serious crimes were subject to trial by jury, justices of the peace pronounced judgement on less important matters, and the simplified procedure guaranteed individual liberty and property.

The renovated judicial system comprised two kinds of jurisdiction: on the one hand were the justices of the peace, and on the other the judges of the common courts. But these two forms of jurisdiction, instead of being superimposed one upon the other, as in the majority of western nations, were distinct, each possessing its court of first instance and its court of appeal, and differing in the way the justices were appointed. The whole structure was crowned by the Senate, which was the Supreme Court of Appeal and controlled the law throughout the Empire.

The justices of the peace had to judge disputes of no great seriousness, of which the value did not exceed 500 roubles, and offences that could be punished by a fine not exceeding 300 roubles or a sentence of at most a year's imprisonment. These justices were elected by the district *zemstvo*, for in order to function satisfactorily they had to know the local population and their habits and customs. The State required two qualifications for candidates: education and wealth, the one ensuring their capacity and the other their independence. However, it was not the Treasury that paid the justices; the Provincial Assemblies which appointed them also fixed the emoluments, and usually their salary amounted to 2,000 roubles a year in the smaller cities and from 4,000 to 5,000 roubles in St Petersburg and Moscow.[1]

Procedure before the justices of the peace was simple and conciliatory. They strove to reason with the parties with a concern for equity rather than for rights. Anyone with a complaint to make addressed himself to the justice of the peace in his own area, either in writing or in person, and the latter would fix a day for the hearing without delay. The sittings, always in public, were marked by a patriarchal good-heartedness which gave the litigants confidence, especially in the country. There was no decorum. The justice had neither robe nor uniform; he presided in a frock-coat or a jacket, just as he felt inclined, but he always wore around his neck a medal on a gilded chain. In a corner of the room was a desk on which were placed the Gospels and the Crucifix. Witnesses swore on the Gospel and kissed the Crucifix before replying to the justice's questions. Their words, like those of the litigants, were summarized in writing, then read over to the interested parties and certified with their signatures. The

[1] From this salary the magistrate paid for the hiring of the court-room, the heating, and the wages of the clerk of the court.

parties put forward their own arguments or were assisted by an attorney. Any adult person had the right to fill this office, but specialists in talking and quibbling were recruited chiefly from among retired employees, former clerks of court and the unemployed secretaries of the region. For them the illiterate moujiks were an easy prey. Whether the cause was good or bad, their interest was to press the plaintiff to lodge an appeal if he had not received satisfaction in the first instance.[1]

In the second instance, the case went before the assembly of justices, which was held every month at the chief town of the Government. The law did not require the presence at this session of all the justices of the Government, but only three of them, one of whom was elected president.[2] The justice of the peace whose decision was in question could not take part in settling the same case. The sittings were public, with a succession of witnesses and pleas. This time an attorney, appointed by the Government, presented his conclusions on criminal matters and certain civil matters. Enlightened by him, the assembly could quash the sentence of the justice of the first instance for reasons of incompetence or formal error. In that event, they sent the dossier forthwith to another, appointed by themselves. Decisions given on appeal by the assembly could only be opposed before the Senate. Procedure in both instances before the justices of the peace was not subject to any stamp duty or tax.

Parallel with this form of jurisdiction were the common courts. They had to deal with more serious matters than those which occupied the justices of the peace. The judges in these courts sat in uniform, and the advocates wore frock-coats. The sittings were always in public and were attended by much display. While the justices of the peace were all elected, the judges of the common courts were chosen from among professional lawyers and appointed by the Emperor. Every court had the right to offer its own candidates to its vacant places, but this candidate had to secure the approval of the

---

[1] One could only lodge an appeal if the value of the dispute exceeded thirty roubles, or the penalty was fifteen roubles or three days' imprisonment.

[2] This system was copied from the meetings of justices of the peace as they functioned in England.

procurator, that is to say the direct agent of the Minister, before soliciting higher approval. The law of 1864 had laid down in principle the irremovability of judges.[1] However, the Government still controlled their promotion or movement. And in a land as vast as Russia, a change of residence was equivalent to exile. Thus, whilst giving up the right to remove the servants of the law, the State held them at its mercy by other threats.

The Minister had his own special representative attached to every court who was subject to immediate removal; the procurator, who supervised the execution of the laws, defended the interests of the State and those of people unable to do so for themselves and inquired into crimes and offences. It was, moreover, from among the procurators that the upper staff of the Bench were often recruited. Alexander Vassilievitch pointed out a disadvantage in this, for a man who was used to regarding the prisoner from the point of view of the prosecution could not, from one day to another, acquire the necessary impartiality of a judge.

There were two instances for the common courts: the District court, having the whole Government under its jurisdiction, and the court of justice, the competence of which extended over several Governments. The judgements given by the District courts, civil or criminal, were subject to appeal before the court of justice, except in cases where decisions were made with the assistance of a jury. These decisions could only be taken to the Court of Appeal.[2] The Senate, set up as a Court of Appeal, was not thoroughly acquainted with the dispute.[3] It examined the judgements of the courts of justice and certain judgements of the District courts from the formal point of view and also as to the interpretation of the

[1] Except if he has committed some crime or some serious offence.

[2] In addition, there were in Russia a certain number of special courts: (1) military courts concerned with offences and crimes committed by military persons or against military persons; (2) ecclesiastical courts which judged disciplinary affairs of the clergy and the matrimonial affairs of private persons; (3) commercial courts, having within their competence commercial affairs in St Petersburg, Moscow, Odessa, Taganrog, Kerch, Kichinev and Archangel; (4) peasant courts, called cantonal courts, and courts for allogeneous peoples, charged with applying, in certain lands, the laws of custom.

[3] The Senate appeals department was divided into two sections: one for civil affairs, the other for criminal affairs.

law. If it was thought necessary to quash a judgement, the case was sent back to another court of appeal.

However, these arrangements had to be modified to take into account the special customs of certain Provinces, especially the frontier Provinces. But it was the law of June 12, 1889, which had caused the most serious disruption to the Russian judicial code by creating cantonal chiefs (*zemskie nachalniki*). Entrusted with supervising the self-government of the peasants, they had in addition received the attributes of justices of the peace. So that, in the Governments where there were cantonal chiefs, judicial power was once more attached to the administration. In the cities instead of justices of the peace there were urban judges, appointed by the Minister of Justice on the proposals of the Marshals of the nobility. Only in the two capitals and six large cities were there elected judges.

In the ordinary courts the defence of private persons was generally assured by sworn advocates (*prisyazhnye poverennye*). There were also notaries to forestall litigation by having deeds, contracts and agreements drawn up in proper fashion. But Russia had no attorneys. It was the advocates who assumed this role in all phases of the proceedings.

Legal expenses were lower in Russia than in other lands. All citations which instituted proceedings or otherwise were drawn up on paper with a 40-kopeck stamp. The proportionate registration fees were 50 kopecks per 100 roubles of the sum in question, and when the dispute could not be valued the court determined the fees. The costs of prosecutions rose to 6 roubles for the convocation and the publication of judgements by default, from 25 kopecks to 1 rouble for the transport and residence of the judges, examining magistrates and local experts, from 25 kopecks to 3 roubles for the compensation of witnesses.

Of course, the advocates' fees were additional to these sums. To be a sworn advocate, it was necessary to have acquired a law-school diploma and to have been called to the bar. The bar in each city elected a council which had the disciplinary power of reprimand, suspension or expulsion over its members. Beginners were subject to a five-year probation before being admitted to the corporate body. In practice, a client rarely dealt with an advocate on the basis of a fixed sum; the fee depended upon the success of the pleading. In a civil case the remuneration amounted, if successful, to 5, 10, or even sometimes 20 per cent of the sum involved. If it was a criminal case, the lighter the penalty inflicted the greater the advocate's remuneration. Alexander Vassilievitch said that the great Russian advocates made fortunes and enjoyed the great respect of the educated public. In this vast empire, without political assemblies, they were the first to speak freely, according to their consciences, and risked endangering their careers by the boldness of their words. In recent years every Russian, no matter what his crime in respect of a private person or the State, had seen a defender stand at his side who dared to oppose the representative of the Government charged with making the accusation.

Before Alexander II's reforms, the investigation of criminal cases was entrusted to the police, who used violence in order to secure statements from suspects. In 1880 the examining magistrates (*sudebnye sledovatli*) made their appearance, but the police continued to encroach on their powers by initiating house searches, preliminary interrogation of witnesses, and sometimes making arrests without warrant. Since the examining magistrates were, according to the law, irremovable, the Ministry got into the habit of entrusting criminal inquiries not to these titular magistrates but to employees in an active capacity, revocable at will. These employees received a miserable salary and were dependent, on the one hand, on the prosecution and the administration, and on the other on the procurators and the provincial Governors.

The laws of 1884 introduced the jury to Russia. Men whose age and wealth satisfied the required conditions for jury service[1] were officially inscribed every year in the general lists. From among these names a district *zemstvo* committee chose those persons most notable for their morality or good sense. Moujiks, small artisans, landed proprietors, aristocrats

[1] To be a juror one had to own 100 dessiatines (about 270 acres) of land in the country, or a house worth 2,000 roubles in the capitals, or 1,000 roubles in a chief town of a Government, or 500 roubles in other localities, or to have a revenue or salary of 500 roubles in the capitals or 200 roubles elsewhere.

and merchants were thus brought together to give their decision on the same case.[1] But, in reality, the final list was drawn up most often on the desk of the District Marshal of the Nobility. Despite the efforts of this representative of the Government, the jurors, drawn by lots from among all the candidates entered in the final list, formed a not very homogeneous group, and their decisions were frequently in contradiction to the law.

In Russell's mind Russia was the land of the knout. He was therefore very surprised to learn that the knout, as a means of punishment, had been forbidden since the early years of Nikolas I's reign and that a ukase of 1863 had similarly suppressed the birch, which the Russian serf had suffered for a long time. Although struck from the penal code, corporal punishment was, it is true, still adhered to traditionally in distant parts of the land. But these were cases too isolated to be worth considering. In its present state the law of the Empire was, according to Alexander Vassilievitch, one of the mildest in Europe. Capital punishment was abolished in Russia in 1753 by the Empress Elizabeth.[2] The only exception to this rule was for attempts upon the life of the sovereign or against the security of the State. So far as secondary political crimes were concerned, the scaffold was usually replaced by deportation and forced labour. When the Government wanted to obtain some spectacular sentence of death for declared enemies of the régime, these were referred to military tribunals, which passed judgement according to martial law. Despite the mildness of the penal code, there were relatively fewer cases of homicide in Russia than in other European countries where the law was more severe. Thus France pronounced 30 sentences of death and 110 sentences of forced labour for life, while in Russia, although the total number of sentences was very much greater, the penalty of forced labour for life, which was the supreme penalty, was pronounced in

[1] Here, for example, is the list of jurors, before drawing lots, in a big bankruptcy case in Moscow: ten *meshchane* (or petit bourgeois), ten peasants, two artisans, one former soldier, one noble and three notable citizens.

[2] However, it is to be noted that the knout, at that time, replaced the axe and the rope. The judge, prevented by law from passing a sentence of death, would condemn a man to a hundred blows of the knout, knowing full well that the culprit would die during the punishment.

only 25 cases during the same period.[1] A ukase of June 12, 1900, had furthermore considerably reduced the number of cases in which deportation could be decided by a court. The days were far off when whole hordes of political prisoners and criminals went off in fetters to the convict prisons of Siberia. Even in 1878 they crossed the Urals in hundreds, famished and in rags, trusting that the end of the journey would prove a recompense.[2]

In fact, these deportees were divided into two main classes: the convicts properly so called (*ssylno katorzhniki*) and those under lighter punishment, the forced-labour columns (*ssylno poselentsy*). In former times the convicts were employed in the hardest tasks in the mines. Those who survived the fatigue and privations of this subterranean life were few. Beaten by the warders, fed on soup made of rubbish, consumed by all sorts of diseases, they almost regretted that they had not been hanged at the end of their trials.[3] Today, on the other hand, the convicts worked in the factories, the salt-mines and quarries or on road construction. According to regulations, they were only kept in prison during the first quarter of their sentence. Afterwards, they passed into the category of forced-labour columns and were free to take lodgings near the camp, outside the barbed wire, on condition that they appeared every day before the prison authorities for control. This permission was often granted for good conduct before the legal period of delay had expired.[4]

For simple deportees discipline was even less harsh. They were only obliged not to leave the domicile to which they had been sent. The police watched them out of the corners of their eyes. Those with means lived on their revenues, rented a house and took their misfortunes patiently. The rest tried to support themselves by practising their former professions,

[1] Figures cited by N. W. Kovalevsky, of the Russian Finance Ministry, in his report of the situation in Russia in 1900.

[2] The figures for 1878 were as follows:

Condemned to forced labour	853
Condemned to simple deportation	9,847
Reintegrated escapees	1,064

[3] See Dostoyevsky's account in *The House of the Dead*.

[4] In order to calculate the period of forced labour, ten months were reckoned as an entire year, which shortened the official duration of the sentence by a sixth.

or by offering their services in the mines and factories on the same level and for the same pay as the free workers. But although the lot of these 'forced settlers' was not at first glance tragic, almost all of them suffered from being so far from their friends, families and the entire world. Though some of them, when their sentences were completed, remained where they were, set up a home and took part in the life of the locality, others, worn out by the monotony of exile, fled.

A fair number of the convicts, moreover, escaped from the prisons despite the vigilance of the warders. To return home the fugitives covered enormous distances across the steppes and frozen forests of the region. Setting out from the depths of Siberia, they tramped for months, begging, stealing and foiling the manœuvres of the police. In their struggle with the authorities they had the help of the common people, for the common people felt the same pity for political deportees and simple criminals, regarding them all as brothers unjustly persecuted by the State. The Siberian peasants who lived in isolated farms, as a matter of custom placed a little food and water in front of their doors each night for these formidable vagabonds. In the towns and villages the passport control made it possible to catch a few of the fugitives. More than ten per cent of those sent each year from Moscow to Siberia were 'reintegrated men'. But there were many who gathered together in bands and wandered about, or were employed in the mines, or laboured in the fields. Pillage, rape and murder flourished in their path.

Having used the deportation of individuals on a wide scale in order to colonize Siberia, the Government, alarmed at the increase in criminal activity in the provinces of Tobolsk and Tomsk, now preferred imprisonment to deportation, but the Russian prisons were inadequate for the new penal policy. Others had to be built very quickly on the model of European prison buildings. To recruit a competent staff and to ameliorate the prisoners' conditions were the intentions of the Ministry of Justice.

'Do you still think we're a barbaric country?' Alexander Vassilievitch asked when he had ended his statement.

'I have never said so!' Russell cried. 'Certainly your penal system is less harsh and more humane than some, but what is so striking to me is the disorder that exists here under an apparent administrative order. You haven't got a law without an exception, nor a liberal institution without someone to watch over it, nor a free citizen without the shadow of a policeman behind him. Every time you describe some generous measure of the Emperor's, I expect some qualification to lessen its effectiveness. You give and you take away again, you loosen the rope and you tighten it again. . . .'

Alexander Vassilievitch began to laugh: 'Don't forget that Russia is in full social evolution. The people who demand freedom are not mature enough to enjoy it without danger. Also the reformers are acting warily, correcting their innovations when they prove in practice to be premature. . . . But in time we'll succeed in consolidating all that. Would you like to see a trial? An advocate friend of mine is pleading for the defence the day after tomorow at a Moscow district court. His client is accused of murdering her husand. It might be interesting.'

Russell agreed. Two days later he passed with Alexander Vassilievitch through the walls of the Kremlin, where, opposite the Arsenal, the imposing white façade of the Palace of Justice rose. They ascended the steps like two ants. The walls drew apart to support an aerial dome in three tiers. Russell felt crushed by the gigantic dimensions of the circular hall, with its Doric columns, its bas-reliefs, paintings, marbles, its hard light and its cold sonorousness. Men with anxious faces were crowded together and murmuring amongst themselves in the antechamber of the law: advocates in white shirt-fronts, clerks in faded uniforms, litigants in fur-lined coats or *tulups*. Alexander Vassilievitch drew Russell into a corridor lit by very deeply set windows, spoke to an usher and pushed open a door. They sat down on one of the benches reserved for the public. Strangers of all classes were talking amongst themselves in respectful expectation.

The hearing had not yet begun. The room was warm and smelt of floor-polish and coal-dust. At the far end, on a three-stepped dais, stood a long table covered with a fringed green cloth. Behind the table were three chairs with carved oak backs. Behind the three chairs was a portrait of Nikolas II in uniform, with the ribbon of the Order of St Andrei round his neck. To the right were two rows of chairs for the jury. In one corner was the procurator's chair, a pulpit and an ikon, and in the other the clerk's table. Near the public was the bench for the accused, polished by use and protected by a barrier of little carved wooden posts.

At last the jury entered, visibly intimidated by their un-accustomed duties. Among them Russell noticed a big bearded merchant, and a bespectacled young man who might be a professor or a doctor. When these representatives of the people's conscience were seated side by side, an usher stood up in the middle of the hall and uttered a few words in a resounding voice. 'The Court!' murmured Alexander Vassilie-vitch. Everyone rose. The president and his two assessors came forward on to the dais. All three were in uniform with gold-embroidered collars. The president was bald and had white side-whiskers. The judges seated themselves in their arm-chairs and the public followed suit to the sounds of shuffling feet and nervous coughing. Then two gendarmes, with swords at their sides, brought the woman prisoner into the box. All eyes were turned towards her, without surprise or reproach, but with a sort of tranquil pity. She was small and thin, with waxen cheeks, and her eyes were dark, deep and gentle. She had cut her husband's throat with a razor while he slept. Under interrogation, she had stated that he had been unfaithful to her, had beaten her and had tried to kill her. The clerk shuffled papers on his table. The jurors were counted; the absent ones were replaced and lots were drawn. . . .

The president placed his hand to his ear so as to hear the comments of his assistants better. Suddenly Russell observed the presence of a cassocked priest on the floor of the court. He was there to swear the jury in. At a gesture from the president he approached the pulpit beneath the ikon, slipped his head, with its long oily black hair, through the opening in a stole, adjusted the sacred ornament on his abdomen, ad-dressed the jurors and explained what he expected of them. Each in turn raised his right hand, with fingers together as when making the sign of the cross, and repeated a formula which Alexander Vassilievitch translated for Russell in a low

voice: 'I promise and I swear, by Almighty God, on the
Gospels and the Cross . . .'

After this ceremony the jurors drew aside to elect their
foreman, then resumed their seats, listened to the advice of
the side-whiskered president, and the trial began. The
woman answered questions in a scarcely audible voice. The
witnesses came and went, the clerk read the accusation, and
the witnesses gave evidence under oath. The proceedings
continued as in Britain. Russell certainly understood nothing
of the words which were exchanged before him, but the
gestures and the facial expressions of the principal persons
helped him to guess their thoughts. There was a report by the
medical expert, an examination by the jury of the exhibits,
crafty questioning of the bewildered witnesses by the procurator and the advocate for the defence, a resounding indictment, and an endless and mawkish counsel's speech. Standing up in his fine black clothes and his stiff white shirt-front,
the defending counsel stretched out a merciful arm towards
the accused and his voice filled with tears. The faces of those
present were filled with gentleness. 'They pity her because
she has committed a murder!' Russell mused, an idea which
seemed to him essentially Russian. The hearing was suspended several times. Finally, the jury retired to deliberate.
Russell was sure of an acquittal, but the woman was sen-
tenced to the loss of rights 'both civil and personal' and to
hard labour for four years. She did not flinch as the president
delivered the verdict. The gendarmes led her away. The
crowd flowed out into the broad flagged corridor. Russell was
disappointed, but as for Alexander Vassilievitch, he reckoned
the sentence was just.

'After all, she did kill her husband!' he said. 'Moreover,
without my friend's speech she would have got double. Let's
go and congratulate him. He deserves it!'

Surrounded by a circle of acquaintances, the advocate was
beaming; he was mopping his brow with a fine cambric
handkerchief.

CHAPTER XI

MOSCOW'S MANY FACES

*The significance of festivals in the daily life of the Russian
people – The blessing of the waters – Tatiana's day – Fasting
and bliny – The Great Lent and the markets – Anathemas –
The melting of the snows – The Day of the Forty Martyrs –
Palm Sunday – Preparations for Easter – Orthodox Easter in
Church and at table*

ONE by one the *traktirs*, shops, monuments, museums
and churches of Moscow yielded their secrets to
Russell. Tatiana Sergeyevna showed him the Tretiakov Gallery, which two rich Muscovite merchants, the
brothers Tretiakov, had given the city in 1882, and which
contained more than 2,000 pictures by Russian painters.
Alexander Vassilievitch acted as his guide to the palaces,
monasteries and cathedrals of the Kremlin, took him to the
top of the Ivan Veliky tower, and led him into the home of the
Romanovs, where nothing had changed, it seemed, since the
time of Mikhail Fedorovitch, the first Tsar of the dynasty.
Paul Egorovitch took him to the Rumiantsev Museum and
the Historical Museum. But to these Russell much preferred
the innumerable aspects of daily life, the interiors glimpsed
through the double ground-floor windows, and contact with
the ordinary man in the street.

Far from the main thoroughfares, the narrow and badly
paved alleyways were a maze, where old and peeling houses
slumbered at the ends of gardens, wooden shanties rotted
behind broken fences, and ill-defined fields opened up,
undulating and powdered with snow, a chapel raised its
bulbous dome above a pile of ramshackle buildings, and a
nobleman's dwelling suddenly appeared with the façade of a
Greek temple, hoar-frost on its columns and two stone lions
flanking the gate. Each building bore a number and the
owner's name legibly on the wall – the Shukin house, the
Tarassov house, and so on. Beside each entrance hung a lantern, which also bore the owner's name, traced in black letters
on the glass. It was the porter's job to keep the lantern going.

This additional lighting was indispensable, for, far from the city centre, the public street-lamps were few.

In fact, there was not just one Moscow, but ten, twenty, thirty Moscows side by side.

There was the Moscow of half-ruined noble families, living far from the Court, with dusty drawing-rooms, chandeliers, portraits of bewigged ancestors, memorials, resentments, debts, silent pride and ragged servants.

There was the Moscow of wealthy tradesmen, of bold industrialists, the kings of cotton, silk, iron, wood or leather, who played at being patrons, built chateaux, subsidized theatrical companies, bought French pictures, took an interest in gastronomy, and gambled away thousands of roubles with a smile, though their grandparents had been simple peasants, with bass *lapti* on their feet, who scarcely knew how to sign their names.

There was the Moscow of the small, corpulent, bearded tradesmen in long greatcoats and squeaky boots, who worked all week in their shops where the pot-bellied samovars shone, went each Saturday to the public baths and every Sunday to mass with their families, who grew indignant when their sons and daughters wished to study instead of remaining in trade and the family tradition.

There was the Moscow of tiny incense-perfumed churches, with their blackened pictures, gentle evening bells, cavernous-voiced priests, frozen beggars, and shawled women, who knelt and beat their foreheads on the stone slabs, kissed all the ikons and knew by heart the list of saints to be invoked in case of illness, theft, pregnancy, dispute or the evil eye.

There was the Moscow of offices, of haggard, badly fed clerks, dressed in faded uniforms, with their crafty struggles for promotion, their scratchy pens, clattering abaci and dim lighting.

There was the Moscow of fashionable salons, where elegant ladies organized meetings for poetry recitals, music, spiritualism and scandal. Reputations were made or destroyed in these salons; the most cutting words were spoken and the most daring intrigues were plotted. Famous beauties played at breaking hearts, and men were banished, fought

Tsarkoe Selo, St Petersburg

Bridge and Church of St Isaac, St Petersburg, with
the monument to Peter the Great

10
Left:
Entran
to the
Palace
of
Tsarko
Selo

Right:
The
Chinese
Theatre
at
Tsarkoe
Selo

Left: On the
banks of the
Neva, St Petersbu
with the
Royal Palace in
the distance

amongst themselves, or committed suicide for them, or forgot them by drinking champagne with the tziganes at the Yar Restaurant.

There was the bright Moscow of the theatres with its permanent idols: Chaliapin, Sobinov, Stanislavsky, Komissarzhevskaya ...

There was the Moscow of the shoemakers, carpenters, glaziers and tailors: poverty, a half-dozen dirty and squalling brats, a pregnant wife, a baby in a packing-case and an ikon in the corner. Great lovers of the balalaïka, the accordion and vodka, these small artisans sang and got drunk on Sunday, and for the rest of the week, taciturn and heavy-headed, brooded over their misfortunes and dreamed of the next Sunday.

There was the Moscow of students, with their meetings, their debates, riots and youthful enthusiasms. They lived poorly several to a room upon the parcels sent them by their parents, earned a few roubles by giving private lessons, worshipped certain professors and detested others, and gazed at their brilliant futures through the smoke of their cardboard-ended cigarettes.

There was suburban Moscow, where the horses sank breast-deep in the snow, where the dogs howled in the white kitchen-gardens, where, behind the Taganka, witches told fortunes, cast spells and mixed powders and philtres; where special bakers cooked *kalach*[1] 'with a handle' for the gilders' workers, so that they should not dirty the bread when grasping it in blackened acid-stinking hands.

There was the Presnia quarter of Moscow, with its dismal factories, its workers housed in barracks, its powerful policemen, its convoys of wagons, its smoke and the racing beat of machinery that made the earth tremble.

There was the Moscow of the Stock Exchange quarter, with its international banks, export stores, warehouses, exchange offices, anxious faces and hands that trembled as they fluttered through the pages of the newspapers or tore off dividend warrants.

There was the Moscow of the popular promenades in the Sokolniki Park, where the merchants still took their marriageable daughters. In the sleigh, hired for the occasion, the

[1] A bread roll in the shape of a padlock.

parents sat on either side of the beautiful dolled-up child, covered in furs and jewels, her cheeks pink from the cold air. On the opposite seat the professional matchmaker (*svakha*) sat enthroned, strong in all the joys conjured up by her intervention. The timid young girl looked neither right nor left, but hundreds of eyes were on her. Young men, walking in the same avenue, scrutinized the living capital offered to their covetous gaze. If one of them should be tempted, he then approached the *svakha* to obtain further details regarding the dowry.

There was the Moscow of the Khitrovka, the centre of drunkenness, robbery, murder and idleness, with its packed night-shelters, liquor-shops, quarrels, summary executions, rags, fog and secret laws.

There was the Moscow of the Trubnaya Square and the adjacent lanes, the quarter for the prostitutes and *maisons de rendezvous*. There was a very elegant example a few steps from the great Hermitage Restaurant, and another, not far away, abutted upon a convent. Because of this the house in question was in keen demand, and its clients had named it Svyatye Nomera, 'the Holy Numbers'. Farther off, in Maly-Kolossov Street, near the Tsvetnoi Boulevard, were squalid brothels that charged only 50 kopecks. The regulation red light shone above their doors.

Though it was almost empty during the week, Trubnaya Square livened up on Sunday mornings. Processions of pedlars came there to sell dogs, cats, rabbits, fighting-cocks, doves, canaries and live fish in buckets. The din of bargaining was interrupted by barks, chirps and bellicose crowings. There were always bird-lovers to buy freedom for the birds — a strange custom which, for Russell, expressed an oppressed people's desire for independence! After a long palaver, the grumbling bird-catcher agreed to the price fixed by his customer, took the money, opened the cage and let the pigeons fly away. All heads were raised joyfully to follow the captives as they flew into the sky towards the Petrovsky Boulevard. But it was a cruel trick, for these were tame pigeons; they settled a little way off and folded their wings, and wisely waited for a small boy to come and collect them and take them back to the vendor to be put on sale again. Towards evening the crowd dispersed and the square returned to its true dimensions; the *likatches* drew up before the Hermitage Restaurant, with its brilliantly lit windows, and on the boulevard the girls of easy virtue appeared in their feathered hats and provocative smiles. The hotel of the 'Holy Number' took in its furtive couples. Champagne was taken up to the rooms. In the convent next door the bells rang slowly.

At dawn, peasants coming from their villages in telegas passed through the city crying: 'Milk! Milk! Who wants milk?' One also met in the streets the vendor of warm drinks, with all his apparatus: an enormous copper boiler in his hand, garlands of bread rolls around his neck, and on his stomach an apron with pockets for carrying the glasses. A knife-grinder passed, carrying his heavy stone and treadle-stand on his shoulder, crying in a raucous voice: 'I sharpen knives, I sharpen scissors!' A Tartar followed him, bowed under the weight of a bundle of carpets and silks; at regular intervals he raised the cry of the dealers of his race: '*Churumburum!*' The people mockingly described this merchant as *knyaz* (prince), for, it was said, in his own country he had only to own thirty sheep to have the right to the title.

Caught by the spell of Moscow, it sometimes seemed to Russell that he was neither altogether in Europe nor altogether in Asia. In the old Russian capital life was regulated by the progress of the seasons, the changes of temperature, the gifts of the earth and the cycle of Orthodox festivals. On January 6, for the Blessing of the Waters, a religious procession went to the banks of the Moskva and halted before a large hole that had been cut in the ice. A bishop celebrated mass in the open air. The choir sang. To the sound of all the bells, a cross was plunged into the cold black water. In a temperature of minus 20°, the crowd watched the ceremony from the bank. When the procession of priests, deacons, banners, crosses and ikons left the spot to return solemnly to the church, there were always a few courageous young fellows who promptly undressed, ran naked to the hole and plunged into the icy water. They came out as red as boiled lobsters, with haggard eyes, shivering limbs and laughter on their lips. Charitable spectators at once rushed towards them, rubbed them, wrapped them in coats and gave them great draughts of vodka. Was there not a popular saying that 'What is health to the Russian is deadly to the foreigner'?[1]

On January 12, 'Tatiana's Day', the students noisily celebrated the anniversary of the founding of Moscow University. After mass in the university church and pompous addresses by the professors, the crowd of young men flowed out into the streets, singing *Gaudeamus* and even the *Marseillaise* at the tops of their voices. The police had been instructed to leave them alone and watched this disturbance of public order with suppressed rage. The festival continued in the Hermitage Restaurant, where the tables had been cleared of their valuable crockery in advance. Those who had money paid for those who had not. Vodka and champagne inflamed their faces. From the Hermitage shouting groups went by sleigh to more distant restaurants, the Yar or the Strelnya. A future judge climbed a palm-tree like a monkey, a future doctor took off his boots and jacket and threw himself into the pool to catch the sterlets by the gills, and future theologians sang with the tzigane chorus. In the artificial caves girls, collected from the Tsvetnoi Boulevard, danced with naked breasts before future engineers who were so drunk that they scarcely saw them. At dawn the staff cleaned up the battlefield, loaded the piles of bodies into sleighs, aired the room and consoled themselves for the damage with the thought that this sort of clientele would not set foot in the place for another year.

A little later, in February, during the first week of Lent, marked by the prohibition of meat-eating (*myasopust*), *bliny* with cream appeared on all tables, accompanied by herrings or caviar. So the days preparatory to the Great Lent became an occasion for gastronomic delights. Pedlars' huts rose on the Devitchy field. Vendors of spiced bread, nuts, hot *bliny*, fish-cakes and sweetmeats, exhibitors of monkeys with their *sharmanka*,[2] story-tellers, accordion and balalaïka players, theatrical companies in motley costume – the whole multitude swirled about, gesticulated and bawled in the frail framework of planks and painted canvas. On the Saturday of the 'great shrovetide' (*shirokaya maslyanitsa*), the Russian

---

[1] *Tchto Russkomu zdorovo, Niemtsou smert.*
[2] Barrel organs.

carnival season was in full swing; the restaurants, circuses, theatres and liquor-shops turned crowds away. On the Taganka side the merchants displayed themselves in rich carriages with their harnesses decorated with paper flowers and ribbons. They promenaded their wives and daughters in all their jewels. Families solemnly greeted each other as they passed.

On Sunday evening the city fell quiet. At twilight, on the banks of the Moskva, between the Moskvoretsky and Ustinsky bridges, rustic sleighs arrived, driven by peasants and overflowing with foodstuffs: barrels of pickled cabbage and salted cucumbers, baskets of dried mushrooms, boxes of chick-peas, jars of various pickles. All these foodstuffs were needed to provision the city for the Great Lent, the first week of which (*syropust*) was dedicated by the Church to vegetables. No more milk, butter or white cheese! Amongst the lowly people and certain great families of believers, these instructions were followed to the letter.

The merchants erected their huts on the embankment in the night and on Monday morning the crowd went down to the Moskva to see the endless rows of tents and shanties stuffed with Christian provisions. Garlands of white, yellow and brown mushrooms hung between the shafts of the sleighs. Nimble hands plunged into casks of brine where gherkins floated among fennel branches and currant leaves. At the end of a vigorous arm swung a whole family of glazed cracknel biscuits, strewn with poppy-seed. Honey oozed from rows of wax. Between two piles of potatoes an artist was selling wood-carvings representing scenes from the holy scriptures, and a colporteur was offering ikons and cheap Bibles.... The Muscovite housewives hurriedly bought the strict foodstuffs which they would need during the long weeks of the Orthodox Great Lent. Then, laden with bundles, baskets and jars, they returned home. But they left again at once so as not to miss the solemn penitential mass, during which the singing of the choirs is always so sad and so beautiful. The bells no longer sounded except at long intervals, deep and funereal. In the nave the priests, in their chasubles of mourning, black with silver embroidery, knelt three times while repeating: 'Lord and Master of my life . . .'

Throughout the first week of the Great Lent, the imperial theatres closed their doors. Profiting by this windfall, foreign actors flowed into Moscow and the public rushed along to their performances.[1] The following Sunday, in the heart of the Kremlin, in the brilliantly lit Cathedral of the Assumption, a very impressive ceremony took place during the mass celebrated by the Bishop himself. To the solemn singing of the choir, a score of priests formed a semicircle around the Bishop. A proto-deacon, with long hair and a haggard face, moved to the middle of the temple and, facing the rapt congregation, called down execration upon the impious and the heretics, on those who did not believe in the resurrection of the dead, the immortality of the soul and the illuminating omnipotence of the Lord, on those who scoffed at the Church, who did not observe the fast ... There were a dozen categories of great sinners. Every time he named one, the proto-deacon took a breath and then cried in a voice of thunder:

'A-na-thema!'

The windows shook. Three times the priests answered in chorus:

'Anathema! Anathema! Anathema;'[2]

A tremor of anguish ran through the congregation, who bowed their heads.

However, the weeks passed and the days lengthened: a very slight warmness, an unusual mildness, and a mysterious gaiety penetrated the air despite the persistent snow. Around Moscow the first buds swelled on the black wet branches. But there was another herald of spring: the rooks came back in groups and made their nests in the gardens. The gutters wore beards of icicles, which the urchins broke off and sucked with delight. On the roofs of some houses, workmen, tied by ropes to the chimneys, plunged their shovels into the snow and cried 'Look out below!' and passers-by flattened themselves against the wall to avoid the avalanche. Often the white mass detached itself and of its own accord fell with a muffled roar.

---

[1] The theatres were closed also during Holy Week and on the eve of the great religious festivals.

[2] In more remote times, the clergy every year launched anathemas upon the heretic Grishka Otrepiev, who had overthrown the Tsar Boris Gudonov, upon Ivan Mazeppa, who had betrayed Peter the Great, on Stenka Razin, 'thief, traitor and infamous creature', and on Pugachev, the 'bloody rebel'.

On both sides of the street rose great banks of dead snow. Sometimes the sky clouded over and flakes whirled through the air. But the end of the winter was at hand.

On March 9, the Day of the Forty Martyrs, the arrival of the larks was the pretext for serving little loaves shaped like birds, with folded wings and eyes made of dried raisins. On the Friday and Saturday before Palm Sunday (the sixth week of the Great Lent), all the willows in the neighbouring country were cut by their owners. A forest of branches with their soft silver-grey catkins moved in convoys in the direction of Moscow and poured into the Red Square. The crenellated fortress walls, the Minin and Pojarsky monuments, and the Cathedral of St Basil were surrounded by fluffy, moving thickets. At the same time balloon-sellers came from every direction, holding their enormous multicoloured wares on a string as they swung to the least breath of wind. Urchins ran amongst the crowd, blowing toy trumpets and swinging hand-rattles. Housewives carefully chose the palms they would take to church to be blessed. On Saturday a strange merry-go-round was organized in front of the Kremlin: gliding over the muddy earth, calashes and landaus went round and round carrying entire beaming families. The horses moved at a walk. The children gazed at the red balloons. In the midst of the immense ring formed by the procession policemen in grey capes were quietly watching from a distance and twirling their moustaches.

On Sunday, after mass, in the humblest homes as well as the noblemen's residences, every ikon had its willow branch. Then began Holy Week, with its deserted squares, its silent bells and its stricter fast. But this somnolence in the city concealed an intense culinary activity. Housewives everywhere were busy organizing the Easter feast. They had to prepare the dough for the *kulich*, the sugared white cheese for the *paskha* and the dyes for the eggs.

The number of eggs bought by the Zubov tribe alone was such that Russell wondered if there were enough hens in the Empire to supply the needs of the population. To colour the shells various powders mixed with boiling water and vinegar were used. The eggs were plunged into the liquid one by one and emerged red, green, blue and yellow. Greased with a scrap of bacon-fat, they shone like jewels. The Zubovs' old *niania* completed the decoration of some of them with a brush. But her hands shook, for she had observed the fast more strictly than her employers, and it had exhausted her nervous strength.

Simultaneously with these activities, there was a general cleaning up in all the rooms. A glazier came to remove the double frames from the windows, and the daylight in the rooms was improved. The gutters dripped. The roadway became clear, turning into a liquid yellowish paste. Sleighs finally gave way to wheeled carriages. The servants polished everything they could lay their hands on. The doorknobs already shone like the Easter eggs; the pendants on the chandeliers were filled with blue lights, and the floors smelt of beeswax. Suddenly a great piece of news passed from mouth to mouth: the ice on the Moskva was breaking.

Russell made his way to the river's edge. Between the embankments a slow break-up was carrying the white blocks along; they swung about, crashed together and crumbled to pieces with a dream-like softness. A crowd of bystanders watched the rising of the waters. The flood threatened some quarters of the city. But everyone was used to it. Everyone looked happy. The great day was drawing near. The Zubovs' *nyanya* sighed deeply, prayed for hours on end before the ikons, and made the sign of the cross over her stomach when she heard it rumble. Tatiana Sergeyevna, Helen and Olga were very busy with their clothes. The dressmaker was late. Would they get their new dresses for Easter? They were to receive them very shortly before the Lord's resurrection.

There was a custom which required that, on the Thursday of Holy Week, each of the faithful should take home with him a little taper which had been lit during mass. A screw of paper surrounded the flame to prevent it from being blown out by the wind during the journey. Innumerable flickering glow-worms thus hurried at the same time through the twilit Moscow streets. As soon as they entered their homes these pious people raised the wax taper and with the black smoke that rose from the wick they traced a cross above the door. Then they rekindled the candles at the ikons. In the Zubov household it was the *nyanya* who performed these rites, on which, she said, the prosperity of the whole house depended. On Easter Saturday, in the street, the majority of passers-by were laden with baskets and boxes. The bakers, overwhelmed with orders, were engulfed in dough and sweetmeats. The *nyanya* decorated the ikons with paper roses, and carried the *paskha*, the eggs and the *kulich* to church, where they were blessed.

For midnight mass the Zubovs and Russell went to the Kremlin. The crowd was so dense within the old crenellated walls that they were unable to get into the Cathedral of the Assumption. Although Alexander Vassilievitch had explained and described the ceremony to him beforehand, Russell was filled with wonder at the ocean of heads that rippled among the reefs of the churches and the palaces. The domes shone far above them in a dark wet mist. But on this evening the stars had come down to earth, for each of the faithful held a wax taper in his hand – a light for every face. The flames flickered in the wind. All classes of the population were represented among those gathered together. Some carried coloured eggs and *paskha* wrapped in paper. Alexander Vassilievitch vanished and soon came back with tapers which he gave to his wife, son-in-law, daughters, son and guest. Russell hunted in his pocket for matches. Tatiana Sergeyevna stopped him. Was he going to commit sacrilege? His neighbour on the left, a robust tradesman, wearing boots and wrapped in a long blue tunic, gave him his own lighted candle. The flame had to pass in this way from one to another like faith in Jesus Christ. The wax sputtered and then burned brightly.

'Thank you,' said Russell.

And as his neighbour looked at him with surprise, he pulled himself together and murmured: '*Spasibo!*'

Tatiana Sergeyevna, and then Helen, came to light their candles from the same bright source, which Russell shielded with his hand. Soon all the members of the Zubov family were lit from below like the ikons. Helen's eyes shone like diamonds. A gilded line emphasized the curve of her cheek. Her lips were smiling with happiness. Everyone around her had a joyful air. People were not praying; they were whispering and jostling with feverish impatience, as they awaited permission to give free expression to their gladness. Distant

singing flowed out through the cathedral doors. A misty
glimmer floated above the entrance. All the candelabra were
lit inside. Russell's candle softened in his grasp. Suddenly
Helen cried 'Look!'

The religious processions emerged simultaneously from all
the Kremlin's churches. Banners, tapers and golden chasubles
formed long and scintillating rivers. Each procession moved
forward through the crowd with a thousand flickering flames.
Priests, deacons and the congregation were seeking Christ
outside the sepulchre in the marvellous certainty of His
resurrection. The choir's powerful singing rose so high and
carried so far that it must have been heard at the ends of the
earth. A star with a fluorescent train leapt into the sky, followed by another. Suddenly everything was lit up. Fire-
works! Golden rain fell upon the domes, catherine wheels
whirled at the top of the towers, and fiery letters – 'X.B.'[1] –
quivered on the palace façades. Under this torrent of light
the whole Kremlin – its domes, crosses, battlements and
columns – quivered like a magic vessel, ready to break from
its moorings and make off into the darkness. The earth
vibrated beneath Russell's feet. An enormous and melodious
sound fell upon his ears. Light silver and heavy bronze, Ivan
Veliky's bells were giving the signal for Christian rejoicing
and all the city's bells replied. Deafened by this uproar,
Russell was astonished to see his neighbour, the tradesman,
turn to him a face that was overwhelmed with thankfulness:

'Khristos voskrese!'[2] said the man.

And Russell felt the touch of a perfumed beard on his
cheek. In his confusion he recalled Alexander Vassilievitch's
advice and stammered:

'Vo istinu voskrese!'[3]

Having exchanged the triple kiss with this stranger, he
turned to the Zubovs, and every member of the family repeated the gesture. Russell repeated: *Khristos voskresse*,
offered his lips and opened his arms. His heart was overflowing with Christian love. As he brushed Helen's smooth cool
cheek with his lips, he felt like an angel amongst angels. All
around them people were embracing, congratulating one
another and offering each other eggs.

[1] 'Christ is risen!'   [2] 'Christ is risen!'   [3] 'Truly He is risen!'

'I am so hungry!' said Alexander Vassilievitch.

That same night, at the Zubovs' home, there was a gigantic supper for many guests. The servants, each of whom had received a little gift (*paskha, kulich,* cheap jewellery), all had merry faces. Russell was much amused by the custom of 'egg fights' among those at table. Each took a coloured hard-boiled egg and, grasping it in his hand, lightly struck the egg held by his neighbour. The one whose egg was broken was out of the game, and the winner at once faced a new adversary, and so on. The experts chose by preference the eggs with pointed ends and held them closely in their hands to lessen the area of impact. At the end of the fight, the host announced the winner, who put his victorious egg aside in anticipation of a further trial and broke another on the edge of his plate for immediate consumption. Pink, yellow or green marbling, due to the colouring matter having penetrated the shell, sometimes marked the plump white surfaces of the shelled eggs. They were salted and munched rapturously. Even those who had taken great care not to observe Lent gave the impression of not having satisfied their hunger for seven weeks.

The eggs gave way to hot and cold *zakuski.* And the hot and cold *zakuski* gave place to the traditional sucking-pig, with its crisp crackling, its half-closed eyes, and a coloured egg in its half-open mouth. Glasses of vodka, zubrovka and pertzovka were the punctuation marks in this long gastronomic sentence. By turns, toasts were drunk to the lady of the house, the host, to the present and absent, to Britain, to Russia, to women in general and pretty women in particular. The *paskha,* in the shape of a truncated pyramid, white and packed with preserved fruits, flavoured with vanilla, the cylindrical *kulich* with its topping of melted sugar, received the praise of the connoisseurs. Supper ended at four in the morning.

The next day Russell was awakened by the melodious ringing of a thousand bells which echoed the good news across the city. On Easter Day in Russia any person could go and ring the bells in the churches, just as he liked. Russian bells were fixed: it was the clapper which made the sound by striking the walls of the bell. The windows shook to this loud but joyful music. The maddened pigeons circled in the blue sky. The sun shone in the puddles. In the middle of the dining-room the table was already prepared for all who came to greet Tatiana Sergeyevna during the day: a sucking-pig, that looked like a brother of the one the night before, slept the sleep of innocence in a field of coloured eggs, charcuterie, caviar, *balyk*, salmon, pickles, *paskha*, *kulich*, and bottles of vodka and wine.

Alexander Vassilievitch had drawn up the list of visits he himself had to pay in the afternoon. A score at least. To miss one of them would have been the greatest discourtesy. Paul Egorovitch and Russell were brought in to accompany him. And so the men hurried through the city from one house to another, and the women received them. They left in a calash. The coachman wore a belt and a new hat. The trotters had carefully plaited tails, black shoes, shining as if with lacquer, and silver harness which caught the smallest ray of sunlight.

At each apartment, where Russell entered behind Alexander Vassilievitch and Paul Egorovitch, he saw the same table, with the same *paskha*, the same sucking-pig, the same *kulich* and the same eggs. A joyful cry invariably greeted the newcomers:

'How kind of you! Come in! *Khristos voskrese!*'

And the lady of the house reached up graciously to Alexander Vassilievitch's silky moustache, while behind him Paul Egorovitch and Russell awaited their turn. Three kisses for each and they passed on at once to serious matters. On pain of upsetting their delightful hostess, they had to taste the sucking-pig, the eggs, the *paskha* and the *kulich* of which she was so proud. At the tenth call the repetition of this menu overwhelmed Russell. Before each table he had the feeling that the Easter dainties of the preceding buffet, led by the sucking-pig on nimble feet, had passed them on the journey, and that he had found them again, inexorable and inexhaustible, in different surroundings and amongst new faces. The eternal piglet watched him fixedly betwixt its golden lids. Russell was reminded of the eye of conscience which followed Cain everywhere. A shiver ran down his back. He held his fork in a feeble hand. His mouth was filled with revolt, but at his side Alexander Vassilievitch and Paul Egorovitch ate with appetite, went into raptures over the quality of the food and drained their glasses. One might have thought it was their first meal since the morning.

At last they left. The open air, the sunlight, and the sound of the bells. Alexander Vassilievitch struck a name from his list and gave a new address to the coachman. They had to cross the whole city, which was in festival array. In the streets were strollers in their Sunday best: the men wore shirts of red, pink, yellow, mauve and blue, and their hair shone with pommade. Their boots were remarkably polished. The women had large flowered skirts, and bright-coloured scarves on their heads. They met, embraced and exchanged Easter eggs. In courtyards and gardens the plaintive sounds of the accordion melted a few sensitive souls, and in the drink-stores laughter could be heard. Each small employer received the congratulations of his staff in his workroom or in his shop, where a big table had been laid beneath the ikon. 'Popes' with high caps and venerable beards passed from one house to another, blessing their parishioners and their food, and drinking a glass of vodka under the fond gaze of the hostess.

A slight jolt. The carriage stopped. Russell, roused from his stupor, followed Alexander Vassilievitch and Paul Egorovitch into a red-carpeted vestibule, passed through open double-doors, saw amid the green plants a crowd of people with glasses in their hands, heard the words *Khristos voskrese*, received three kisses, six kisses, a dozen kisses, and allowed himself to be led to the table where the piglet awaited him with an Easter egg between its teeth.

The next day, although the time of fasting was over, Russell put himself on a diet.

CHAPTER XII

THE TSAR AND HIS ENTOURAGE

*Visit to St Petersburg – The building of the city – Its appear-
ance to a newcomer – A military parade – The life of the
Imperial Family – The Court staff – The Emperor's day at
Tsarskoe-Selo – The ceremony of Easter greetings to the
Emperor and Empress – A ball at the Winter Palace – The
high society of St Petersburg – The clubs of the two capitals –
Artistic movements in Russia*

ALEXANDER VASSILIEVITCH had to go to St Petersburg on
business and Russell decided to go with him: 400 miles
by railway in a straight line, and a 12-hour journey. Before they left, the family gathered beneath the ikon. They all
sat with bowed heads for a moment's meditation; then there
was a great noise of chairs being pushed back. They all rose
and embraced under the tranquil gaze of the holy picture.

Alexander Vassilievitch preferred to travel by day so that
Russell might admire the landscape. But in fact the landscape
was nothing remarkable. After leaving Moscow by the Nikolas
Station, the train rolled rapidly along between bare plains,
copses of puny trees, muddy marshlands and dreary peat-
bogs. The villages were half-submerged in mud. The roads
were tracks of brownish refuse, cut by ruts and broken by
puddles. As the train approached the Tver the scene became
even more desolate: a featureless plain, stumps of trees instead of stunted forests, a network of channels full of dirty
water, and all around slabs of peat piled up in the shape of
coffins. Afterwards came thick-set pines and birches with
trunks as white as dried bones. In the pastures were window-
less huts for storing hay. There were houses built of wood
from foundation to roof, grouped around a well, and a rustic
church with a gold-studded blue dome; a level-crossing with
its woman keeper, booted, and wearing a scarf over her head.
Then there were more marshes.

Alexander Vassilievitch explained to Russell that St Petersburg had been built, by order of Peter the Great, on a spongy,
sodden plain at the mouth of the Neva. At this point there

had once stood a Swedish fortress, which the Emperor had razed in 1702. The following year (May 16, 1703) he laid the first stone of the new Russian capital, which he said would be a window to the West. His ambition was to build a city as quickly as one built a house.

Forty thousand workers were employed on this superhuman task in an unhealthy climate. The soil was so soft that for the foundations they had to bring material in sacks from far away. As there were no stones in the vicinity, the captains of all the ships on Lake Ladoga and the drivers of all wagons bringing goods to St Petersburg were ordered to carry a load of stone that was fixed in advance, and to put themselves at the disposal of the commissioner in charge of the building. The majority of the buildings were raised upon piles. To drain the marshes, canals were dug that ran out of the river and returned to it. The congestion of workers was such that they lacked both lodging and food. The weakest died for want of care. The rest arrived in convoys from the far ends of the Empire. If Peter the Great was harsh towards the serfs, he was no less so towards the great. A ukase ordered 350 noble families and as many merchant and artisan families to take up residence in St Petersburg and to build their homes there in accordance with plans already drawn up and approved by the Tsar. He himself had been installed in a modest dwelling since 1703, while awaiting the completion of the Summer Palace. The city was solemnly raised in 1712 to the rank of court residence, and in order to give it the importance of a national sanctuary, the Tsar had the bones of St Alexander Nevsky taken there in 1724.

Forced to abandon their comfortable Moscow habits for the new life in a land 'rich in tears and marshes', the Emperor's familiars resigned themselves to this change of residence as to an undeserved exile. Then, as St Petersburg grew in size and splendour, thousands of 'volunteers' flowed there to seek their fortunes in trade and government service. Now in this strange region where the sky was pale green, where the poor grass was mixed with heath and moss, where the bristling pine and the melancholy larch predominated, where the exhalations of stagnant water filled the air with dampness, penetrated the houses and pierced a man to the marrow, there

rose an artificial city, systematic and cold. One and a half
million inhabitants lived there in the shadow of the sovereign.
All the ministries, all the administrative departments, and all
the aristocratic circles were gathered together in a foggy
corner of land. No Russian was ever out of his element when
he arrived in Moscow for the first time, but everyone was so
when arriving for the first time in St Petersburg. They did not
feel at home, though they felt to some extent in Europe. Thus
it was, paradoxically, from the least Russian city in the whole
of Russia that since Peter the Great the Romanov dynasty
had governed the nation. Alexander Vassilievitch said that
this psychological error might have grave consequences in
the years to come.

'A Tsar ought to live at the heart of the nation. And the
heart of the nation is not St Petersburg with its straight vistas,
its fog, its uniforms, its arrogance and red tape; it is patriarchal and gaudy Moscow, where everything is simple, traditional and charming! Do you know why the St Petersburgers
don't like us? Because, without daring to say so, they envy
us. . . !'

At these words the engine emitted a distressful whistle.
They had arrived at Bologoye. Alexander Vassilievitch remembered that there was an excellent buffet there and persuaded Russell that a *borsch* and *pirozhk* would do them both
good.

        ❋   ❋   ❋   ❋

The Hotel de l'Europe at St Petersburg was like any first-
class hotel in any other capital in the world. Alexander
Vassilievitch and Russell took rooms with windows that
looked out on to the Nevsky Prospect. The next morning they
set out in a cab to reconnoitre the City. Protected by the
leather hood of the carriage, Russell listened to the beat of
the raindrops above his head. In the rain and the mist, St
Petersburg seemed to emerge, all streaming with water, from
a deep swamp. Trails of dampness impregnated the walls. In
the air there floated a strange smell of smoke, decay, sea salt
and carbolic. The streets were wide and perfectly straight,
without a tree or a hoarding. Stone façades of imposing
dimensions were everywhere. On the pavements the pedes-

trians moved along elbow to elbow with the same automatic sort of walk. Black umbrellas swayed above their heads. Their faces were pale and anxious. No one strolled or gazed into the shop windows, or stopped to exchange a few words with a stranger; they passed straight on, as if forced along by a fixed idea. Carriages with rubber-tyred wheels rolled along silently on the wet roadway and threw up sprays of dirty water when they passed through the puddles.

The Nevsky Prospect began at the monument to St Alexander Nevsky and stretched for two and a half miles to the Admiralty building, the gilded spire of which pierced the mist above the river. This triumphal route, nearly forty yards wide, was flanked with palaces, churches, government offices and shops: the Anichkov Palace, the residence of the Dowager Empress Marie Fedorovna, the Imperial Library, the Gostiny Dvor, a sort of vaulted arcade with low-built shops and a crowd of silent buyers, the municipal Duma with its granite steps, and the Kazan Cathedral with a colonnade copied from St Peter's in Rome. Alexander Vassilievitch showed Russell that the ikonostasis and balustrade of this cathedral were of solid silver and that the metal used in it had been recaptured by the Don Cossacks from the soldiers of Napoleon's army after the latter had pillaged Moscow's churches. Amongst other marvels, the Cathedral contained the miraculous picture of the Virgin of Kazan, French flags, Imperial eagles, the keys of twenty-eight foreign cities and Marshal Davout's baton. At Alexander Vassilievitch's instructions, the carriage turned slowly left, into the great Morskaya. With its luxury shops, its private hotels and its fashionable restaurants, this artery was the rendezvous for the elegant strollers of St Petersburg. Russell could have believed himself in Paris, in the Rue de la Paix, if a spectacle of Asiatic richness had not suddenly taken his attention. The great Morskaya opened out on to an immense square, or more exactly on to twin squares, one of which surrounded the Imperial Council building and the other the overwhelming St Isaac's Cathedral, built of marble and granite, decorated with monolithic columns and crowned with golden domes. Between these two gigantic buildings – the profane and the sacred – stood the equestrian statue of Nikolas I in the uniform of the

Knights Guards. His wife and three daughters had posed for
the effigies of Justice, Strength, Wisdom and Religion which
encircled the pedestal. Never had a family portrait a less
familiar air!

What a contrast there was between this conventional and
ponderous work and Falconnet's statue of Peter the Great,
situated 500 yards away in a great square near the Senate and
the Synod! The bronze Tsar, dressed as a Roman Emperor,
was forcing his mount to rear on a rock above the abyss. He
hurled defiance at the waters of the Neva, at the pestilential
marshlands, at the whole Russian nation; he held out an arm,
gave the command, and on this desert shore a capital was
born. On the plinth were these words: 'To Peter the First –
Catherine the Second'. The high figure of the monarch was
wrapped in mist. Drops of water streamed over his bronze
face. Pushkin had celebrated the statue in a poem and
Alexander Vassilievitch translated a few of its lines for
Russell's benefit:

> . . . and in thy hold
> A curb of iron, thou sat'st of old
> O'er Russia, on her haunches rearing!

Military music sounded afar off; fifes and drums. Soldiers
marched past in a near-by street, striking the muddy surface
with their boots. All the statues of the emperors must have
quivered with satisfaction. The coachman cracked his whip.
The horses moved off. The line of the embankment appeared.
This was the pride of St Petersburg: a dike of Finnish pink
granite hemmed in the Neva which was here as wide as an
arm of the sea. On the flat and glaucous water lay steamships,
lighters, sailing-boats and rowing-boats. Cranes lowered their
black arms over cargoes of cases and barrels. There were
whistle-blasts, jets of smoke, and the nonchalant coming and
going of stevedores around the merchandise. . . .

Opposite, on the northern shore, was the Cathedral of St
Peter and St Paul, its belfry topped by a thin golden spire,
overlooking the sinister walls of the fortress. This northern
shore was divided into numerous islands by the arms of the
river. The first of these islands was occupied by the St Peter
and St Paul fortress, a prison of dank dungeons where – like

so many other political prisoners – Dostoyevsky spent some months while awaiting trial and deportation in irons to Siberia. On the second island, Vassili Ostrov, rose the University buildings, the Academy of Sciences, the Academy of Fine Arts, the Naval Academy, the Mining Academy, and various scholastic establishments. But Alexander Vassilievitch said that this student city was much less lively than the Latin quarter in Paris. Here a uniformed youth, serious, careworn and generally poor, lived in a boredom of rectilinear vistas and sumptuous barracks built by the emperors for the education of their best subjects. To the north were smaller and less populous islands: the Island of the Apothecaries, with its botanical gardens; the Kamerny Island, with its Church of the Nativity of John the Baptist, Summer Theatre and rich villas; the Ielagin Island, with its palace and fine oak-trees; the Krestovsky Island, with castle, gardens and yacht club; the Petrovsky Island, favoured by Peter the Great, and its park, which was laid out according to his own directions. . . .

In summer, according to Alexander Vassilievitch, all these verdant islands were invaded by city-dwellers hungry for space and fresh air. Restaurants, bandstands, and café-concerts opened up in the groves. The air was alive with the continuous sound of singing and laughter. Crowds turned up to see the sun set in the Gulf of Finland and rise almost at once in the east in the glow of morning, for that was the season of the white nights, of the midnight sun. . . .

But St Petersburg spread its holiday resorts far beyond these islands – as far as Oranienbaum, Peterhof, Gatchina, Pavlovsk and Tsarskoe-Selo, some of these localites having been founded by Peter the Great and others by his successors. Alexander III was fond of Gatchina; Peter the Great had a predilection for Peterhof, where he had two residences built for him by Leblond, named Marly and Mon Plaisir. As to the reigning sovereign, Nikolas II, he retired either to Peterhof or Tsarskoe-Selo with the beginning of the fine weather. At the moment he was still at St Petersburg, and so was all the high aristocracy of which his entourage was composed.

Having passed along the enormous Admiralty building, the carriage turned right into the Winter Palace Square. In the

centre stood Alexander's column, a prodigious monolith of
pink granite, surmounted by an angel bearing a cross. Russell
was able to catch only a glimpse of the monument, the top of
which was lost in mist. The carriage was already making a
wide curve; they returned towards the river and ran up the
Court Embankment. The walls of the Winter Palace
stretched out of sight: they had a brownish-ochre tint, and
were heavy with ornaments and statues. Then came the
Hermitage Palace, the barracks of the Preobrazhensky Regiment, the Grand Duke Alexandrovitch's palace, the Grand
Duke Mikhael Nikolayevitch's palace, the Marble Palace and
other dwellings belonging to the principal families of the
Russian nobility. It seemed to Russell that they were driving
through a rainy Olympus. High dignitaries in uniforms that
were studded with decorations and great ladies in diadems
lived behind the windows at which he dared to gaze as he
passed. He told Alexander Vassilievitch that he would give a
lot to be able to attend a ball at the Winter Palace, but
Alexander Vassilievitch replied that all the money in the
world could not buy him such a favour. If Russell would like
to look at the Tsar and his suite from afar, he would have to
be content with attending a military review on the parade
ground.

'Do you think you could get two good seats in a stand?'
Russell asked.

'I don't know at all,' said Alexander Vassilievitch. 'But I
have influential connections in St Petersburg. I'll try. . . .'

The carriage took a turning and drove back to the city,
passing in front of the Pavlovsky barracks. Then came the
Imperial stables, the Imperial stud, the Mikhail Theatre, and
once again the Nevsky Prospect, a wide misty corridor between two rows of grey façades. In Moscow Russell had
never felt such a penetrating atmosphere of absolute sovereignty. Here the palaces, barracks and ministries jostled one
another. One man in three was in uniform. Each of them
lived with the thought of the Tsar above him. Everything
belonged to the Tsar, from the stones to the souls of men.

'When will there be a review on the parade ground?'
Russell asked.

'Next Sunday,' said Alexander Vassilievitch.

During the next few days, while Alexander Vassilievitch hurried from office to office on his affairs, Russell conscientiously visited the city's principal churches and the Hermitage Museum, which was crammed with wonderful paintings. He went at a steady pace from Rembrandt to Rubens, from Claude Lorrain to Raphael, and from Tintoretto to Chardin. But all these splendid things did not turn him from his fixed idea: he wanted to see the Tsar and his army. At last, on Saturday evening, Alexander Vassilievitch brought the good news: one of his friends, Count Alexis Mikhailovitch Radionov, had got him two seats in the back row of a stand.

'Now we have only to hope for good weather,' said Russell.

'The weather will be good,' said Alexander Vassilievitch; 'that's certain.'

'Why?'

'Haven't you heard of the Tsar's sunshine?'

Russell shook his head. Perhaps, indeed, in this strange land the sun itself was under the Emperor's orders.

*   *   *   *

The sun emerged from the mist just as Alexander Vassilievitch and Russell settled into their seats in one of the high stands kept for the public on the left of the imperial pavilion. An elegant company was assembled there, elbow to elbow, and knee to knee. The women's filmy attire shone out against the dark mass of uniforms and jackets. The silence was filled with innumerable murmurings. On the parade ground the whole guard was assembled in living, quivering immobility. The regiments were like wide bands of varied colours sewn end to end and spangled here and there by the glitter of swords and bayonets. Farther off, at the edge of the parade ground, the crowd seethed dimly. All of a sudden a cry ran from mouth to mouth: 'There he is!'

The Emperor on horseback appeared very far away at the corner of the parade ground. As he came into sight the flags trembled and the music broke out, throwing to the heavens the first notes of *God Save the Tsar*. Nikolas II came on at a gentle gallop along the front of his troops. As he came closer Russell could see his features more clearly. He was of medium height, slender and well proportioned. He wore the white tunic of the Knights Guards, and over it the blue ribbon of the Order of St Andrei. A helmet, topped by the two-headed eagle, stood above his pale face, with its short, round beard. His horse had a light, almost dancing pace. A scarlet cloth covered the saddle. Behind the Tsar came his escort, in uniforms of red, green, white and blue, in helmets, fur caps and plumes, with crosses, medals and fringed epaulettes. A few foreign officers were among the cohort of Russian generals. As he came level with each regiment, the Tsar cried: 'Zdorovo rebyata!' ('Greetings, children!') And each regiment replied in chorus: 'Zdravie zhelaem, Vashe Imperatorskoe Velitchestvo!' ('Good health, Your Imperial Majesty!') The Empress followed in an open carriage drawn by six horses. A great stir greeted her arrival before the tribunes. She took her place in the central pavilion. Around her were other members of the Imperial Family, dignitaries, ministers and courtiers. Nikolas II halted without dismounting. His horse tossed its head up and down. A deafening salvo resounded and the parade began.

The red lines of the Cossacks of the escort moved off first, preceded by their fanfare. The infantry followed in compact masses: first came the Preobrazhensky and Semionovsky Regiments; then the Pavlovsky Regiment, wearing the high gilded mitre of Frederick the Great's grenadiers. The marks of bullets were still to be seen on the oldest headgear, which were real museum pieces. But it was customary to make holes in the metal of the helmets to perpetuate the memory of earlier struggles. The Pavlovsky held their rifles at a slant with two hands, as if for a bayonet charge. The other regiments made their appearance in parade order, dressed in green and divided at intervals by the markers' little pennants. Before passing in front of the Tsar they changed to parade step. The artillery arrived next, at the trot. Scarcely had silence returned than an order sounded in the distance.

The cavalry! Over the whole length of the parade ground, a wall of men and horses emerged from the dust: Knights Guards in silver breastplates, Horse Guards in golden breastplates, yellow Cuirassiers and blue Cuirassiers, the Empress's Uhlans armed with lances bearing pennants with their colours, Horse Grenadiers with chenille helmets ending in a strip of yellow and red material floating in the wind, the Emperor's Hussars in gold-embroidered vermilion tunics, blue breeches and white dolmans with black fur on the shoulders, the Emperor's Cossacks in purple tunics, bearing lances, the Heir Apparent's Cossacks in light blue uniform. ... The torrent rolled along to the very foot of the tribunes. The ladies made a movement of recoil, as if they were afraid of being run down by the wave. The Tsar's hand went to his helmet. But at the instant they reached the imperial pavilion, the riders stopped dead; then, starting an elegant curve, they made off along the platforms reserved for the guests. The weather was clear and Russell already saw a line of silky cruppers drawing away, their tails beating the air. He wanted to applaud, but the crowd kept quiet. In the distance shrill bugle-calls vibrated.

Alexander Vassilievitch murmured: 'A very fine parade. It couldn't have been better even in Moscow.'

On returning to their hotel, Russell's legs were stiff and his back ached as if he had been on a horse all morning.

That same evening Alexander Vassilievitch had invited Count Alexis Mikhailovitch Radionov to dinner; he was the friend who had got them the seats at the review, and Russell had the honour of being introduced to this eminent person in the restaurant of the Hotel de l'Europe. Without a definite job at Court, Alexis Mikhailovitch Radionov was present nevertheless at all official receptions, and was delighted to tell Russell about the life of the Imperial Family and its entourage.

According to this expert in etiquette, there was no court in Europe where the staff was as varied and the hierarchy as complicated as in the Russian Court. At the head of the whole palace administration was the Minister of the Imperial Court. Below him were the Grand Marshal of the Court, the Grand Chamberlain of the Court, and the Grand Master of the Court, who formed the upper level of the pyramid, with the Cup-Bearer, the Esquire Trenchant, the Master of the Horse and the Master of the Hunt. Almost all these gentlemen were state officials of the second class (privy councillors, or generals of infantry, cavalry or artillery) and had the right as such to the title 'Your High Excellency'. The state officials of the next class (privy councillors and councillors of state) performed the functions of Marshal of the Court, Grand Master of Ceremonies, Master of the Court, Chamberlain, Equerry and Huntsman, and were addressed as 'Your Excellency'. Lesser functions were those of Masters of Ceremonies, Gentlemen of the Chamber, and so on.

The female staff at court was smaller and less varied. The Empress's court consisted of a Grand Mistress, and several ladies of honour and maids of honour. The lesser courts, those of the Grand Duchesses, consisted of a smaller number of ladies and maids of honour.

These arrangements dated from the time of Alexander III, who had a taste for display. Nikolas II, on the other hand, was simpler. Temperamentally modest and indecisive, and by choice a solitary, he spent as little time as possible at St Petersburg, where the excitement upset him, and preferred to live quietly with his family at Peterhof or Tsarskoe-Selo. The Empress Alexandra Fedorovna, who was impressionable and uncommunicative, shared her husband's feelings and was only really happy when away from the crowd and among her four daughters. At this date, 1903, the eldest, Olga Nikolayevna, was eight years old; then came Tatiana Nikolayevna, six; Maria Nikolayevna, four, and Anastasia Nikolayevna, two.[1]

At Tsarskoe-Selo there were two principal palaces: the Catherine Palace (the old palace), which was used for big dinners, receptions and ceremonies, and the Alexander Palace (the new palace), where the Emperor led a steady patriarchal life amongst his own folk. Rising at eight o'clock, he bathed in a leisurely fashion, and breakfasted alone (tea with milk, and rolls or biscuits) in the rosewood room. If the Empress was awake by this time, he took his meal with her in their room. Immediately afterwards he went to his office to listen to various reports. First came the duty A.D.C., the Grand Marshal of the Court and the Palace Commander. The Grand Marshal discussed only questions concerning ceremonial, but the Commander, who was personally responsible for the Tsar's safety, brought political and police matters to his attention. After the Commander came ministers or high officials

[1]The Grand Duke Alexis Nikolayevitch was born later, on July 30, 1904.

summoned from St Petersburg. When these audiences were over, the Emperor took a walk in the park with his dogs. Then he usually ate a snack – *borsch, kasha, kvass*; these eatables (*proba*) were brought him in a covered dish by a warrant-officer. After midday he received visitors of less importance. Lunch was served at one o'clock. The menus were prepared three days in advance by the staff of the Marshal of the Court and submitted to the Empress, who approved or modified them as she thought fit. Lunch – to which came mostly a few of the Tsar's friends – comprised four courses besides *hors-d'œuvre*. Nikolas II ate moderately, preferred the Russian cuisine, often asked for sucking-pig with horseradish, never ate fresh caviar (having once suffered serious indigestion from having taken an excessive quantity), drank a glass of vodka before sitting down to table, and during a meal preferred to drink port.

After lunch he returned to work until half-past three; again he walked in the park, and at five o'clock took tea with the Empress, while he browsed in Russian and foreign newspapers. From six till eight there were further audiences. Dinner was at eight, with five courses. At about half-past nine Nikolas II retired to his office once more, examined a few dossiers, then rejoined the Empress and ended the evening chatting or reading aloud at her side. When she was not with her husband, the Empress spent her time at embroidery, talking to her ladies of honour or walking in the park with her children.

This timetable was modified, of course, on days of religious or military ceremony.

To ensure the safety of the sovereign, the Palace Commander had the following under his orders: (1) His Majesty's personal escort and the combined battalion of the Guard, which together provided the sentries within the palace and the park; (2) the palace police, who watched the neighbouring streets and, in accordance with a register, supervised the comings and goings of persons summoned to an audience; (3) the first railway battalion, which kept watch on the line from St Petersburg to Tsarskoe-Selo; (4) the duty guard, entrusted with the protection of the Imperial Family on its journeys.

Nikolas II's closest relatives, Grand Dukes and Grand

Duchesses frequently came to Tsarskoe-Selo on friendly or formal visits. The Dowager Empress usually resided at Gachina. But she never failed to join her son for Easter. On Easter Sunday the Emperor's entourage gathered to offer him their greetings. From ten in the morning the rooms of the Alexander Palace were full of people. Then the various court services in full dress passed one after the other into the drawing-room where the Tsar and Tsarina stood. First, the priests and cantors of the Imperial Chapel moved forward in their gold-braided crimson caftans. Behind them came the gardeners with baskets of flowers and fruit, the members of the palace farriery with the Grand Farrier leading, the fourriers of the chamber in vermilion uniform and white stockings, the officiating priests in scarlet, the couriers in black and their hats ornamented with ostrich plumes in the imperial colours, the Arabs in turbans with oriental shawls over their shoulders, the butlers, the cooks, the scullions, and the lesser kitchen staff. These had scarcely retired bowing when the Master of the Horse brought the officers of equitation and harnessing before the Tsar, the elegant Italian halberdier in elk-skin breeches, with gold-embroidered white jacket and varnished boots. Behind him, as if for contrast, came the coachmen in long wadded greatcoats with pleated backs, tied with silk scarves; numerous medals shone on their broad chests, and their hair, which was cut in the Russian style, glistened with oil. The stablemen and washers followed in their footsteps. They soon gave place to the huntsmen, guards and beaters of the Imperial Hunt. Next came the Palace Commander's men and the Tsarskoe-Selo police, and the heads and deputy heads of all departments of the court administration. Hundreds of visitors thus filed into the room which was decorated with enormous sheafs of lilac and roses. In the middle stood the Emperor in full uniform, but simple and smiling. The Empress sat at his side in an armchair. The Minister of the Imperial Court, the Grand Mistress of the Court, the ladies and maids of honour and a few members of the suite stood behind them. Baskets of coloured eggs stood on the long tables. Each employee, whatever his rank, advanced to the Emperor.

'*Khristos voskrese*,' said Nikolas II.

'Vo istinu voskresse,' was the reply.

Then the Emperor and his subject kissed three times. After a deep bow, the palace servant approached the Empress, who offered him an Easter egg and said: 'Khristos voskrese.'

The servant replied: 'Vo istinu voskrese,' took the egg and kissed the Empress's hand.

The eggs for those of lower rank were large and of fine porcelain and came from the imperial factories. The dignitaries had the right to smaller eggs of various stones from the Urals cut in the imperial factory at Peterhof. The Dowager Empress received staff greetings in a near-by room. At the end of the ceremony, Their Majesties went to the Library to hear the choir of the Imperial Chapel. Count Radionov reckoned that in two days more than 1,600 persons passed before Nikolas II in this way.

However, it was not on this occasion that the Court could be seen in all its splendour. Whoever wished to see St Petersburg high society around its master could not do better than be present at a grand ball at the Winter Palace. The season of grand balls was over, and Russell had to make do with Radionov's enthusiastic description of them.

From early in the day the heralds of the Imperial Household ran through the city bearing from house to house the list of those invited that evening. Usually everyone had known the date of the ball for a long time, but the official invitation was an order given on the same day. According to etiquette, it freed one from all previous engagements to private persons and relieved one even of the duties of mourning. The loss of one's dearest did not exempt one from appearing at this function. Moreover, no woman could appear before the Emperor and Empress in black, except when the deceased was a kinsman of the royal family.

The opening of the ball was timed for nine o'clock, but the guests had to be assembled well in advance, to await the entrance of the Tsar. Lines of sleighs and carriages glided towards the brilliantly lit palace from all parts of the city. Shawl-covered figures, wrapped in fur-lined coats, crowded upon the snow-covered steps. Having taken their masters to their destination, the coachmen crowded around the fires that had been lit in the corrugated-iron shelters. While this bivouac swelled in the frozen square, furs fell from the naked shoulders in the glittering marble and crystal vestibule. A procession of uniforms and dresses with trains, diadems and decorations, swords and fans, spread into the great gallery and ascended the staircase of honour between two rows of Knights Guards, motionless giants in breastplates and feathered helmets. In the immense White Room the statues looked down upon a landscape of palms and roses. The crowd of guests undulated gently under the lights of the chandeliers, and all eyes were already fixed on the doors through which the Emperor would enter.

In the first ranks of notable persons were the old 'portrait' ladies, so called because they wore upon their corsages a miniature of their sovereign framed with brilliants. They were zealous guardians of etiquette and living chronicles of Court life, and they cast a strict eye upon the bevy of maids of honour, who were recognizable by the diamond monogram of the reigning Empress on their left shoulders. These maids of honour were chosen from families of exceptional merit or of high birth. Their prestige was great in St Petersburg society. But most of them paled before the famous beauties of the capital. Graceful young women, crowned with plumes and jewels, passed through the hall in a wave of rustling materials. Men of all ages crowded around them. Amongst their admirers were ancient and worn-out dignitaries of the Court, ministers, and chamberlains with the golden key on their backs. All the serious servants of the Empire were decorated with broad ribbons, studded with decorations, so that there was not an empty space on their breasts. By contrast, their age gave even greater presence to the young officers of the élite regiments: the Knights Guards and the Horse Guards, who carried their massive eagle-crowned helmets in the crook of their arms, the Lancers with their red breastplates, the Hussars of the Guard with white gold-braided dolmans, and the wasp-waisted Circassian Princes with damascene daggers.

From minute to minute, curiosity, impatience, and a kind of anxiety grew amongst the Tsar's guests. Then it was nine o'clock and all movement suddenly froze, conversations stopped one by one, and the main door opened its two leaves.

In the deathly silence a loud voice cried: 'His Imperial Majesty!'

The Emperor came forward in uniform, escorted by all the members of his family, each in the place assigned to him by the degree of his kinship. The orchestra, grouped in a thicket of green plants, launched upon the opening bars of the traditional polonaise. The Grand Marshal and the Grand Mistress of the Court led the procession. The Emperor gave his hand to one of the Grand Duchesses, and the Empress gave hers to the doyen of the Diplomatic Corps. The other couples formed up in their turn and circled the hall with measured tread. This graceful musical promenade was followed by quadrilles, waltzes, and mazurkas. . . . Alexis Mikhailovitch Radionov flushed as he recalled the excitement of the ball:

'What dresses, my dear fellow! What jewels! Every diadem, every necklace is worth a hundred thousand roubles! A simple ribbon is held by a plaque of precious stones worth a fortune! Some apparently plain robes cost more than the dalmatics and brocades of gold and silver! But all this is nothing compared with the fancy-dress balls which are also held in the Winter Palace. On the last occasion, Their Majesties appeared in Russian costumes of the seventeenth century, like those worn by the tsars and tsarinas before Peter the Great. It was a riot of brilliants, pearls, precious stones, silks, velvet and rare furs. The Empress's robe itself weighed two pouds (over 70 lb.). Her long cloth-of-gold cloak was fastened across the breast with a clasp of enormous rubies, undoubtedly the finest in the Imperial Treasury. These clothes were as stiff as a suit of armour, and our beloved sovereigns looked just like the ancient ikons!'

❈   ❈   ❈   ❈

From Alexis Mikhailovitch Radionov's tales and Alexander Vassilievitch's comments, it did not take Russell long to realize that St Petersburg high society was very different from that of Moscow. In the imperial capital, social circles were stricter than anywhere else. A man could achieve a brilliant career in the service of the State, become a general, a privy councillor, or even a minister, but the doors of certain salons would still be closed to him if he was not well born or if he had compromised himself by a misalliance. A certain diplomat, who had been officially received by the Emperor, was ignored by the noble families of the Empire for this reason. On the other hand, the same families would suddenly take a fancy to some young man of no standing, because he was obsequious and witty. He would be pushed along, encouraged, and put on the road to success.

But the leading part played by aristocratic circles seemed less strange to Russell than the part played by the clubs, the number of which was incalculable. But whereas in England a club was a place where men escaped from their wives, in Russia clubs mostly had a family character.

In St Petersburg every class of society had its club. At the top was the Imperial Yacht Club on the Morskaya. It had only 150 members and was regarded as the most aristocratic in the capital: the Grand Dukes, the high dignitaries of the Court, and the Tsar's aides-de-camp formed its nucleus. A few foreign diplomats were admitted to it temporarily. How many men, strolling along the Morskaya, cast an envious glance at the sanctuary where the most famous servants of the Empire were gathered! A man who had hitherto been quite unassuming and kindly became a monument of coldness, self-importance and authority if, after secret scrutiny, he was considered worthy to belong to the élite of the Imperial Yacht Club. From one day to the next he became dogmatic about everything, with the assurance of a minister. He would say: 'The Yacht Club thinks this . . .' or 'The Yacht Club reckons . . .' Such vanity was not unfounded, for most people to be found there were familiars of the Emperor. Thanks to their connections, the members of the Yacht Club could aspire to the most distinguished careers. It was in these rooms that the candidates for important administrative posts, for the honorary Court functions, and for command of the Guards regiments, were recruited. Here, as in the army, *esprit de corps* implied a robust unity of thought, responsibility and sentiment.

The English Club (founded in 1770 with the approval of Catherine II) was once the choice of political men: affairs of State were discussed there between games of chess. With time it had lost its air of great wisdom, but the number of its members was still limited, and many men grew old and embittered before they achieved the honour of becoming one of them. Neither musical evenings nor balls were given there, for the members preferred good food and cards.

The New Club (*Novyi Klub*), recently founded at the instance of the Grand Duke Vladimir, was more modern in spirit than the English Club, its neighbour on the Court Embankment. At the New Club the rich young men crowded together: one gambled there for high stakes, retailed the latest gossip from behind the scenes, from antechambers and alcoves, and in the long run one acquired an unquestionable stamp of elegance. Women were not admitted to this establishment – where, nevertheless, their praises were sung – except on a few great occasions.

The River Yacht Club (*Retchnoi Yacht Klub*) was restricted mainly to sportsmen. Its members went in for yachting and even tennis. Many foreign yachtsmen were members.

The other clubs, where ladies were admitted, either to special evenings or in the normal way, were the Noble Assembly (*Blagorodnye Sobranie*) which in days gone by had received illustrious foreign musicians, such as Rubini, Alboni and Liszt; the Arts Society of St Petersburg, devoted to theatrical performances, *tableaux vivants* and sing-songs; the Dance Society, a name which describes its activities; the Commercial Club, which was a meeting-place of wholesalers; the Merchants' Club, where the wives of these gentlemen displayed an ostentatious luxury; the Shop Assistants' Club, where only employees were received; and so on.

To balance this mass of Petersburgian clubs, Alexander Vassilievitch named some Muscovite clubs: the English Club, as aristocratic as its namesake in the capital, the Nobles' Club, the Merchants' Club, the German Club, the Arts Club, the Musical Circle ... But in Moscow the clubs were not so open to women as they were in St Petersburg.

If these two great cities were rivals in worldliness, they were equally so in matters of art and literature. It seemed to Russell that in cultured Russian society the passion for poetry, novels, the theatre, music and painting was more intense and more sincere than among the same social groups in England and France. It is true, of course, that public enthusiasm is not always evidence of good taste. The pompous Munich style had its admirers. But the rich Moscow merchants, Shchukin and Morozov, were already buying impressionist canvases which nobody wanted in Paris. Thanks to them the names of Manet, Monet, Renoir and Cézanne were better known in Russia than in France. Another rich Moscow merchant, Ostrukhov, was devoting part of his wealth to acquiring old ikons. Yet another, Soldatenkov, spent his money unstintingly to facilitate the publication at a very low price of the books necessary to the country's intellectual development. As to the brothers Tretiakov, who were enthusiastic collectors, Moscow was indebted to them for the largest collection of contemporary Russian pictures.

In St Petersburg, Serge Diaghilev and the painters Somov and Benois founded the review *Mir Iskusstva* (*The World of Art*, 1897), while another review, *Novy Poryt* (*The New Way*), brought the thinkers and philosophers of the younger generation together. Tolstoy and Chekov still dominated the novel and the theatre, but on all sides people of new and fiery talent were rising, bursting with daring comments and getting together in coteries, clubs and schools. The poets of Moscow gathered around Briussov, those of St Petersburg around Zinaida Hippius, Merezhkhovsky and Fedor Sologub. The general public was not very well informed about the different theories which stirred the writers known as 'modern', but the whole of Russia's cultured society lived in a state of creative fever. Hundreds of students would sacrifice all their savings to hear Chaliapin or Sobinov, or to be present at a performance at the Arts Theatre, or to be captivated once again by the bitter and tragic voice of Komissarzhevskaya. A frenzied love of the theatre seemed to Russell one of the main traits of the Russian character. Families in comfortable circumstances took their children to the opera and ballet while they were still very young, and 'to play at theatre' was the favourite pastime of every schoolboy.

In the previous century, parallel with the great imperial theatres, gentlemen had founded private theatres where actors who were the slaves of their talents performed. About 1825 a Moscow merchant named Varguin had organized a company in his own house which, as it developed, had

11 Nikolas II
and the Empress
Alexandra in
the robes of
the Tsars and
Tsarinas before
the times of
Peter the Great

low: The Winter Palace, St Petersburg, on the occasion of a ball

12 Nizhni-Novgorod with the barges gathering on the waterfront

A street scene in Nizhni-Novgorod

assumed the name of the Maly Theatre (Little Theatre). This stage was to produce the finest works of Russian dramatic art: *The Misfortune of having Too Much Sense*, by Griboyedov, who depicted the noble officials in all their dullness and servility, Gogol's *Revizor*, a violent satire on the ways of the Government, plays by Ostrovsky, in which the author denounced the brutality, ignorance and cupidity of the merchants, and the dramas of Tolstoy.... There was a saying among the students that 'one learns science at the University and life at the Little Theatre'.

At the beginning of the twentieth century there were five public theatres in Russia directly dependent upon the Imperial Government: they were attached to the Ministry of the Court. In St Petersburg: the Marie Theatre[1] (opera and ballet), the Alexandra Theatre (drama and comedy), the Mikhail Theatre (where there was a permanent French company and where, in the Russian language, only classics were usually presented). In Moscow: the Grand Theatre (opera and ballet) and the Little Theatre, which has been mentioned above.[2] The nobles and dignitaries of the Empire reckoned that their presence at ballet and opera at the Marie Theatre was both a privilege and an obligation. For performances on Tuesdays and Fridays (opera) and on Sundays (opera in the afternoons, ballet in the evening) one could, with a little luck, obtain tickets at the box office, or with greater certainty (and by paying rather more) from the numerous people who loitered around the building with tickets for resale. On other days almost all the seats were reserved by season-ticket. The Russian aristocracy, faithful to the Marie Theatre, appreciated also the French plays at the Mikhail Theatre. The Alexandra Theatre, on the other hand, was frequented by the lesser nobility, the intellectuals, officials, merchants and students.

In 1883 Tsar Alexander III had finally abolished the monopoly of the imperial theatres, opening the way to private enterprise in the drama. At once many companies were formed in the two capitals: the Korch Theatre in Moscow, the

[1] As an indication, the Marie Theatre had 2,000 seats, and the price of first-tier boxes was 16 roubles 10 for the ballet and 19 roubles 40 for operas.
[2] The Little Theatre was burnt down in 1901.

Suvorin Theatre in St Petersburg. Mamontov, a business man, decided to reform the Russian opera which was in danger of being stifled by conventions. He gave his patronage to Mussorgsky, from whom the 'connoisseurs' turned away ironically, helped Rimsky-Korsakov to force *Snegurotchka*, *Tsar Saltan* and *Le Coq d'Or* upon the public, and gave encouragement to Chaliapin, who had been dismissed from the Marie Theatre for 'incompetence'. Another melomaniac, Belayev, organized chamber-music evenings at his own home. The principal habitués of this little circle were Rimsky-Korsakov, Borodin, Glazunov, Blumenfeld. . . .

Meanwhile, the real reform of the stage was prepared at a restaurant in Moscow. There, on June 22, 1897, the young actor and prime mover, Stanislavsky, met the dramatist Nemirovitch-Danchenko, and during a heated argument laid down the conditions for the rebirth of the Russian theatre. From their discussion the famous Moscow Arts Theatre was born, and it was a Moscow merchant, Sava Morozov, who financed this revolutionary enterprise. The new building of the Moscow Arts Theatre was inaugurated in 1902 as a result of his subsidy. But the St Petersburgers realized this time that the Muscovites had completed a stage in the competition between the two cities. Alexis Mikhailovitch Radionov declared that Moscow had turned it to good account, but that did not prevent him from insisting on keeping Zubov and Russell at St Petersburg.

'Why are you in such a hurry to catch the train?' he asked. 'In a few days we shall be celebrating the bicentenary of the foundation of St Petersburg. You really must be there. Their Majesties are going to inaugurate the Troïtsky Bridge over the Neva opposite the Peter and Paul fortress.'

Dazzled by this prospect, Russell hoped for a moment that Alexander Vassilievitch would agree to prolong their stay in the capital, but the latter excused himself on the ground that urgent business was calling him back to Moscow.

CHAPTER XIII

THE PEASANTS

Life in the country – Interior of an isba *– The bath-houses – Village festivals – Dances, songs and costumes – Making* lapti *– A pedlar – Origins of the moujik – The* mir *in relation to the communal council – The moujik at home: patriarchal and other customs – Marriage rites – Nuptial laments – Work in the home – Seasonal migrations of the moujiks – Their primitive piety – The* Beguny *sect – Various superstitions – Russian folklore – Popular sayings – The political education of agricultural workers – Agrarian troubles*

WHEN the fine weather began Moscow took on a new look. Even the plainest women managed to greet the sunshine with bright-coloured kerchiefs and skirts. Soldiers and students sported their summer outfits. There were white shirts and helmets everywhere. Many men had their heads shaved.

It was regarded as good form to have a villa on the outskirts of Moscow, and the Zubovs had one. With the month of July the whole family moved there, and Russell went with them. The Zubovs' country house was both charming and decrepit; the walls were cream, with a touch of pink; there was a pillared flight of steps, a large garden, a birch wood, a pond, a kitchen garden, an aviary, a playing-field and swings for the children. The days were pleasantly spent in walks, fishing-parties, croquet matches and charades.

The tea ceremony played a very important part in the life of a Russian family on holiday. Tatiana Sergeyevna, seated at the end of the table beside the samovar, presided over the handing round. Having prepared a very strong infusion in the teapot, she poured the dark and scented essence into cups for the ladies and glasses for the men, and diluted it with boiling water from the samovar. If one asked for a second cup, the lady of the house rinsed the cup and dried it with a little embroidered cloth before refilling it in the same way. On the table were fruit, jams, honey, patisseries, slices of watermelon and small jugs of soft drinks. This meal lasted from four till six in the afternoon.

Alexander Vassilievitch and Paul Egorovitch were often obliged to return to Moscow on business. As they accompanied the men to the little station, the women pitied them for having to leave for the difficulties, the heat and worries of the city. But actually this feminine pity was slightly qualified by the idea that perhaps, after working hours, the two men would find distraction with the tzigane singers. For greater convenience Tatiana Sergeyevna had brought only half her staff to the country. Thus the husbands would not be without help in Moscow. After three or four days away, they returned, weary, important and happy, to the verdant retreat where the ladies awaited them, smiling, in their floral gowns. When rain threatened, the men played billiards in the Russian fashion. Parties with neighbours were sometimes organized on the veranda.

When he could escape from social obligations, Russell went for walks in the country. Paul Egorovitch Sychkin gladly went with him on these excursions. As they moved away from the railways the two men moved backwards in time. In one hour's walking from the comfortable Zubov villa there began the crude, disturbing, attractive world of the Russian moujiks. From one visit to another Russell learned to know them better.

All the villages resembled one another: a little church with a bulbous steeple, a well, some geese, some hens scratching in the dust, sunflowers lifting their great yellow heads above a fence, and a few cabins of logs that were fitted closely together and made draught-proof with oakum packing. Inside was a small single room with a large stove, all smoke-blackened, with benches along the wall, a table and, in the corner, lit by night-lights, the holy pictures to which the visitor had to bow before greeting the master of the house. The best place to sleep was the one reserved by the moujik for himself, on the oven: it was warm there in winter and cool in summer. Sometimes he took his wife there with him, or a sick child. But mostly the women, girls and boys slept on the floor on piles of rags, or in the barn. It was not the custom to undress for the night, but the men took off their boots or bark sandals to air their feet. The flies loved this dim menagerie-like stench: they buzzed in swarms around the copper samovar. Earthenware plates, wooden spoons, goat-skins hanging from nails, everything there was wretched.

But in Russia every village of any importance had its bath-house. The population crowded there on the eve of a feast day. In these steam baths men and women sweated separately until they almost swooned, flogged themselves to stimulate circulation, and scratched and scoured themselves with pitiless frenzy. Afterwards, in the winter, the more courageous ones rolled in the snow; in the summer they all dressed again and, made thirsty by such violent sweating, went to a traktir to quench it.

A religious festival was always accompanied by a copious meal. The members of a family gathered together at the home of the grandfather or father whom they had left in order to set up homes of their own. Now that the tribe was together again for a few hours, it showed its gratitude to the head of the tribe by eating heavily and drinking hard. Besides the relatives, there were friends, pilgrims, neighbours, and beggars, 'sent by the Lord'. Russian hospitality was no legend and its gastronomic character was confirmed by numerous proverbs such as: *Chto v pechi, to na stol mechi* (Bring to the table everything you can find in the oven); *Ne krasna izba uglami, a krasna pirogami* (The house is not made beautiful by its rooms but by its pies). The very word hospitality in Russian, *khlebosolstvo*, was derived from two words: *khleb* and *sol*, bread and salt. The poorest peasants saved their money to be able, on certain dates, to organize serious feasting. These feasts usually lasted the whole day. They ate, drank, went out to stretch their limbs and get some air, and then sat down to table again with a new appetite. While the old folk gorged and groaned with pleasure, the young ones amused themselves in the meadow. The band consisted invariably of an accordion and a balalaïka, a species of mandolin with a triangular body. The girls, holding hands, formed *khorovody*, in other words, they danced around and sang popular songs. The boys, not far away, with jovial faces and bent knees, frenziedly flung one leg out after another to the maddening beat of a *trepak* or a *cossack*. Sometimes the bolder boys attempted to hug a girl. Then there were shouts, excited laughter and such vigorous rebuffs that the gallant fellow would find himself on his back in the grass. Around the swings (*kacheli*), an indispensable item at every celebration, there was much shouting and laughter. Peasant women sat astride the plank that hung on ropes. At each end of this small bench, stout young fellows set it swinging to and fro by flexing and straightening their knees alternately.

For holidays the women dressed in the *sarafan*, a brightly coloured frock with shoulder-straps, covering an embroidered shirt. Some of them wore the *kakochuik*, a red or blue diadem ornamented with glass trinkets. Others wore simple scarves knotted over their heads. Around their necks hung long necklets of multicoloured beads. The men had cut their hair as if with a basin. The young men were beardless, but the old men wore full beards; all of them wore blouse-shaped cotton shirts that buttoned at the side and hung outside, linen or wool trousers that were stuffed into their boots. For the moujik a fine pair of boots was a sign of elegance. The poorest made do with *lapti*, a sort of sandal made of the plaited bark of lime-trees.

In June the whole village joined forces to cut down some limes in the vicinity. Next began the delicate operation of detaching the first two layers of bark. When the weather was warm and humid the tree could be stripped easily, but in cold and dry weather there was no sap in the fibres, and even with an axe it was difficult to separate the superimposed layers. Each of these layers had its use in the peasant's domestic economy. The first skin was used for roofing houses; the second skin, taken mainly from young lime-trees, was put into water and was left soaking all the summer. When winter began it was piled up in a warm room, and when thoroughly dried was cut into strips and plaited to make *lapti*. A moujik often used two or three pairs of *lapti* a week. He liked this kind of footwear, which left his feet free, did not retain moisture for long and cost nothing.

No village festival was complete without a pedlar, or *korobeinik*.[1] An indefatigable walker, the *korobeinik* came

[1] From the word *korob* = a box.

from distant places, carrying an enormous black bundle strapped to his shoulders. He was always dressed in a black frock-coat of an antiquated shape, a black waistcoat decorated with metal or glass buttons, black trousers and a cap with a black peak. Sometimes the man had a horse and cart to transport his goods, in which case he slowly walked the roads beside his horse. He had scarcely arrived in some hamlet when the whole population hurried out to meet him. The women stood enraptured at the cretonnes and the brilliantly coloured prints which he spread before them. One of them, with flushed cheeks and eyes shining covetously, tried on a necklace of glass beads, while another, clinging to a pair of green ear-rings, plunged her hand into the piles of multi-coloured ribbons, and a third begged the pedlar to accept a roll of thread, which she herself had plaited, in exchange for a little ikon. But the pedlar was not listening, being too occupied in negotiating the sale of a silk belt to a rich, bearded, paunchy moujik. Paul Egorovitch, who watched such an incident with Russell, translated the conversation.

'Well!' cried the moujik in an assured voice, 'shall we shake hands on it?'

'Add another 50 kopecks,' the pedlar begged, bowing low, 'Christ is my witness that even so I shall get nothing out of this but our friendship.'

'Enough of these lies! I'm certain you're robbing me of a rouble.'

'If I robbed all my customers of roubles I should now be a merchant in Moscow,' the pedlar replied, winking maliciously.

'Very well, then. Let's split the difference. I'll give you another twenty-five kopecks!'

'One feather more or less makes no difference to a pillow! Make it thirty-five kopecks and it's yours!'

Meanwhile some urchins were prowling around the spiced and sugared buns, longingly fingering the wonderful whistles cut in the shape of birds, horses or serpents, or sniffing the air near the piles of caramels screwed up in shiny paper. The pedlar unwrapped vessels of coloured wood, books, ikons, kerchiefs or *lubochnye kartiny*, a 'tuppence coloured' sheet of pictures representing the generals Ermolov and Skobelev surrounded by mythological figures, the Tsar, the Tsarina, or the torment of sinners in Hell.

After the pedlar's departure, the objects he had sold apparently lost half their attraction in the hands of their owners. The colours faded, the laughter died out, and everyday life was resumed.

＊ ＊ ＊ ＊

Once there had been two kinds of serfs: those who were tied to the soil (*krepostnye*) and those who were tied to the master (*dvorovye*). The *dvorovye* were not involved in agriculture, but served in the master's house as porters, cooks, valets and coachmen. They could be sold at any moment and into no matter what conditions. The *krepostnye*, however, could not be removed from the soil they cultivated, and if the proprietor sold them properly, they passed under the authority of the purchaser without the boundaries of their fields being affected by it. Thus in the course of centuries the idea had taken deep root in the minds of the moujiks that the land was theirs, although their persons belonged to the master. The master could deprive them of everything except the land.[1] When, on February 19, 1861, Alexander II promulgated the law emancipating the serfs, the latter received the news with a joy that was mixed with anxiety. According to this law, the *dvorovye* must, for two more years, either pay a fee to the master (30 roubles per man and 10 roubles per woman), or guarantee him personal service. After this brief interval they were free but, of course, received no share of the land. Thus a class of permanent servants was created. The treatment of the *krepostnye*, on the other hand, was inspired by the anxiety both to give land to former serfs and to safeguard, as far as possible, the right of the owners. The latter therefore found that they were forced to give the moujiks a part of their domains, but subject to compensation in accordance with a scale annexed to the act. The application of these extremely complex terms was entrusted to an arbitrator, chosen from amongst the nobility. The latter's decisions could be submitted to a special court composed of the nobles

[1] The Russian peasants were enslaved and tied to the master's land only at the end of the sixteenth century by a decision of the Tsar Boris Gudonov.

of the Government. And it was the Senate, the noble assembly *par excellence*, which judged the differences in the last resort. This aspect of the reform aroused the suspicions of the moujiks; dimly convinced that they were the owners of the plots they cultivated, they were astonished that they now had to pay for them. Doubtless the owners had distorted the Emperor's generous ideas! One day the truth would out! The Tsar would issue a new 'ukase', written 'in letters of gold', to make clear that he gave the moujiks both their liberty and their land.

But the years passed; the 'ukase in letters of gold' was slow in appearing, and the moujiks reckoned that, although they were freed from bodily servitude, other restraints weighed upon them. In fact, to make it possible for them to acquire their enclosures and portions (*nadel*) rapidly, the State had granted them long-term loans. It was the State which, in their stead, had paid the purchase price (*obrok*) to the landowners in letters of credit. Afterwards, the State turned to the moujiks to claim an annual payment of six kopecks for every rouble advanced, the capital being fully redeemed in forty-nine years. Thereafter every connection was broken between the former masters and the peasants. But the latter remained debtors to the State which, to secure its debt, imposed responsibility for payment upon the commune, represented by the popular assembly known as the *mir*. Formerly, it had been the master who had accepted the responsibility for tax collection: if he was harsh he flogged the negligent payer, but ended by sending the taxes where they were intended; if he was a good man, he might pay the debt himself out of laziness or pity. But the *mir* was intractable. This assembly of peasants accepted no excuses from their fellows who, by misfortune or mistake, jeopardized the interests of the community. According to Paul Egorovitch Sychkin, many moujiks, overwhelmed by care, felt a nostalgia for the days of serfdom. Once they had been like children, without rights, vaguely oblivious and without initiative; but now they had become adults overnight, with instructions to steer their own way through life. 'Things were better in the masters' days,' the old folk said. 'At least, we didn't have to worry about the future. We were sure of eating our fill. The master did the thinking for us. . . .'

On the other hand, the young folk had already adapted themselves to the new situation. At present every peasant owned a plot of land but, at the same time, as a member of the commune, he was co-proprietor of an inalienable communal plot, the control of which rested with the *mir*.

The *mir*, or *skhod*, was a popular body which met at the request of any member of the commune. If two peasants had a disagreement, they went at once to the *starosta*, the elected leader of the village; and if the *starosta* did not succeed in conciliating the two points of view, they declared: '*Mir nass rassudit!*' ('The *mir* will judge between us.') At these words the *starosta* was obliged to call the *mir* together. An urchin ran off and stopped at every house, every enclosure and every crossing, to summon the peasants. An hour or two later the *mir*, meeting in the *starosta*'s *izba*, listened to the two parties and, after some discussion, gave judgement that was immediately enforcible.

The *mir* also met to hear Government communications, to concern itself with the guardianship of minors, to share out the taxes which fell upon the village and to distribute amongst the peasants the land that belonged to the commune. Of this land there were three categories: rich, medium and poor. Each of these categories was itself divided into as many plots as there were members of the *mir*: lots were drawn and each peasant received a piece of each kind of soil. Woodlands and other outlying parts were not shared out. In practice, this parcelling-up sometimes posed insoluble problems, and plaintiffs went to a higher level, the *volost*, a sort of council comprising the elected representatives of several communes (one representative for every ten households). The *volost*, presided over by a *starchina*, had a permanent council, the *volost*'s regency, and a court composed of three elected judges. A cantonal chief, or *zemskii nachalnik*, watched closely on behalf of the Government the use which the moujiks made of their new-found freedom.[1]

The institution of the *mir* was, in fact, inspired by the customs of Russian peasant families. These families, with their patriarchal traditions, were *mirs* in miniature. Supreme authority belonged to the father or the grandfather, so long

[1] See the earlier chapter on local government in Russia.

as he kept his wits. Often, after marriage, the sons remained with their parents. Thus several households lived under the same roof and worked in the same field. Such cohabitation was not without its consequences. It was not seldom that an 'old one', still in his prime, coveted his daughter-in-law, who was always before his eyes. It was generally when the son left to do his military service that the father replaced him beside the young forsaken wife. Accustomed to this kind of abuse, the people described them by the generic word *snokhach-estvo* (from *snokha*, daughter-in-law). There is an anecdote about this sort of thing. In the Government of Voronezh the moujiks had bought a bell, but, when they came to hang it in the belfry their combined efforts were not enough. Persuaded that the bell was weighed down by the sins of the men who were trying to get it into position, the village 'pope' ordered all those whose feelings for their daughters-in-law were too great to withdraw. To everyone's astonishment, half the helpers let go their ropes. That the mothers-in-law should be shrewish was inevitable in such circumstances. The young husband, in any case, beat his wife shamelessly, and she was not ashamed of being beaten. If her husband did not thrash her from time to time, she felt that he did not love her very much.

When a moujik reckoned that the time had come for his son to marry, he began to question the boy about his preferences. If the boy hesitated the father gave him the choice of a certain number of girls he had sorted out. Once the decision was taken, father and mother appointed a professional matchmaker (*svakha*) to act as go-between with the parents of the future wife; or sometimes an elderly aunt was entrusted with the negotiations.

'Would you like an alliance with such-and-such?' the matchmaker would ask.

The young girl's parents would refuse with a sigh or reply unambiguously that the alliance would not be disagreeable.

The samovar then appeared on the table, and the terms of the deal were discussed at once: the size of the dowry, where the household would be set up, and various other promises. The matchmaker drank her tea from the saucer with a piece of sugar in her cheek. Her ear registered the least word, and her sharp glance took in the contents of the *izba*. After her departure the parents called in the fiancée and told her of the proposals of which she had been the object. Even if the news overwhelmed her with joy, she had, according to tradition, to show despair. However, if she was really desperate, her cries and her sobs had a more sincere quality and in that case her relations would be convinced. Forced marriages were increasingly rare in the country.

When there was nothing more to discuss, the fathers of the betrothed met for a last time and set a seal on the arrangement by wrapping their hands in their coats and striking them together; the purpose of this was symbolically to ensure that the couple should not lack cloth for their garments. Afterwards, the girl's parents blessed the couple with the family ikon.

Well before the wedding ceremony the young woman renounced the innocent pleasures of her youth and wept openly with her friends. Together they sewed the trousseau while singing old laments about a brutal husband, a licentious father-in-law, a hateful mother-in-law, and sisters-in-law with the tongues of serpents. Certain phrases in these laments (*svadebnye plachi*) were ritual and were passed on from one marriage to another. The fiancée begged those who were nearest to her not to hand her over to 'wicked strangers', but to leave her free, 'whether it be a cold winter, or a fine spring, or a warm summer'. These groans and sighs reached their paroxysm on the *devichnik*, the last evening the girl spent in her parents' house. She bade farewell to the beribboned hair of a virgin and asked her mother to remove it from her unruly little head. If she wept too much, her friends entreated her to be quiet, but the old women advised her, on the contrary, not to restrain her tears: 'Weep your fill at table or you will weep in the stable.'

An unchanging ritual required that the girl should grieve in this way until the moment when the wedding procession left for the church: was she not on the point of leaving her well-loved parents? But once the religious ceremony was ended, she must not spill a tear for fear of vexing her new family and her young husband. At the church itself, the witnesses followed with interest the way in which the couple behaved before the altar, for it was said that the one who first set foot on the carpet was certain of dominating the other. The flames of the candles which the couple held in their hands were also watched, in order to foresee which of them would survive the other. Pages took turns in holding crowns above the heads of the young couple. The priest, serious and with huge beard, gave them the rings, ordered them to exchange a kiss, to drink wine from the same cup and to follow him three times round the altar with their hands tied together. Incense was burning in the censer which the *dyakony* was swinging. A peasant choir sang with angelic voices. And everything ended in an enormous meal in one house or the other. The 'pope' was, of course, at the feast. The young couple did not eat, but had to embrace each time their health was drunk. As it was customary that neither food nor drink should be lacking from a wedding feast, the rejoicings went on for several days and the moujiks were in debt for a long time.

*   *   *   *

Since the emancipation, young couples had showed an increasing tendency to set up home away from their kinsfolk. Married or not, while he lived in the paternal home the peasant took no part in the communal assembly. But as soon as he set up house for himself and his wife, he became the head of a family and took part in the deliberations of the *mir*, with the same rights and duties as his father. Despite the recent sharing-out of the land, the majority of moujiks could not extract all that was necessary for subsistence from its cultivation. To add to their comforts, they worked at home as a family during the long winter months. This small home industry was known in Russia as 'bush industry' (*kustarnaya promyshlennast*). Seven or eight million peasants were thus employed for the coldest part of the year. The most varied objects came from their hands. There were as many specialities as there were provinces! Wooden spoons, knives and forks, baskets, plaited footwear, and cloth made of rushes (*rogozhi*), were made principally in the Nizhny-Novgorod region. At Yaroslav and Kostroma thread and cloth were

made from flax, Vladimir was famous for silk goods, Vologda
and Balaghna for their lace, Vyatka and Perm for leatherwork,
Kursk for religious imagery, the Government of Moscow for
its toys, that of Tula for its harmonicas (the simplest costing
five kopecks and the most luxurious 250 roubles) and for its
magnificent samovars. A Russian proverb said: 'One does not
go to Tula with one's samovar (V *Tulu samovarom ne
ezdyat*).'

Because rural industry was so widespread in Russia, a
swarm of agents went through the country buying the products wholesale. Each merchant – or *prassol* – confined his
activities to a fixed district comprising several villages. Knowing the population thoroughly, he shared in the intimate life
of the moujiks, lent them money, gave them limited credit,
even provided the necessary raw material for their labours,
and always arranged to monopolize their output at a paltry
price. If, distrusting him, the peasants went to the nearest
town to try and sell their merchandise on better terms, they
found other *prasol* there who invariably offered them lower
prices than had been offered by their usual *prasol*. Faced
with this secret union of merchants, the unfortunate rural
craftsmen had to give in. In the smoky *izba*, men, women
and young children toiled together: one carved a wooden
bowl and another decorated it with a large brush dipped in
a pot of paint. Grandfather snored as he slept on his stove. A
girl sang, seated beside the window which was covered with
frost-flowers. Snow blocked the doorway.

When the spring came the *kustarniki* did their accounts
and saw that they had not gained much: only some 50 to 70
roubles a year.

There was another means by which peasants could aug-
ment their income. Often, when the weather turned bad,
they left their hamlets to seek work elsewhere. This migratory movement reflected a vague need for expansion in the
restless spirit of the moujik. His homeland, the *matushka
Rus* (our Little Mother Russia), was so big that wherever
he went he could be certain of finding a land belonging to
the same *batyushka Gosudar* (the Emperor, our Little
Father) and the same holy Russian cross shining above an
Orthodox church. The less adventurous were content to go

to the city, with their horses and sleighs, to secure a police permit to be a sleigh-driver for the winter. Others crossed Russia in every direction, buying shoddy goods in one village to resell them in another. Others, still, ended their journeys in a factory, in a naval yard, near a railway under construction, at the bottom of a mine, on the shore of a lake full of fish, or as shepherds in the steppes of the Government of Orenburg. Children of fourteen, who had set out from Tver, got as far as the shores of the Sea of Azov. People from the Government of Nizhny-Novgorod laboured on the Kama, or the Don, or in Western Siberia, while stoneworkers, who were natives of the Government of Orel, were at work paving the streets of Moscow, like those from Baku, Saratov and Batum.

Distances were of no account to these permanent nomads, for there was no reason why their wills should become exhausted while there was still no obstacle in sight. The level horizon was a permanent incitement to go on. According to Paul Egorovitch Sychkin, the statisticians reckoned that the number of peasants who left their homes every year was six millions. Roused by fabulous stories, they left in search of adventure, marching towards a land of abundance and sunshine. Was it not said that in some provinces they paid 1 rouble 50 kopecks for a day's work? Russell had already seen groups of migrating peasants marching along the railway line with sacks on their backs and scythes over their shoulders. If, when they reached the end of their journey, they did not find anyone to hire them as they had hoped, they set forth again undiscouraged and passed into the next Government. Some returned home for the harvest, others worked far from their own villages until the end of the autumn. But all, on their return, had to confess that the savings they brought back were very small. Paul Egorovitch, who loved figures, revealed to Russell that in 1895, for example, of 55,500 workers who had left for the Government of Kherson, 83·6 per cent had arrived on foot. The time they had taken to cover this distance represented 12,500,000 working days. After deduction for expenses en route, their average wages, for the whole duration of the summer, was 13 kopecks a day!

Back in his own hamlet, the migratory moujik gladly related what he had seen and what he had heard during his journey. But even those who only half-believed him did not grudge him his inventions, for the Russian mind is well trained to the love of stories.

＊　＊　＊　＊

Paul Egorovitch Sychkin was definite on one point: the moujik got his taste for marvels from reading the sacred books. In most of the *isbas* profane pictures, cut from old illustrated periodicals, were stuck on the wall beside the ikons, and on a shelf there was always a dusty and mildewed Bible smelling of leather and incense. For a short while there had been a primary school in certain villages of the region. However, nine times out of ten the little moujik learned to read more or less at home from the Gospels, the book of martyrs and the psalter. Fed on biblical legends, he was accustomed to living in daily communication with God and his Saints. As he grew up he associated them with his own life. He tried to understand them better. And by dint of interpreting and commenting upon their messages in his own fashion, he passed gently and unconsciously into heresy. His religion seemed to be simultaneously a fidelity to the unchangeable rituals and a constant individual creation.

There were a few Old Believers in one of the villages which Russell had visited with Sychkin. As members of the *Beguny* sect, they rejected the official Gospels, corrected by the Patriarch Nikhon in the seventeenth century. A pious member of this brotherhood had been entrusted with copying out, for the use of his companions, the books that were still filled with 'sacred mistakes'.

Superficially the life of the dissenters closely resembled that of other moujiks. They worked in the fields, married and had children. Their doctrines certainly forbade them to frequent the church, to prostrate themselves before the holy images dishonoured by Nikhon, or to use incense and candles; but in fact the long prayers they said together in an *isba* did not prevent them from being present regularly at the Orthodox service. There they were distinguished by their behaviour during mass, saying *Issus* instead of *Iissus* (for Jesus), crossing themselves with two fingers instead of three, and not follow-

3 A peasant family at table

A young peasant conscript leaves to join the army

14 *Left:* Emigrants at Chelyabinsk Station

Volga steamship

Russian emigrants at the station at Samara

ing the rest of the congregation in the repetition of the cry
Allelujah!

As old age approached, the *Beguny* stopped going to
church and began a new kind of existence: they ate apart
from the family, from bowls with their own wooden spoons.
Then the need to save their own souls became so pressing
that they fled from home, never to return. Doubtless they
went to join other old folk in the forest, in order to devote
their last days to contemplating God. It was said that there
were monasteries of Old Believers hidden among the ancient
trees, far from any road and from anyone's gaze. There the
Beguny lived on fresh water, bread and incantations, and in
a state of ecstasy allowed their bodies to be devoured by
insects.

In fact, the Russian peasant was ready to believe anything.
For his religion was less a moral matter than a mystery. It
was not in obedience to the precepts of Christ that he was
patient, docile, hospitable and charitable, but from a natural
inclination to be indulgent. This quite evangelical kindness
did not prevent him, if he was deceitful, envious or de-
bauched, from sincerely asking for the blessing of a certain
saint for the success of his ventures. Having only a dim idea
of evil, he sought powerful accomplices in heaven. Thus the
horse-thieves confided their expeditions to St Nikolas, and
usurers recommended their transactions to St Akim. According to Paul Egorovitch, of the candles that burned in the
church beneath the ikons, two-thirds at least were evidence of some bargaining with the higher powers ruling the
earth.

These higher powers were either Christian or pagan
according to circumstances. Despite the new school and its
bespectacled teacher, despite the resounding voice of the
'pope', age-old superstitions combined to torment the Russian peasant's soul. He gladly sought a supernatural explanation of the smallest event in his life. Wherever he turned the
universe seemed to him to be peopled with good or evil
spirits. Even the advanced moujiks, who pretended to despise
these legends, did not like to go out at night near cemeteries
or old mills.

In the forest lived the *leshii*, a spirit with a bluish skin, protruding eyes and long hair. This spirit protected criminals, imitated birdsong and wandered through his realm laughing, whistling and clapping his hands. The echo was of his making. A mocking creature, he often amused himself by leading men astray in the woods. To counter his tricks, one had to wear one's jacket back to front and to put one's left boot on the right foot. His brother of the plain was the *polevik*. The *vodyanoi* was the spirit of the waters. Every river, every stream, every pond had its own spirit, old, hideous and green bearded. When he was well disposed, he was pleased to guide the fish into the fishermen's nets. But if he was in a bad humour, he tore the traps and the lines, raised storms, sank ships and smashed dikes. When he was drunk he made the rivers overflow. In the depths of the waters there also lived the water-sprites, or *rusalki*, beautiful naked girls with skin the colour of moonlight, silken hair and emerald eyes. They so charmed the passers-by with their laughter and songs that some of them would drown themselves for the *rusalkis'* sake. The *vedmy*, or sorcerers, were stunted, wicked, toothless women, who gave themselves to black magic, travelling by night on brooms and casting spells. There was also the *baba-yaga*, a repugnant hook-nosed creature which moved about, seated on a mortar, with a pestle in its right hand to force a way, and a broom in its left hand to efface the signs of its passage. As all Russian children knew, it lived in a mobile *isba*, mounted on chicken's feet. This dwelling had neither doors nor windows. There was a terrible black cat in its yard.

Of course, the moujik's house itself was full of little spirits, who hid in the chimney, under the soil or amongst the beams. Their leader was the *domovoi*, old and dishevelled, with a hairy body and a tail. He protected the family, shared in its daily life, amused himself in provoking a sleeper's snores, tangling a flirtatious woman's hair, hiding the master's boots, maddening the hens, and breaking the leg of a bench; but on the other hand he often healed the sick and appeased domestic quarrels. His comrade in the farmyard was called the *dvorovoi*, the one in the stable the *konyushennik* (at night he plaited the mane of his favourite horse), and the one in the bath-house the *bannik*. The girls questioned the *bannik* about their future while they exposed their naked backs to him through the half-open door at midnight; if he scratched them they could expect the worst, and if he caressed them life would be sweet. But the *bannik* detested young women in childbed, who were generally transferred to the hut reserved for ablutions, if there was no place in the *isba*. Everyone knew that it was dangerous to leave them alone with the *bannik*.

To these deities of a rudimentary mythology were added all the spirits of the departed, who returned to earth to help the living or to complicate their tasks. The *tchur*, or dead ancestor, had the right to special veneration. The children unconsciously invoked him when, playing tag, they called out on touching 'home': *Chur menya!'* – in other words, 'Ancestor, protect me!' As to the custom of taking burning coals from the old hearth into a new house, this symbolized the passage of the spirits of the ancestors from one dwelling to the other.

✿   ✿   ✿   ✿

Russell was particularly interested in popular sayings, of which Paul Egorovitch provided the translations. The majority of them were involved in rhymes or in amusing consonances. They illustrated the fatalism of the Russian peasant, his slowness and his great laziness: '*Pospeshish lyndhei nasmeshish!*' (If you hurry, you will make people laugh!) '*Tishe edesh, dalshe budesh!*' (Go slowly, you will go farther!) Other proverbs refer to the poverty of the countryside: 'No one knows (*vedaet*) how the poor dine (*obedaet*).' 'Bread and water (*voda*), those are our food (*eda*).' 'Bread and *kvas*, that's all there is at home (*u nas*).' '*Stichi da kasha, pishcha nasha.*' (Cabbage soup and gruel, that's our food.) The protest against the inequality of men was expressed as follows: 'In the forest the trees are unequal, and in the world so are men.' 'If there were no bast shoes, there would be no velvet clothes.' 'We all look at the same sun, but we don't eat the same dinner.' Evidently no Tsar was able to come to the aid of his people, for *do Boga vysoko, do Tsarya daleko!*' (God is too high and the Tsar is too far away!) As to the judge, he is too aware of the power of money

to take the part of the moujik: *'Karman sukh, sudya glukh!'*
(If the pocket is empty, the judge is deaf.) 'The law is like the
helm (*dychlo*), it goes wherever you turn it (*vyshlo*)'. In con-
clusion, all the moujiks saw themselves in the favourite Volga
boatmen's proverb: 'Pull on your rope (*lyamka*) until they dig
your grave (*yamka*).'

The more Russell discussed the Russian peasant with his
hosts, the less clear his picture of the peasant became. Sometimes he saw the moujik as a sort of primitive Christian with
an aura of innocence, and sometimes as an idle brute, illiterate, crafty and cruel. In fact, the Russians themselves could
not agree about him. For the Slavophils, the *narodniki*, the
moujik's rough exterior, hid great virtues which would ex-
pand, sooner or later, under the sun of liberty. For the 'wes-
terners' he was, on the other hand, an eternal lesser creature,
incapable of setting the general interest above his particular
interest, and opposed to all progress and change. Angel or
beast, he represented an immense, elusive and uncontrollable
power. Everyone felt that the future of Russia would perhaps
have the strange face of a little moujik with a red beard, a
flat nose, a low brow and a childish look. Paul Egorovitch
Sychkin told how revolutionary circles attached an overwhelming importance to the political education of the land-
worker. Already, the majority of the peasants, even those
whose sons did not go to school, knew the meaning of the
words 'socialism' and 'capitalism'. Into the bands of pilgrims who marched towards the holy city of Kiev slipped the
apostles of the Marxist religion, disguised as beggars, pedlars
or tramps. They loitered at the crossroads and at the outskirts
of the forests to indoctrinate the passers-by. They set themselves up in the village as tailors, healers and menders; they
made friends with the teachers and the inn-keepers; they distributed leaflets and booklets amongst the young people who
were hungry for learning. Their lesson was always the same:
although the land had been distributed, the moujiks would
remain impoverished so long as they did not recover from
their masters the goods which the masters had unjustly kept;
as to the Tsar, it was absolutely necessary that he should be
elected by universal suffrage and his power limited by a constitution. Actually, the peasants were not interested in the

way in which the Tsar would be elected or the nation governed. Of all the ideas which the commercial travellers of socialism showed them, they remembered that which was of the most benefit to themselves. From the moment I become poor, I have the right to appropriate those things of which the rich have too many. Sometimes a group of policemen hurriedly went to a village to arrest an agitator. But he always disappeared before their arrival.

The year 1902 had been marked by many agrarian troubles in the Governments of Poltava and Kharkhov. A *pomieshik*,[1] a friend of the Zubovs, had had his barns pillaged by rioters the previous year. He told Russell about his misfortunes. He had noticed for some weeks that the moujiks had been holding secret assemblies, whispering amongst themselves whilst casting sidelong glances at his house. One day they came in a crowd to demand the return of his corn: 'If you don't give it to us, the men from the next village will take it! Now, you know us and you know that we love you very much! You must give us preference!' And, while the *pomieshik* protested, they all ran off to his barns. There they began to quarrel amongst themselves. After a little while, one of the thieves came back to find the *pomieshik*: 'I beseech you, *barin*, to help us to divide it up. It is quite disorderly: some are taking too much and others have nothing!' But the *pomieshik* refused to preside over his own pillage and the man went away crest-fallen. In the barns they were knocking one another over and struggling amongst themselves. Those who had succeeded in filling their sacks made off, bent under their loot. Others at once took their places. The next day was a disappointing one for the looters. A detachment of police arrived in the village with a telega full of rods. The moujiks hastened to return the stolen corn to the *pomeshchik* and actually asked him for a receipt!

All lootings did not end in this simple fashion: horses were stolen, and mills and barns were set on fire, but those truly responsible for the disorders mostly escaped the police. Sychkin reckoned the lot of the moujik must be quickly eased if the growth of brigandage in the country was to be stopped. But as he looked out upon the limitless cornfields, the pretty

[1] Landed proprietor.

green-domed churches, the trembling birch-woods, the peasants with their kind, sunburnt faces and the Zubov family taking tea on the veranda, it was difficult for Russell to believe that there was a greater threat to the social order in Russia than anywhere else.

CHAPTER XIV

NIZHNY-NOVGOROD

*The fair: men, animals and goods – The different races which
form the Russian people – The position of the Jews – Pogroms
– Foreigners in Russia*

BAEDEKER was categorical; a conscientious visitor must
visit the Nizhny-Novgorod fair, which was held every
year from July 15 till September 10. All the races of
Russia met there in a turmoil of trading. Nizhny-Novgorod was
only eleven hours from Moscow by express train, which
stopped at Pavlov, the station close to the Zubov property.
Alexander Vassilievitch decided that he would take his guest
on this trip, while Sychkin would stay with the women in the
country. They took the sleeping-car. The compartment was
luxurious. At each end of the corridor were perfectly appointed toilets. A samovar steamed in a recess which served
as a kitchen. One had only to summon the attendant and he
would serve tea at any hour. Very pleased with such comfort,
Russell wanted to take a look at the third class.

Though he disapproved of his companion's curiosity,
Alexander Vassilievitch went with him through the corridors
to the poorest part of the train. They came to a halt in a
wagon littered with sordid packages, among which drifted
travellers like bundles of rags. Shapeless women with red
scarves over their heads and their hands folded on their
stomachs, scabby brats tottering with fatigue, and moujiks
with straw-coloured hair and weatherbeaten skin, filthy with
dirt and sweat, but with the gentle eyes of cattle. An acrid
human stench rose to Russell's nostrils and he beat a hasty
retreat.

When he got back to his compartment, he confessed to
Alexander Vassilievitch the distress he felt at seeing again the
crude juxtaposition of riches and poverty in Russia. To dis-
tract him from these thoughts, Alexander Vassilievitch began
to explain the Nizhny-Novgorod fair. From 1641 the principal
fair in the region was held in the neighbourhood of the

convent of St Macaire, seventy versts from Nizhny-Novgorod, on the property of a landowner who took a fee from the merchants. But in 1816 a fire destroyed the huts and Alexander I, seeking new sources of revenue, ordered that the fair should be transferred to the plain between the Volga and the Oka. This site was always flooded, and to put the matter right the Government put some gigantic works in hand, which, under the direction of General Augustin de Bétancourt, went on until 1822 and cost more than 3,000,000 roubles. The ground-level was raised about ten feet and supported by freestone; an immense sewer was constructed underneath and the drainage ran out into the Volga. The Nizhny-Novgorod fair was important because it took place at the intersection of two great waterways, where the trade of East and West met. Of course, the turnover of this extraordinary bazaar dropped somewhat following the development of the railways, but it still amounted to between 165 and 200 million roubles for the merchandise brought in, and between 150 and 185 million roubles for the merchandise sold. As for the population of Nizhny, which normally numbered 89,000 inhabitants, it was swollen by 400,000 visitors from the second half of July.

Although this information had prepared him to some extent, Russell was astonished the next day when he approached the town which Alexander Vassilievitch had described. After leaving their baggage at the Post Hotel, the two men took a cab for a quick visit to the old city of Nizhny-Novgorod, with its kremlin, monasteries, cathedrals, churches and park. Then, from the top of a hill, they looked down upon the strange sight of the fair. It stood in the triangle where the Volga and the Oka met. In the foreground lay a fleet of vessels with wide square bows and a forest of masts. Farther off, in midstream more slender ships were moored together, forming veritable islands surmounted by masts and ropes. Then, beyond a stretch of calm water, ill-matched hulls were lined up, showing battered tarpaulins and limp sails, while a crowd of stevedores swarmed in a morass of bluish mud. These vessels, barges and junks had brought tea from Kiakhta, iron from the Urals, cashmere goods from Persia, furs from Siberia and dried fish from the Caspian Sea.

A wooden bridge crowded with pedestrians, horses and

carriages spanned the Oka and connected the old city with the fair. But seen from afar this wide bridge seemed pointless, for the boats around it were so closely packed that one could, by leaping from one to another, cross the river without wetting one's feet. Beyond the green roofs of the bazaar lay another stretch of water, shining like a stream of mercury: the Volga. The horizon was as infinite as that of the sea. Into the warm air, redolent with the odour of fish and of tar, rose the hum of voices. All the dialects of Russia and Asia met at this spot.

Alexander Vassilievitch ordered the driver to go on. The carriage descended a short and steep road, and then started across the plank bridge. Caught between traps, calashes and droshkis, they progressed slowly, while coming to meet them were a variety of signs, pinnacles, hangings, glassware, fragments of the alphabet, Asiatic smiles and Russian beards. They left the carriage where the crowd was thickest.

The fair consisted of an inner and an outer part. The inner part consisted of covered markets (*ambars*) of one or two floors, constructed for the most part of stone, beside the wide roads that intersected at right angles. In this section 3,000 shops displayed jewellery, goldsmith's work, silks, clocks, and various knick-knacks.[1] Around this vast market lay another, the outer market, more irregular and more animated than the first. In it were 4,000 wooden huts. At the shop-doors were merchants of all kinds and races: Chinese in gleaming silk and skull-caps, with pigtails hanging down their backs; velvet-eyed Persians with hooked noses; moustached Turks in fezes, shaven-headed Kalmuks, Jews in long and filthy greatcoats, Circassians, Armenians, Poles . . .

Each row (or *ryad*) was devoted to a different trade. There was the Petersburgskaya, crammed with glassware and crude pottery, and the Alexander Nevsky, which was restricted to wooden chests painted in varied colours, with tinplated fittings. These two arteries ended at the Alexander Nevsky Cathedral, under the guardian shadow of which was an avalanche of spoons, jugs and pots. Not far away was the bell market with its heavy bronze-ware hanging from the scaffold-

[1] The *ambarres* belonged to the Crown and their rents totalled 500,000 roubles a year.

ing in order of size. Anyone who wanted to could ring them by striking the tongue against the bell; bending their heads and shutting their eyes, the ringers listened to the thunder of the bell with an air as pleased as if they were listening to birdsong. Without allowing Russell time to pause amongst these melomaniacs with such strong ear-drums, Alexander Vassilievitch led him through the jumble of races and voices, and the mixture of odours, to a site west of the Siberian landing-stage, where the tea depots lay.

The bales of tea, piled up to a great height, were covered with tarpaulins. The sellers lived in the vicinity of their treasure, in huts made of matting. Alexander Vassilievitch explained to Russell that the tea that came from China by the land route (caravan tea) was reckoned to be better than the tea that came by sea, because the aroma had not been weakened or denatured by damp. In reality, however, the caravan tea did not always follow the land route from the Chinese frontier and from Perm to Nizhny-Novgorod it was carried by ship on the Kama and Volga. Known also as 'Russian tea', it was carried in little boxes that were sewn up in skins, with the hair turned inwards to prevent the perfume from escaping. Compressed tea in tablets (*plitochnyi chai*) was also sold, and even a coarse tea in heavy bricks (*kirpichnyi chai*) which had to be broken with an axe before use. The Kalmuks and Caucasians drank it with milk, butter, salt and pepper. All the tea-buyers were provided with a little teapot, so that they might taste it before giving their orders. The foreign merchant, seated in his matting shelter, always had a steaming samovar at his side. He tossed into the teapot a pinch of the sample chosen by the customer and poured over it a reasonable quantity of boiling water. In the largest booths the circle of experts plunged their noses into the heaps of tea and exchanged views in a subdued voice.

Behind the tea depot stretched the depot for undressed skins, the sale of which was entirely in the hands of Tartars and Kirghiz. A sharp and nauseous smell hung over the thousands of hairy hides to which the tails of horses and horns of cattle were still attached. A little farther off, in contrast to these lowly skins, were the luxury pelts: the dead white of bear, the speckled white of ermine, the silver glint of blue fox, the tawny yellow of polecat, the ash of squirrel, and the regal sable, a velvety dark brown. But Alexander Vassilievitch was already drawing Russell on, for there were so many things to see. Soon they were stumbling over hillocks of slippers, *lapti* and boots, over a whole landscape of nuts, pistaches and raisins, over a multicoloured expanse of Persian carpets, along the gallery of carriages ('Drozhki, tarantass for sale!') or among the fine collection of Kirghiz, Cossack and Arab horses that were whinnying with fear in the faces of the passers-by. As they passed in front of a thriving textile shop, Russell commented on the dexterity of the book-keepers, whose fingers flew to and fro on the abaci. In Russian commercial houses all calculations had been done on these apparently rudimentary machines for hundreds of years.[1] The abacus was a rectangular frame with several transverse metal rods on which wooden beads were threaded. The beads on the first row were the units, those on the second row were the tens, those on the third row the hundreds, and so forth. There was a row for the *poltinniki* (50 kopecks) and a row for the kopecks. By moving these beads from left to right, the experts carried out the four forms of arithmetic at prodigious speed and, it is said, they could do the same for even more complicated calculations. Whereas a religious silence reigned in the accounts offices of all other parts of Europe, here the employees lived amidst the happy clatter of beads. The best abaci, which were much sought after for the quality of their wood, were made by the house of Svietchnikov. Alexander Vassilievitch claimed that there were virtuosos with the abacus, to whom additions, subtractions and multiplications were as pleasant to listen to as music.

Another feature of the Nizhny fair was the market for Ural iron. It took place on the long sandy island of Peski, which was reached by a bridge of boats. There, along a stretch of one kilometre, under shelter or in the open, mountains of iron were piled up in the form of sheets, bars, anvils, screws, forks, nails, ladles, buckets, wheelbarrows, choppers, pans, bolts.... These metal articles amounted in value to about

---

[1] Used since time immemorial by the Chinese and the Tartars, the abacus was introduced into Russia by the Mongols towards the end of the Middle Ages.

twenty-five million roubles a year. On the same sandbank were interminable lines of boats laden with dried or salted fish. Swarms of beggars crowded along the bank; to secure a way through the fishermen threw them a few damaged herrings.

It was strange that there was no quay for discharging cargoes. The Volga and the Oka ran through the land as freely as at the creation of the world. Steamboats and great tubby barges loaded and unloaded their goods beside the banks of clay or sand. A few cranes puffed about near the bigger vessels. Heralded by bugle-blasts, wagons rolled along the rails across the port, while among them squeezed the muscular stevedores of Nizhny, called *kryuchniki*, or 'human hooks', bent double under their enormous loads. All had sinister faces, with swollen purple nostrils, beards that were soaked in sweat and alcohol, and drunkards' eyes that were sunk in a network of wrinkles as deep as scars. Their clothes were very scanty: trousers of thin grey cloth, strips of filthy linen for socks, and blouses of a strange rose-coloured cretonne, soaked by rain and sweat, torn, vainglorious and revolting. . . .

❊   ❊   ❊   ❊

When they returned to the hotel that evening Russell felt overwhelmed not only by the diversity of the goods he had seen but also by the variety of human types which formed the Nizhny crowd. How could the Russian people maintain an apparent political unity with such an amalgam of races, traditions, religions and dialects? Alexander Vassilievitch's answer to this question was simply that it was a miracle. The cement which held the disparate elements of the Russian nation together was their love for the Tsar, but this love was controlled by a vigilant police force.

'Russia is a puzzle, and a puzzle that involves also a framework,' said Alexander Vassilievitch. 'Take away the framework and the whole lot falls apart!'

To convince his questioner, he named the various ethnic groups within the Empire which totalled 129,000,000 inhabitants at the 1897 census, and 135,000,000 according to the latest forecasts. Of this immense total the Great Russians (about 55,000,000) formed the Russian nation properly so called. Vigorous, thick-set, with blue or brown eyes, and with thick, curly, light chestnut hair, they were nonchalant, showed their unconcern with a smile, a shrug and the word *nitchevo* (meaning 'nothing'), and attributed their virtues and faults to the 'richness of their nature' (*shirokaya natura*). The Little Russians (about 23,000,000) inhabited mainly the Governments of Kiev, Kharkov, Chernigov and Poltava. Of more slender appearance than the Great Russians, with brown complexions and dark eyes, they were famous for their fierce attachment to the language, traditions and history of their province – Ukraine – which has a magnificent folklore. The White Russians (4,500,000) occupied the Governments of Grodno, Smolensk, Vitebsk, Minsk and Mogilev, but according to Alexander Vassilievitch they were so poor and so wild that villages of more than ten huts were rare in their land.

Like the two great races previously named, the White Russians were Orthodox. The Poles (9,000,000) were Catholic. The Lithuanians, together with the Latvians, formed a branch of the Indo-European family (5,000,000), but the Lithuanians were mostly Catholic and the Latvians were Lutheran. The Finns and Estonians (6,000,000) were also Lutherans. As for the eastern races, they were innumerable: Tartars, Turkmens, Kirghiz, Bashkirs, Buryats, Tungus. . . . To these were added all the populations and religions of the Caucasus: Circassians, Georgians Mingrelians, Khevzurs, Karbadins, Ossetians, Chechens, Lezgins, Armenians. . . .

Different statues existed for diverse groups, such as the Finns, who enjoyed a special juridical position, and the Cossacks, both of whom formed a class apart, with rights, privileges and some sort of self-government. As to the nomad tribes and the savages of the north and east of the Empire, the State only required that they should recognize Russian sovereignty, but otherwise left them to live their own lives according to the customs of the steppes. Alexander Vassilievitch had reached this point in his exposition when Russell asked him about the exact condition of the Jews in Russia. Alexander Vassilievitch's face clouded over at once. His questioner had touched upon a sore point. He clicked his tongue sadly and said:

'You must understand us. . . .'

After which he admitted that the Jews in Russia had suffered 'a few restrictive measures'.[1] They could not live where they liked, nor change their residence freely. By law they were allowed to settle permanently only in the western and southwestern Governments of European Russia. An exception was made for Jewish merchants in the first guild (those who payed the highest tax), for Jews who had completed a higher education, and for those who practised certain professions 'necessary to society'. On the other hand, there were severe restrictions on the right of Jews to acquire landed property, enter State service, participate in the election of town representatives, or enrol in a public educational institution. Of their total number of students, Russian universities admitted Jews to the extent of only between three and ten per cent, and the proportion admitted to the secondary schools was the same. Alexander Vassilievitch deplored the distressing situation of the Jews in Russia, but to him it seemed difficult to give them greater freedom.

'Our people are too poorly educated, too simple, too credulous! If the Jews were to spread through the country all our moujiks would be ruined in a few years. Every time a *prassol* Jew appears in a small town or in a fairground the roubles change hands. Our crafty fox makes nothing and sells nothing; he acts as an intermediary and takes a commission. Or worse, he advances money at a usurious rate.... The peasant doesn't understand the lender's talk at all, signs the papers and does not even dream that he will have to lay out money for interest, and there he is, suddenly caught, struck all of a heap, stripped of everything.... Even if we offered the Jews the opportunity to live like us, they wouldn't want to. They have their own practices. They stick close together around their rabbis. Their lives are so closely moulded by religion that to some extent they are afraid of progress and the future....'

'What happens to the status of a Jew in Russia if he should be baptized a Christian?' Russell asked.

---

[1] It was only in 1769 that, for the first time, the Jews were authorized to settle in Russia in certain Governments. But the Jewish question was not really raised until after the annexation of Poland, where the Jews were very numerous.

'Everything would be different!' Alexander Vassilievitch cried gaily. 'In the eyes of the law he would be no longer a Jew, an allogeneous type, but a citizen like the rest, a son of the great orthodox fatherland!'

'But the faults for which you blame his race will not have been effaced by conversion. He will not be less eager for gain, for example, nor less crafty!'

'Who knows?' Alexander Vassilievitch sighed. And he fell silent, with a frown of irritation and distrust.

'Why don't you admit, then, that in Russia you don't like the Jews very much?' Russell answered smiling.

Alexander Vassilievitch shot him a challenging glance:

'Yes, my dear sir. But we are careful in our dealings with them. We will gradually give them the equality of rights they ask for – when they have become Russian at heart, and when they have shown a desire to leave their ghettoes. That will take years, centuries perhaps. . . .'

While Alexander Vassilievitch was speaking, Russell mused upon the anti-Jewish riots at Balta and Tchernigov, and the terrible Kichinev *pogrom* that had broken out on Easter Day that year.[1] Encouraged by the authorities, a crowd of intoxicated hooligans had pillaged, demolished and set fire to the Jewish dwellings for forty-eight hours; 130 persons were killed or seriously injured and 500 slightly injured. The Minister Plehve, who was obviously the instigator of the *pogrom*, forbade the Russian newspapers to mention it; but everyone in Russia knew about this sorry affair.

'The trouble with the Jews,' Alexander Vassilievitch went on, 'is that almost all of them have the revolutionary spirit. They would like to overthrow the régime and dismember Russia.'[2]

'Isn't that what was said in the proclamations distributed at Kichinev?' Russell murmured.

Alexander Vassilievitch pretended not to hear.

[1] April 8–21, 1903.
[2] Since his accession to power, Plehve had exasperated the national minorities continuously: Jews, Poles, Finns, Armenians. The Kichinev *pogrom* was followed, on August 29, by one at Gomel, directly supported by the troops. Plehve was assassinated on July 15, 1904. But the *pogroms* broke out again, here and there, with 'the black centuries' as the prime movers.

'I hate violence,' he said, 'whether from the right or left. Now this is strange! We have been to the fair, we were in a good humour, we began to speak of the Jewish problem, and everything becomes dark and sad and anxious! However, when you remember the Dreyfus affair, are you in the West entitled to reproach us for anti-semitism?'

'There is one difference,' Russell replied. 'I imagine that in Russia Dreyfus would not have been able to get his trial reviewed.'

'That's true,' Alexander Vassilievitch conceded. 'Here the authorities never admit a mistake. That's because of the size of the country. There are so many people to watch over. If France and Britain were bigger they would be less liberal. . . . Yet I don't think there's a nation in the world more open to foreign penetration than is Russia!'

At these words Russell gave a start: he remembered his passport troubles and the fuss at the customs.

'Oh, yes!' Alexander Vassilievitch went on. 'There are certain formalities for foreigners who want to cross the Russian frontiers of course, but once in Russia they are very nearly our equals. To encourage foreign scholars, artists and technicians to settle in Russia, Peter the Great and his successors gave them land, tax exemptions and privileges. Today Russia not only offers foreigners the complete protection of the administration and the courts, but even allows them certain political rights. Thus a foreigner can occupy certain posts in the State service, get himself registered as member of a professional body, purchase a commercial or industrial licence, acquire landed property, be a merchant of one or other guild, build a factory,[1] obtain the rank of notable citizen in his own right and afterwards hereditary, and finally can ask for naturalization after five years' residence in Russia – or even less. Isn't that simple and practical and generous? There are complete colonies of Germans in Russia; since the reign of Catherine II, they have lived beside the Volga, in Crimea and in the Governments of Ekaterinoslav and Kherson. You would be astonished at the number of Frenchmen who have settled in St Petersburg and Moscow and have made their

[1] Restriction of the right to devote oneself to commerce or industry existed only for foreign Jews.

fortunes there. Our governesses, fashions and sympathies are all French. . . .'

He grew excited as he spoke, and suddenly, with tears in his eyes, he grasped Russell's hand on the table:

'You know what's in my mind, Ivan Pavlovitch? Why don't you stay in Russia?'

Russell smiled and shook his head.

CHAPTER XV

THE VOLGA

The burlaki *or Volga boatmen, their work and customs – Visit
to Samara – Kumys – The preparation of caviar – Russell finds
a happy ending to his long stay in Russia*

H AVING visited Nizhny-Novgorod, it was difficult to resist
the temptation to go down the Volga by ship. It was
Alexander Vassilievitch's view that the journey should
extend at least as far as Samara, if not Astrakhan: three days
down-river and four days up. Having made this decision, he
telegraphed his wife, suggesting that she should join them,
and forty-eight hours later Tatiana Sergeyevna reached
Nizhny-Novgorod with her two daughters, her son and her
son-in-law.

Several shipping companies maintained the river service:
the Volga Company, the Caucasus and Mercury Company,
the Samoliot Company, and the Nadezhda Company. All the
passenger vessels were steamships, with two decks, large
paddle-wheels and tall smoke-stacks; they had comfortable
cabins, electric lighting, restaurants, saloons and bathrooms.
The trip to Samara cost 9 roubles 30 kopecks first-class, and
6 roubles in second. The fares to Astrakhan (six days) were
21 roubles and 13 roubles 50 kopecks respectively.

Alexander Vassilievitch selected an attractive steamer,
very white and very new, that belonged to the Samoliot
Company. The voyage began. At the third stroke of the bell
the steamer drew slowly away from the shore, with its pon-
toon of rotten planks, low houses and a few waving girls in red
blouses. Then it described a circle, beating the water with its
paddle-wheels, and turned its back on the city. The Volga
widened. Its yellow flood seemed slow at the banks and rapid
in midstream. At the stern, near the engine-room, the outcasts
among the travellers were crowded together, a mass of
ragged creatures drinking their soup from old jam-jars. They
went from one town to another along the river without definite
purpose and without real hope. From the upper deck, which

was restricted to the first class, the sandy banks could be seen lying upon their chalk foundations like the layers of a cake. Little churches with blue roofs, miniature kremlins in rose-coloured brick, gilded crosses, wooden cottages, white and pillared villages proliferated. Then came velvety green strips of forest, a pale beach, trails of mist and finally the twilight. A balalaïka was playing on the deck occupied by the poorer passengers.

Because of frequent changes of depth, the ships could not always turn to starboard. Thus, when two ships were about to pass, the sailors on each of them waved flags by day, or lanterns by night, to signal the side on which passing was possible.

Russell was very impatient to see the famous Volga boat-men, the *burlaki*, whose poverty, it was said was so great and whose songs were so beautiful. Alexander Vassilievitch re-strained his impatience: the *burlaki* were disappearing. The progress of steam navigation had practically destroyed their work. But shortly before reaching Issady, Russell caught sight of a band of haulers, dragging an enormous barge against the current. All the passengers on the steamer imme-diately lined the rails. Paul Egorovitch Sychkin lent Russell his field-glasses.

A band of ragged creatures was marching slowly and pain-fully along the bank. A cable linked them to the mast of the vessel which they had taken in tow. The end of this cable was fitted with leather straps, distributed in pairs, each with a short stick attached. The *burlaki* were harnessed to the straps and brought all their weight to bear upon the stick which was level with their belts. The vessel was of medium size, and one row of *burlaki* was enough to move it. Had the load been greater, a second row would undoubtedly have been needed. The men followed one another in single file. A muffled and vaguely rhythmical chant accompanied their efforts. They put their right feet forward in unison, but the load they drew was so heavy that they could not advance their left feet in the same way and had to be content to bring them level with the right. A forward thrust of the chest, a powerful lean of the shoulder, and once more all the right feet moved in the mud of the little road. The song's monotonous rhythm controlled

their step so strictly that, according to Alexander Vassilievitch, it was impossible for a *burlak* to slow his pace without
hindering all his companions.

When the wind was in their favour the *burlaki* could cover
thirty to thirty-five versts a day, but when the wind blew
against them they covered only a few versts between sunrise
and nightfall. Their system of haulage varied according to
the nature of the terrain. When the banks became steep and
covered with forests, the *burlaki* gave up towing the ships
from the bank by ropes. They took two little boats into the
middle of the river and dropped an anchor there. To this
anchor a long cable was attached, the free end of which was
taken to the deck of the ship being towed. Then all the
burlaki assembled on the deck, gripped the rope and hauled
until the heavy vessel moved up to the anchor. Having
reached this point, the little boats went to cast the anchor
farther away and the manœuvre was then repeated.

Like many Russian workers, the *burlaki* framed an *artel*.
The total strength of the *artel* varied with the size of the ship
to be towed. For the biggest the team sometimes numbered
150 or 200 men. Once the group was organized, the *burlaki*
chose their cook, a task that usually fell to a boy of ten to
thirteen years. He prepared for all of them an abundant but
invariable diet: cabbage soup and buckwheat gruel. Having
elected their cook, the *burlaki* met again to choose the
strongest man to lead them; they called him 'old one' or
stavosta. The *stavosta* marched at the head of the team and
gave the orders, and by his courage was an example to them
all. The least robust members of the *artel* came at the tail of
the formation and saw that the cable did not catch on any
obstacle as they passed. To tow a cargo ship the *burlaki* were
assisted by a pilot, or *botsman* (derived from the English
word 'boatman'), who knew every turn in the bed of the
Volga. The sandbanks in the stream shifted so frequently that
the pilot had to be able to discern these changes of depth by
nothing more than the colour and transparency of the water.
He was better paid than his comrades of the *artel*, and distinguished by a fine red shirt and high leather boots.

The *burlaki*'s day began before sunrise. At eight in the
morning they breakfasted, then they worked until two

o'clock; a short halt for dinner and once again the whole crew applied themselves to the straps; when the first stars began to shine the Volga boatmen dropped the rope at last, ate their soup, lay down fully dressed on the earth or in their boat, and slept the sleep of beasts. Uncommon strength and inexhaustible lungs were required. The most widespread disease amongst the *burlaki* was tuberculosis. Whoever fell sick during a towing job was unlucky: he was given his pay and passport forthwith, and was abandoned on the bank.

Normally, the *burlaki* had to complete the haul from Astrakhan to Nizhny-Novgorod in seventy to seventy-three days in order to be at the fair by July 20. The proprietor of the merchandise carried in the vessel grew increasingly impatient as the date drew near, and the *artel* strove to keep to the agreed time. Towards the end of the journey the men scarcely slept; they were dazed, their legs trembled and their throats were raw with dust. Having reached Nizhny-Novgorod they drank away their meagre pay in the drinking-dens and when the hauling season ended found themselves as poor as ever. Russell was astonished that any people, although primitive, ignorant and illiterate, should be forced into a form of labour which could normally be done by beasts of burden.

'Go and tell them then!' cried Alexander Vassilievitch. 'You see what they say! Those fellows are savages. The *Volga matushka* (little Mother Volga) is their homeland, and they love it jealously and fiercely! Steamships and tugs are for them objects of superstitious hate. They even detest the new roads! The poorer the land and the less cultivated it is, the more they feel at home! But don't worry, the Volga boatmen will soon be no more than a musical memory! And sentimental people will regret their passing!'

❊   ❊   ❊   ❊

The next morning the ship approached the port of Kazan. A veil of dust concealed the city proper. Around the quay stretched a miserable sort of camp, frequented by beggars, sailors and Tartar merchants. Some offered boxes of caviar, others leather slippers, water-melons, curdled milk, cold chickens, and pigs' hearts in bowls. The passing of a suburban tram occasionally stirred this stagnant hole to life. There was a halt of three hours and then the steamer sounded its whistle once again, puffed, and beat the dirty water into a white foam.

Russell had the strange feeling that, like the ship that carried him, he had broken his ties with the real world. His will, his identity, and even his intelligence had dissolved in the slow strength of the Volga. He lived from one vista to another, from meal to meal, from smile to smile. Space had no limits. His eyes followed the quivering wave which fell away from the ship and lost sight of it long before it had touched the shore. Over there were villages, dunes, churches, moujiks. . . . When they reached a port a horde of swarthy Asiatics and peasant women with swollen bosoms beneath their coloured blouses dashed in the direction of the engine-room. A rich merchant came up on to the first-class deck with his wife, who was dressed in rustling silks. Russell observed the comings and goings of the passengers out of the corner of his eye. In this little floating world only one face seemed pleasing: Helen's. Why was it that this young lady was even more attractive on the water than on the land? The reflections from the river gave her a disturbing charm. She had only to say a few words to Russell, or to hand him a glass of tea, or to breathe a sigh as she gazed at the horizon, and he felt as if lifted up on wings.

After three days' sailing the steppe widened out and then closed in again; the river lapped at a village, rounded a smooth curve and the first houses of Samara came into view. White cube-like villas shone in their dark terraced gardens. But the landing-stage was only a long strip of mud, strewn with bundles, barrels and sacks. A band of ragged men were shouting abuse at one another as they floundered about in the mud. Steamships puffed about, beating the water with their giant wheels, and around them the little boats danced like nut-shells in the oily eddies. An enormous steamer, rather like those on the Mississippi, drew away from the pier to make way for the newcomer of the same company. Farther off some barges glided along in single file, drawn by tugs that were as black as crows.

There was a halt of three and a half hours. Alexander Vassilievitch decided to use it for a visit to the city. All its streets intersected at right angles. The wooden houses seemed blackened as if by fire, while the houses built of stone were covered with white plaster. The air was filled with a blinding hot dust, like that of the African deserts. On both sides of the main thoroughfare – the only one that was paved – rose the private mansions of the richest corn merchants in the region. A tramway passed through the built-up area from one end to the other, but turkeys were pecking between the rails. At the foot of the monument to Alexander II some urchins were playing a game of chance in which they spun a plate that was covered with numbers. In Dvorianskaya Street, Russell noticed some prettily decorated windows. It was there too that he met his first Russian camels, hairless and melancholy, with soft humps, a feminine gaze and a light tread. But Alexander Vassilievitch would not let him spend his time dreaming of caravan trips; he was anxious to visit a *kumys* house. The family was divided between two *isvostchiks*, and to the sound of little bells they set off for Annayevo on the hill. During the journey Russell learned that *kumys*, the great speciality of Samara, was a drink made from fermented and gasified mare's milk. A tonic drink *par excellence*, it worked wonders with anaemia cases.

When he had swallowed his glass of *kumys* Russell did feel a deep sense of well-being; opposite him Helen leaned her pretty profile over a cup filled with a white liquid with bluish shadows. Seated around the table, the other members of the family were discussing whether they would stay at Samara or continue their journey to Astrakhan. Alexander Vassilievitch favoured a radical solution:

'Who would be satisfied with a half-Volga when he has the chance of doing the whole thing? We ought to go as far as the Caspian Sea, to the very sources of caviar! Do you know, Ivan Pavlovitch, how caviar is made?

'No,' Russell stammered, for his mind was really elsewhere.

'Very well, I'll explain.'

Lost in his happy daydream, Russell vaguely heard that there were several sorts of caviar (*ikra*). Fresh caviar or grainy caviar, which was obtained by cleaning the sturgeon's eggs in a sieve in order to separate the adhering fibres; afterwards they were laid out to drain for twenty-four hours on a sieve or in a cloth; finally they were put into drums. Pressed caviar was made the same way, except that it was then kneaded by hand in pickling brine and twisted in linen sacks before being stored in barrels. A third kind of caviar was subjected to salting and drying. Finally, the experts at Astrakhan and the fishing-ports of the Caspian Sea had themselves served with sturgeon's eggs taken straight from the fish's belly, before their eyes, and whipped up in a glass of water.

'A feast for a king!' Alexander Vassilievitch exclaimed. 'I'll make you taste them all. Do you know how many eggs a large sturgeon has in its entrails? Three million! . . . . So it's settled? We're going on to Astrakhan?'

'Why not?' cried Russell enthusiastically.

In his present state of mind he would have accompanied the Zubovs to the antipodes. They returned to the ship in haste. Helen was radiant. That evening, as usual, the family gathered on deck to watch the last gleams of daylight. Sunsets on the Volga were reputed to be the most beautiful in the world, like those seen on the Nile. The horizon flamed, the banks were no more than an intangible coppery dust, while golden shivers ran through the green water. Russell was watching Helen and, with the other travellers, repeated:

'It's wonderful! It's divine!'

Alexander Vassilievitch had caviar served for supper. Then they returned on deck.

The sky was filled with stars. Men were singing on the deck below. The paddle-wheels threw up cascades of diamonds on the black water. The Zubovs, excited with the beauty of it all, sank into a row of deck-chairs. But Helen soon left her parents and went to lean upon the rails. Russell went to join her. She gazed straight ahead and her face showed happiness. The shores of the Volga could be seen no more. A warm scent rose from the young girl's hair, and Russell found the courage to tell her that he loved her.

Three months later he married her in Moscow. As from that day, daily life in Russia would have no more secrets for him.

BIBLIOGRAPHY

The bibliography of a subject as broad as daily life in Russia at the beginning of the twentieth century should comprise all the memoirs of the survivors of the Tsarist regime, all the modern historical, ethnographical and political treatises, all the periodicals of the time, and even all the novels and stories that portray the habits of the different social classes of Russia on the eve of the revolution. But I have restricted myself to recording here the principal works I consulted in the course of my labours.

[PUBLISHER'S NOTE: Very few of these works are available in English translation, but these are separately noted.]

A. WORKS IN FRENCH OR TRANSLATED INTO FRENCH FROM THE RUSSIAN

BAEDEKER (K.): *La Russie. Manuel du Voyageur.*
BEUCLER (André): *Paysages et Villes russes.*
BOGDANOVITCH: *Journal.*
BOMPARD (Maurice): *Mon Ambassade en Russie, 1903–1908.*
BRIAN-CHANINOV (N.): *Histoire de Russie.*
Capitales du Monde…
DELINES (Michel): *Russie, nos Alliés chez eux.*
GAUTIER (Théophile): *Voyage en Russie.*
GILLARD (Pierre): *Le Tragique Destin de Nicolas II et de sa famille.*
GOURFINKEL (Nina): *Théâtre russe contemporain.*
GRUNWALD (Constantin de): *Quand la Russie avait des saints.*
GUÉRASSIMOV (General): *Tsarisme et Terrorisme.*
HOFMANN (M.): *Histoire de la Littérature russe.*
HOFMANN (R.): *Un Siècle d'Opéra russe.*
JACQMIN (Paul) and d'ESTAINTOT (René): *Droits des Patrons et des Ouvriers.*
KARSAVINA: *Ballets russes.*
KOBÉLIATSKY: *Recueil complet de Législation industrielle.*
KOVALEVSKY (M. W. de): *La Russie à la Fin du XIXᵉ siècle.*
KOZLIANINNOFF (Colonel W.): *Manuel commémoratif de la Garde à cheval.*
LABRY (Raoul): *Autour du Moujik.*
LACROIX (Frédéric): *Les Mystères de la Russie.*
LAPORTE (Maurice): *Histoire de l'Okhrana.*
LÉONIDOV (L. D.): *La Rampe et la Vie.*

LEROY-BEAULIEU (Anatole): *L'Empire des Tsars et les Russes* (articles from *Revue des Deux Mondes*).

LOREY (Doctor G.): *L'Hospice des Enfants trouvés de Moscou.*

LOUKINE (Rotislas): *Mythologie russe.*

LOUKOMSKI (G. K.): *La Vie et les Mœurs en Russie.*

MARIE DE RUSSIE (S. A. I.): *Éducation d'une Princesse.*

MICHAGUINE-SKRYDLOFF (Prince): *Russie blanche et Russie rouge.*

MILIOUKOV (Paul), SEIGNOBOS (Ch.) and EISENMANN (L.): *Histoire de Russie.*

MORIN (Jean): *Mes souvenirs sur la Russie des Tsars* (La Bibliothèque mondiale).

NAZAREVSKI (V. V.): *Histoire de Moscou.*

PALÉOLOGUE (Maurice): *La Russie des Tsars.*

PINOTEAU (Robert): *La Russie d'hier et d'aujourd'hui.*

ROUET DE JOURNEL (M.-J.): *Monachisme et monastères russes.*

SALOMON (Ch.) and LEBLANC (Léon): *La Loi russe du 2–15 juin sur les Accidents du Travail.*

SÉMENOFF (E.): *Une Page de la Contre-Révolution russe: les Pogroms.*

SÉRAPHIM (Métropolite): *L'Église orthodoxe.*

SILVESTRE (Armand): *La Russie.*

SOUVORINE (Alexis): *Journal intime.*

SPIRIDOVITCH (General Alexandre): *Histoire du Terrorisme russe.—Les Dernières Années de la Cour de Tsarskoïé-Sélo.*

Tablettes gastronomiques de Saint-Pétersbourg, rédigées par un amateur.

TSAKNI (N.): *La Russie sectaire.*

VASILI (Count P.): *La Sainte-Russie.*

VIROUBOVA (Anna): *Souvenirs de ma Vie.*

VOLKOV (Alexis): *Souvenirs d'un valet de Chambre de la Tsarine Alexandra Feodorovna.*

WASSILIEFF (A. T.): *Police russe et Révolution.*

WEIDLÉ (Wladimir): *La Russie absente et présente.*

WRANGEL (N.): *Souvenirs du Baron N. Wrangel; du Servage au Bolchevisme.*

ZAVARZINE (General): *Souvenirs d'un Chef de l'Okhrana.*

B. WORKS AVAILABLE IN ENGLISH

CUSTINE (Marquis de): *Russia in 1839.*

KLEINMICHEL (Countess): *Memoirs of a Shipwrecked World.*

KROPOTKIN (Prince): *The Terror in Russia.*

PLATONOV (S.): *History of Russia.*

RADZIWILL (Princess): *The Taint of the Romanovs.*
SOKOLOV (Y.): *Russian Folklore.*
STANISLAVSKY (C.): *My Life.*

C. WORKS IN RUSSIAN

(Titles translated here for convenience)

ASTROV (N. I.): *Memoirs.*
BRUCHTEIN (A.): *Pages from the Past.*
BURYCHKIN (P. A.): *The Merchants' Moscow.*
CHMELEV (I.): *A Nobleman's Summer.*
DEMENTIEV (E. M.): *The Factory, what it gives and what it takes.*
FENIN (A. I.): *Memoirs of an Engineer.*
GRINEVICH (V.): *Workers' Movement in Russia.*
GERASIMOV (V.): *A Russian Worker's Life.*
GILIAROVSKY (V. L.): *Moscow and the Muscovites.*
History of the U.S.S.R. in the 19th Century.
IANIUL (I. I.): *Memoirs of a Factory Inspector.*
LUGININ: *The Artels and the Cooperative Movement.*
SEREBROV (A.): *The Time and the Man.*
SOBOTOVITCH (I. and E.): *Moscow from a River Omnibus.*
SYTIN (P.): *History of the Moscow Streets.*
TELECHOV (N.): *A Writer's Notebook.*
TOUGAN-BARANOVSKY: *The Russian Workshop.*

INDEX

Abacus, 33, 160, 219
Address bureaux, 135–6
Advocates, 151–2
Alexander II, 129, 131, 136–7, 147, 200
Alexander III, 129, 139, 179, 184
Ambars (covered markets), 217
Apprentices
   in bath-houses and restaurants, 54–56
   in Cossack regiments, 125
Architecture, 14, 20, 63, 156, 177
Army
   barracks, 123
   food, 123
   life and training, 108 fol.
   military courts, 150n, 153
   officers' status in 'table of ranks', 127
   organization and hierarchy, 115–17
   parades, 181–2
   pay, 120, 123
   uniforms, 114–15, 121, 123–4, 182–3, 188
   weapons, 121, 123n, 125
Arsheen (measurement unit), 10, 23
Art, 159, 191–2
Artels (artisans' communities), 98–9, 228–9

Baby-hiring, 61
Balalaïka players, 122–3, 161, 164, 197, 227
Ballet and ballet schools, 41–2, 193
Banishment, 138, 154
Baptism, 75–6
   of foundlings, 105
   as sole registration of persons, 67
Bath-attendants ('bathers'), 52–4
Bath-houses, 51–4
Bazaars, 36
Beards and moustaches, 19, 31, 36, 100, 198
Beggars, 58, 60–1, 86, 101
Beguny (religious sect): *see* Old Believers
Beloriztsy (religious sect), 79

Bird-catchers, 162
Bliny (pancakes), 26, 164
Borsch (soup), 26, 27
Botsman (ship's pilot), 228
Boyars, 128
Bribery, 136
Brothels, 162
Bund, the (league of Jewish workers), 98
Burlaki: see Volga boatmen
'Bush industry', 205–6

Cadets, Army, 108 fol.
Calashes (carriages), 31, 33, 167
Calendar, 21
Camels, 231
Capital punishment, 138, 153
Catholic Church
   divergences between Catholic and Orthodox Churches, 68, 74–6, 83, 84n
   membership of, 221
Cavalry training, 108–15, 122–3: *see also* Cossacks
Caviar, 231–2
Censorship
   postal, 139–40
   of Press and books, 141–4
Chaliapin, Fyodor, 28, 161, 192
Chancellor of the Empire, 127
Charitable societies, 101–2
Chekhov, Anton, 28, 44
Children
   as apprentices, 54–6 *passim*
   attendance at factory schools, 96
   employment regulations, 89, 97
   as foundlings, 102–7
   hiring of babies, 61
   as thieves and prostitutes, 61
Chin ('table of ranks'), 127–8
Choirs
   Army, 118
   Church, 82
Churches and cathedrals, 20, 21, 86, 160, 166, 167, 170, 177–9 *passim*
Church membership, 74
Church vestments, 83, 84n

Cities, 15
Clothing prices (for workers), 96
Clubs, 26, 46–7, 190–1
Coachmen, 45–6, 47, 55–6
Cock-fighting, 56, 162
Communal assemblies (of peasants), 134–5
Conscription, 115–16
Constantin, Grand Duke, 73
Convents, 21n, 216
Conveyances: see Calashes; Droshkis; Landaus; Motor-cars; Sleighs; Troikas
Convicts, 154–5
Co-operative movement, 98–9
Copiers (of plays etc.), 60
Cossacks, 117n, 124–6, 221
Costume, 17, 31
  of children's nurses, 32
  of peasant women, 198
  of priests, 83n
  of sleigh drivers, 18
  see also Uniforms
Court of Appeal, 135
Court staff, etiquette and ceremonial, 183–9
'Crabs' (tailors), 60
Crime and punishment, 57–61, 138, 153–5
Crows (in Moscow), 38
Customs formalities, 13–14

Death penalty: see Capital punishment
Decorations, 120
Deportation, 138, 154
Diaghilev, Serge, 192
Divorce and annulment of marriage, 67
Dostoyevsky, Fyodor, 69n, 72n, 73, 154n, 179
Drama, 28, 43–4, 192–3
Droshkis, 217
Drunkenness, 92, 99–100, 161, 164
Dukhobory (religious sect), 79
Duma, the, 145–6
Dzhigitovka (Cossacks' acrobatics), 125

Easter ceremonies and customs, 67, 84–5, 167–73, 186–7
Ecclesiastical courts, 150n
Education, 31, 96, 134
Egorov Restaurant (Moscow), 56

Electoral qualifications, 133n, 145n
Electric lighting, 21, 36
Elizavetgrad Cavalry School, 108–114
Entertainments: see Ballet; Music; Opera; Salomonsky Circus; Theatres
Estonians in Russia, 221
Ethnic groups, 220–3

Factories, 87
  children in, 89
  dormitories and living quarters in, 90–6
  medical services in, 89–90
  women in, 89
  working hours and holidays, 87–8
Fairs, 215–20
Fast-days, 68, 105, 164–5
Feast-days and festivals, 81, 84–5, 163–73, 197–8
Finns in Russia, 221
Fire brigades, 37–8
Food and drink, 14, 25–8, 30, 35–7 passim, 46–7, 95, 100, 111, 123, 165, 167, 171, 172–3, 194–5, 199, 231
Forced labour, 153–5
Foreigners in Russia, 31, 224–5
Forenames custom, 24
Foundlings, 102–7
Francophiles, Russians as, 225
French language, cuisine and fashions, 22, 26, 225
Frenchmen in Russia, 224–5

Gastronomic Notebooks of St Petersburg, 26
Germans in Russia, 224
Gogol, Nikolas, 73
Golubiatnia Restaurant (Moscow), 56
Gorki, Maxim, 57n
Government administration, 127 fol., 132 fol.
Great Lent, the, 164 fol.
'Great Russians', 220–1
Guilds, merchants', 131
Gymnasia (schools), 31

Hermitage Restaurant (Moscow), 55, 56, 164
Hiring of labour, 58
Holidays (official non-working days), 81, 88

Holy Synod, 21, 67, 69, 73, 74, 78, 135
'Honorary cornets' (senior Army cadets), 108–9
Horses, 31, 33–4
cavalry, 111, 121*n*
Cossacks', 124–6 *passim*
fire brigades', 38
Hospitality as Russian characteristic, 24 fol., 197
Hospitals and asylums, 101
for factory workers, 90
Moscow Foundling Hospital, 102–107
Hotel de l'Europe (St Petersburg), 176
Hotels, 17, 21, 176
Household management, 30, 32
Houses, naming customs, 159

Iberian Chapel (Moscow), 20
Ikons, 63–6
in churches, 83
in law courts, 157
in restaurants, 56
Illegitimacy, 103–4, 106–7
Industrial accident insurance, 89
Ironwork, 219–20

Jews
banned from the Okhrana, 139
as nobility, 130
persecution and status of, 222–4
workers' league, 98
Judges, 147–8, 149–50
Julian calendar, Russia's adherence to, 21
Junkers (officer cadets), 108 fol.
Jury system, 152–3, 157–8
Justices of the peace, 147–9

Kalach (bread roll), 161
Kammerpages (Pages of the Chamber), 115
Kamorki (workers' dwellings), 90–6
Kasha (gruel), 27
Kazan, 229–30
Cathedral, 21*n*, 177
Kchessinskaya, Matilda, 28, 42
Kharkov, population of, 15*n*
Khitrov market, 56–62, 162
Khlysty (religious sect), 79
Khomiakov, Alexey, 73

Kiev
metropolitan of, 70
pilgrimages to, 80
population of, 15*n*
saints' relics at, 81
Kinzhal (dagger), 125
Kireyevsky, Ivan, 73
Knout, the, 153
Komissarzhevskaya, Theodore, 161, 192
Kopeck, value of, 10
Krasnaya ploshchad, meaning of, 20
Kremlin, the (Moscow), 19–20
Kruychniki (stevedores), 220
Kulibyaki (composite dish), 26, 46–7
Kulich (brioche), 26, 67, 85, 167, 169, 171, 172
Kumys (mares' milk), 231

Landaus, 31, 167
Lapsha (vermicelli dish), 57
Lapti (footwear), 53, 198
Latvians in Russia, 221
Lava (Cossack charge), 126
Lavra: see Monasteries
Law, 147 fol.: *see also* Advocates; Court of Appeal; Judges; Jury system; Justices of the peace; Magistrates; Okhrana; Police
Leontiev, Constantin, 73
Likatch (coachmen), 45–6
Literature, 191–2
Lithuanians in Russia, 221
'Little Russians', 221
Lodz, population of, 15*n*
Lubochnye kartiny (pictorial sheet), 199–200

Magistrates, 152
Makhorka (tobacco), 59
Mares' milk, 231
Markets, 35–7, 56–62, 162, 217
Marriage rites and customs, 84, 203–205
Marxist indoctrination, 98, 212–14
Matchmakers, professional, 162, 203–204
Medals and decorations, 120
Medical services in factories, 89–90
Merchants, 46–7, 131
Merzavchik ('little rascal': small vodka bottle), 100
Meshchane (petit bourgeoisie), 131
Messenger services, 37

Metropolitans, 70
Military parades, 181–2
Military schools, 108–14
Minin, Kuzma, 21, 66
Mir (peasants' assembly), 134, 201–2
Molokany (religious sect), 79
Monakhi (monks), 69–73
Monasteries and convents, 21*n*, 69,
   71–3
Money units, 10
Monferrand, Richard de, 64*n*
Monks, 69–73
Moscow, 8, 18–19, 159 fol.
   charitable societies in, 101
   citizens' migration to St Peters-
      burg, 175–6
   Foundling Hospital, 102–7
   metropolitan of, 70
   Minin and Pojarsky as liberators of,
      (1612), 21, 66
   number of electors, 133
   population of, 15*n*, 133
   rivalry with St Petersburg, 28, 41,
      175, 191
   suburbs, 100
   university, 164
   see also under Churches and
      cathedrals; Hotels; Restaurants;
      Theatres
Moscow Arts Theatre, 39, 43–5, 194
Moskva (river), 17–18
   and the Great Lent, 165
   religious ceremony at, 163
Motor-cars, 31
Moujiks: *see* Peasants
Multi-racial elements, 220–5
Museums, 159
Music and musicians, 41, 47, 49, 181,
   191, 193, 194
Mythology, 208–11

Nadiel (peasants' land-plots), 131
Nemets (foreigners), 31, 224–5
Nemirovitch-Danchenko, 43, 194
Nemolyakhi (religious sect), 79
Nevsky, Alexander, 175
   monument to, 177
   order of, 120
Nevsky Prospect (St Petersburg),
   176–7, 180
Newspapers, 32, 141–3
Night-shelters, 58–61
Nikhon, Patriarch, 77, 208
Nikolas II, Tsar, 7, 14, 179, 181 fol.

Nizhny-Novgorod, 215 fol.
   the fair, 216–20
Nobility, 127 fol., 160
   palaces of, 180
Nuns, 82*n*, 86
Nurses, children's, 23–4, 32, 168, 169
Nyanyas: see Nurses, children's

Obrok (peasants' land-purchase price),
   131–2, 201
Odessa, population of, 15*n*
Okhotny Ryad (market), 36–7
Okhrana (secret police), 136–40
Old Believers (religious sect), 74, 77–
   79, 208–9
Opera, 193–4 *passim*
Opolchenie (territorial army reserve),
   115–16
Optina Pustyn (monastery), 71–3
Orthodox Church, 14
   baptismal and communion rites,
      75–6
   choirs, 82
   divergences between Orthodox and
      Catholic Churches, 68, 74–6, 83,
      84*n*
   foundation and history, 73–4
   hierarchy, 69–70
   marriage rites, 84
   the mass, 82–3
   relations with the Tsars, 73–4
   ritual, 63–8, 75–6, 83–6
   saints, 80–1
   as sole registrar of births, marriages
      and deaths, 67
   see also Fast-days; Feast-days and
      festivals; Monks; Nuns; Priests

Pages, Corps of, 114–15
Pages of the Chamber, 115
Palaces, 179, 180, 184
Parks, 33–4, 47, 161–2
Pashka (cheese cake), 26, 67, 85, 167,
   169, 171, 172
Passports, 13–14
Pavlova, Anna, 28
Peasants, 131–2
   communal assemblies of, 133–5,
      201–2
   drinking habits, 99–100
   as factory workers, 92–3
   home industries, 205–6
   marriage customs, 203–5
   Marxist indoctrination of, 212–14

as migratory workers, 206–8
religious and superstitious beliefs, 208–11
as serfs 200–1
village life of, 196–200
Pedlars and street-vendors, 162, 164–165, 167, 198–200
Personal names customs, 24–5
Pertsovka (peppered vodka), 26
Peter the Great, 128–9
  and foreigners, 224
  and founding of St Petersburg, 175
  and Petrovsky Island, 179
  residences of, 179
  statue of, 178
Petrovsky Island (St Petersburg), 179
Petrovsky Park (Moscow), 33–4, 47
Philippov Café (Moscow), 35
Physical characteristics of Russians, 17
Piety as Russian characteristic, 76–9
Pilgrims, religious, 79–80, 86, 212
Plays: *see* Drama
Pogroms, 223
Poles in Russia, 139, 221, 222 *n*
Police, 58, 59, 132–5 *passim*, 152
  see also Okhrana
Pood (unit of weight), 10
Population statistics, 15, 220–1
Pozharnaya Ploshchad (Red Square), 20
Prazdnik: see Feast-days
Prefectural cities, 132
Prepodobnye (saints), 80–1
Press and book censorship, 141–4
Priests, 67–71, 83 *n*
Prisons, 155, 178–9
Prosfors (ritual loaves), 67
Prostitution, 61, 162
Proverbs, 197, 211–12
Publishing, 143–4: *see also* Newspapers
Punishment: *see* Crime and punishment
Pustyn (hermitage), 71

Racial elements, diversity of, 220–5
Railways, 13–16, 214
'Ranks, table of', 127–8
Receivers of stolen goods, 60
Red Square (Moscow), 19
  meaning of name, 20
Registration of births, marriages and deaths, 67

Religion: see Catholic Church; Church membership; Orthodox Church
Religious sects, 74, 77–9, 208–9
Rents of workers' dwellings, 95
Restaurants and cafés, 35, 44, 45, 47–9, 55–6, 58–9, 161
Revolutionaries, 137, 139
Riga, population of, 15 *n*
Roads, 16
Rouble, value of, 10
Rural industries, 205–6
Russo-Japanese War, 7
Ryady bazaars, 36

Sagene (measurement unit), 10
St Basil's Cathedral, 20, 167
St Petersburg, 28
  cathedrals, 177, 178
  charitable societies in, 101
  foundation and history of, 174 fol.
  Hotel de l'Europe, 176
  metropolitan of, 70
  Muscovites' migration to, 175–6
  population of, 15 *n*
  rivalry with Moscow, 28, 41, 175, 191
  as Tsar's favoured residence, 20, 175
Saints, Russian, 80–1
Salaries: *see* Wages and salaries
Salomonsky Circus, 39
Salons, 160–1
Salutation customs, 24
Samara, 226, 230–1
Samovars, 14, 206
  meaning of name, 27
Sarafan (women's dress), 198
Schools, 31;
  in factories, 96
  peasants', 134
'Second-rate animals' (junior Army cadets), 108–10
Secret agents, 139–40
Senate, the, 135
Separation of powers, 147
Serfdom, 14–15, 131–2, 200–1
Servants, domestic, 23
  wages, 30
Shashka (sword), 125
Shipping companies, 226
Shops and shopping, 17, 33, 35–6, 217–18
  shop signs, 19

Siberia, forced labour in, 154–5
Skakung (religious sect), 79
Skating, 34–5
Skit (hermitage), 71
Skoptsky (religious sect), 79
Slavyansky-Bazar Hotel (Moscow), 21, 56
Sleighs, 18–19, 30, 33, 40, 207
Smoking, 27–8, 37, 59
Sobinov, Leonid, 28, 161, 192
Social classes, 61–2, 127 fol.
Sokolniki Park (Moscow), 161–2
Soloviov, Vladimir, 73
Spirits, belief in, 209–10
Stanislavsky, Constantin, 43–4, 57n, 161, 194
Starets (elderly monks), 72–3
Staroveri: see Old Believers
Steamships, 226–7, 230
Stevedores, 220
Strakhov, Nikolay, 73
Stranniki (religious sect), 79
Street life, 19
Strelnya Restaurant (Moscow), 44, 45, 47–9, 56
Strikes, industrial, 97
Students, 161, 179
Sunflower seeds as food, 100–1
Superstition, 209–11
Svakha: see Matchmakers, professional

Tailors, 54, 60, 113
Tea and tea drinking, 14, 27, 56, 123, 195–6, 203, 215, 218
Telephone service, 17
Territorial Army Reserve, 115
Testov's Restaurant (Moscow), 55, 56
Theatres, 39–45, 166n, 192–4
Thieves, 57, 60
Tipping customs, 54, 55, 136
Titles and forms of address, 127 fol.
Tobacco-smoking, 27–8, 37, 59
Tolstoy, Leo 73, 144
Tradesmen and industrialists, 160–1
Traktirs: see Restaurants and cafés
Travel regulations, 13–14
Troikas, 34
Trubnaya Square (Moscow), 162–3
Tsar, the
    and the administration, 128
    and the boyars, 128
    and the censorship, 145
    and the Church, 73–4
    and the Duma, 145n
    and the Easter greetings ceremony, 186–7
    and St Petersburg, 20, 175, 179–80
    uniform of, 121, 182
    see also Alexander II; Alexander III; Nikolas II; Court staff, etiquette and ceremonial
Tuberculosis, 229
Tulups (overcoats), 19, 54
Tverskaya Street (Moscow), 19, 37
Tzigane musicians and singers, 47–9

Uniforms, 17
    Army, 121, 123–4, 182–3, 188
    cadets', 114–15
    coachmen's, 33
    Cossacks', 124
    Guards officers', 119, 121
    railway staffs', 14
    theatre attendants', 40
    Tsar's, 121, 182
Universities, 164, 179
Unmarried mothers, care of, 106–7
Uryadniki: see Police

Vaccination, 106
Verchok (measurement unit), 10
Verjbolovo (Wirballen), 14, 21–2
Verst (measurement unit), 10
Vestments, church, 83, 84n
Village life, 196–200
Vodka, 25–7, 123
    state monopoly in and peasants' consumption of, 99–100
Volga (river), 226 fol.
Volga boatmen, 227–9
Volost (peasants' assembly), 132, 134

Wages and salaries
    Army pay, 120, 123
    of ballet dancers, 42
    of factory workers, 88
    of justices of the peace, 148
    of servants, 30
Waiters, 48, 55–6
Warsaw, population of, 15n
Weapons, 121, 123n, 125
Weights and measures, 10
Wet nurses for foundlings, 104–7
White Russians, 221
Wine-drinking, 26, 28, 35, 111
Winter Palace (St Petersburg), 180
    balls at, 187–9

Wirballen (Verjbolov), 14, 21–2
Witches, 161
Women
    in factories, 89, 92, 97
    peasants' costume, 198
    as railway gate-watchers, 17
    smoking habits of, 27
Workers' assistance associations, 97
Workers' dwellings, 90–6
Working conditions and hours
    of bath-attendants, 52–4

    in factories, 87 fol.
    of tailors, 60
    of waiters, 55–6
    see also Peasants

Yar Restaurant (Moscow), 47, 56, 161

Zakuski (hors-d'œuvres), 25
Zemstvos (Government assemblies), 133
Zubrovka (variety of vodka), 26–7